# Basic Weight Training
# *for* Men and Women

## SIXTH EDITION

## Thomas D. Fahey
California State University

Boston   Burr Ridge, IL   Du                                      San Francisco   St. Louis
Bangkok   Bogotá   Carac                                  on   Madrid   Mexico City
Milan   Montreal   New Delhi   Santiago   Seoul   Singapore   Sydney   Taipei   Toronto

*To my father, the Old Carioca*

Published by McGraw-Hill, an imprint of The McGraw-Hill Companies, Inc.,
1221 Avenue of the Americas, New York, NY 10020. Copyright © 2007. All rights reserved.
No part of this publication may be reproduced or distributed in any form or by any
means, or stored in a database or retrieval system, without the prior written consent of
The McGraw-Hill Companies, Inc., including, but not limited to, in any network or other
electronic storage or transmission, or broadcast for distance learning.

This book is printed on acid-free paper.

1 2 3 4 5 6 7 8 9 0 DOC / DOC 0 9 8 7 6

ISBN-13 978-0-07-304688-4    ISBN-10 0-07-304688-4

Vice President and Editor in Chief: *Emily Barrosse*
Publisher: *William R. Glass*
Senior Sponsoring Editor: *Christopher Johnson*
Director of Development: *Kathleen Engelberg*
Developmental Editor: *Beth Baugh, Carlisle Publishing Services*
Development Editor for Technology: *Julia D. Ersery*
Executive Marketing Manager: *Pamela S. Cooper*
Project Manager: *Brett Coker*
Manuscript Editor: *Mary Roybal*
Design Manager and Cover Designer: *Preston Thomas*
Text Designers: *Terri Wright, Jenny El-Shamy*
Art Editor: *Ayelet Arbel*
Illustrators: *John and Judy Waller, Susan Seed*
Manager, Photo Research: *Brian J. Pecko*
Senior Production Supervisor: *Richard DeVitto*
Media Producer: *Michele Borrelli*
Composition: *10/12 Times Roman by Carlisle Publishing Services*
Printing: *45# New Era Matte by R. R. Donnelley & Sons*
Cover image: *Stockbyte/Superstock*

**Library of Congress Cataloging-in-Publication Data**

Fahey, Thomas D. (Thomas Davin), 1947–
    Basic weight training for men & women / Thomas D. Fahey. — 6th ed.
        p. cm.
    Includes bibliographical references and index.
ISBN 978-0-07-304688-4  ISBN 0-07-304688-4
    1. Weight training. I. Title.
GV546.F25 2006
613.7'13—dc22                                                        2005053132

The Internet addresses listed in the text were accurate at the time of publication. The
inclusion of a Web site does not indicate an endorsement by the authors or McGraw-Hill, and
McGraw-Hill does not guarantee the accuracy of the information presented at these sites.

www.mhhe.com

# Contents

**8   Developing the Back and Neck  108**

**9   Developing the Abdominal Muscles  126**

## 11  Exercises to Develop Speed and Power  157

# Preface

WEIGHT TRAINING IS A WORLDWIDE OBSESSION. FROM IPANEMA TO IOWA, PEOPLE OF ALL ages lift weights hoping to build firm, healthy-looking bodies. Sports scientists, athletes, and coaches have developed increasingly sophisticated methods for improving strength and performance through training and nutrition. Unfortunately, these concepts sometimes are difficult for the average person to implement. *Basic Weight Training for Men and Women* is a primer on this enjoyable and beneficial activity. I've tried to furnish the most up-to-date information simply, without a lot of scientific jargon.

The sixth edition of *Basic Weight Training for Men and Women* includes many new features that make this text the best and most comprehensive beginning weight-training book on the market. In this edition, photographs of college students demonstrating the exercises replace the line drawings used in earlier editions. The Healthy Highlight boxes have been updated to include commentary on topics such as diet, burning calories, the debatable benefits of stretching, training large and small muscles, and strength training for women. Each chapter presents the most important and up-to-date weight-training exercises that can be done with free weights and on the 17 most popular exercise machines found in schools and health clubs in the United States. Also included are the latest diet and exercise guidelines found in the *Dietary Guidelines for Americans 2005,* issued by the U.S. Department of Agriculture (USDA) and the Department of Health and Human Services (DHHS), as well as exercise recommendations from the U.S. Surgeon General.

New sections discuss exercise and disability, weight training and children, body building, how to do weight training at home, and how to integrate power training into workouts. A new appendix featuring the skeletal system complements the appendix featuring the muscular system. Also new to this edition is a chapter on drugs and supplements, with information on anabolic–androgenic steroids, growth hormone, IGF-1,

DHEA and androstenedione, insulin, clenbuterol, myostatin blockers, creatine mono-hydrate, HMB, amphetamines, caffeine, and weight-loss supplements. An extensive list of updated references on topics ranging from resistance training to fad diets to aging has been added, and the glossary has been revised to reflect new terminology used through-out the book. Combined with the chapters from the previous edition on exercise tech-niques, program design, sports nutrition, plyometric and speed exercises, strength testing with norms, and basic exercise physiology and biomechanics of weight training, this new material makes *Basic Weight Training for Men and Women* a comprehensive and highly usable manual for students of weight training.

## ORGANIZATION

Chapters 1 through 5 provide the basic principles of weight training—the practical and scientific bases of the activity. I've tried to translate the latest information from the sports-medicine literature into language that is clear to the average person. Chapters 6 through 10 describe the various major exercises (using free weights, weight machines, or your own body weight) that make up almost all weight programs. Chapter 11 is unique among weight-training books. It teaches the principles for increasing running speed and power for basic movements using techniques developed by Eastern European sports scientists and coaches. Chapter 12 presents important information from sports nutritionists on diet and weight control, separating fact from fiction in this controversial area. Chapter 13 dis-cusses drugs and supplements used by some weight trainers. Appendix 1 illustrates the muscular system, and Appendix 2 illustrates the skeletal system. Appendix 3 lists exer-cises important for the most popular sports and also lists specific exercises for the differ-ent muscular areas of the body. Appendix 4 presents procedures and norms used in popular strength tests.

## NEW TO THIS EDITION

Each chapter includes topics that either are new to this edition or are discussed in greater detail than in the previous edition. Following are the new or expanded topics by chapter.

**Chapter 1:**   **Basic Weight Training**  Brief history of weight training • Latest USDA/DHHS recommendations for diet and exercise • Social benefits of exercise • Weight training and Metabolic Syndrome • Exercise and disability • Weight training for children • List of weight-training and fitness Web sites

**Chapter 2:**   **Weight Training and Your Body**  Expanded discussion of the relation be-tween muscles and the skeleton • Definition of terms used to describe motions used in exercise or movement skills • Effects of aging on women versus men in masters weight lifting

**Chapter 3:**   **Weight Training Guidelines**  Training guidelines for long-lasting fitness development • More on the latest USDA/DHHS recommendations for diet and exercise

**Chapter 4:  How Weight Training Improves Your Body** Signs of overtraining • Dynamic exercise

**Chapter 5:  Getting Started: The Basics** Weight belts and injury • Use of exercise balls, medicine balls, and lifting stones • Importance of training large muscles before small muscles • Using paused reps in workouts • Training for body building, strength, and power • Exercising at home

**Chapter 6:  Developing the Chest and Shoulders** Proper hand and arm position while exercising • Revised information and techniques for chest and shoulder exercises • Tips for building chest muscles • Rotator-cuff exercises and preventing rotator-cuff injury

**Chapter 7:  Developing the Arms** Revised techniques for dumbbell curls • New techniques for pole curls, pole twists, and wrist curls

**Chapter 8:  Developing the Back and Neck** Research on women and multiple sets • Expanded discussion of building back muscles • New back exercises and techniques • Importance of doing neck exercises correctly

**Chapter 9:  Developing the Abdominal Muscles** Abdominal fat and muscles • Why you shouldn't do sit-ups • Safe, effective exercises for the abdominal muscles • The core and the kinetic chain • Harnessing metabolism to fight abdominal fat • Role of weight training, aerobics, interval training, and diet in managing abdominal fat • Sample workout to improve appearance of abdomen

**Chapter 10: Developing the Lower Body** New and revised exercises and techniques for developing the lower body • New information on functional training machines

**Chapter 11: Exercises to Develop Speed and Power** Upper- and lower-body plyometrics • Debatable benefits of stretching before exercise • New and revised basic speed and power exercises • Integrating power into workouts • Peak-power weight training

**Chapter 12: Nutrition for Weight Training** New USDA/DHHS diet and exercise recommendations • Burning extra calories through weight training • How to read a food label to choose healthy foods

**Chapter 13: Ergogenic Aids: Drugs and Supplements** Expanded discussion of the effects and health risks of anabolic steroids, growth hormone, IGF-1, amphetamines, clenbuterol, GHB, insulin, and cocaine • Overview of popular supplements and drugs used by weight trainers, including creatine monohydrate, HMB, myostatin blockers, and weight-loss drugs

## SUCCESSFUL FEATURES

*Basic Weight Training for Men and Women* has many features that make it unique among weight-training books. It contains the latest information from the medical, exercise physiology, and sports medicine literature, presented in a manner that is easy to understand. Topics include health benefits of weight training for adults and children, osteoporosis, sports nutrition, eating disorders, basic muscle physiology, weight control, building speed and power through plyometric and speed exercises, body-building secrets for toning, and drugs and supplements. Every exercise is described in detail, and most are accompanied by photographs clearly demonstrating the techniques.

- ◆ **Illustrations** The photographs in *Basic Weight Training for Men and Women* complement the text. Adding a "how-to" dimension to the discussions, they emphasize correct technique to help you gain the greatest benefit from your workout.

- ◆ **Healthy Highlight** By focusing on the many health benefits of weight training, this feature offers motivation throughout the book. Topics include effects of aging on women versus men in masters weight lifting, signs of overtraining, the importance of training large muscles before small muscles, women and multiple sets, the debatable benefits of stretching, and burning extra calories through weight training.

- ◆ **Fact or Fiction?** This feature highlights common misconceptions about weight training and sets the record straight. It addresses questions such as these: Is it true that weight training offers no cardiovascular benefits? Does weight training make you muscle-bound? Is it important to wear a weight-lifting belt while working with weights? Do women gain excessive bulk when they weight-train?

- ◆ **Caution** Caution boxes appear throughout the book to help you avoid injury and to promote awareness of safety concerns during weight training. Following are a few examples of cautions from the book:
  - Weight training should be part of a general program that includes sensible diet and aerobic exercise.
  - To prevent excessive muscle bulk, do more repetitions and use less weight, or do only a few repetitions and use more weight.
  - Never bounce at the bottom of a squat—this could injure the ligaments of your knee.
  - Always maintain control of the spine when doing plyometric and speed exercises.

- ◆ **Glossary** The Glossary at the end of the book features the important terms used throughout the text and gives clear definitions. It can be used for quick reference and for study. Glossary terms are set in boldface the first time they appear in the text.

- ◆ **Workout Card** Attached to the back inside cover of this book is a workout card to use for your personalized workout program. You can photocopy the workout card before you start and update it as you progress.

## SUPPLEMENTS

Supplements are available for both instructors and students using *Basic Weight Training for Men and Women*. An Instructor's Resource CD-ROM includes an image bank, a set of PowerPoint slides, and a test bank. At the book's Web site, instructors can access the image bank and PowerPoint slides as well as Web links and exercise programs. The PowerPoint slides, Web links, and exercise programs are also available to students at the Web site. Contact your McGraw-Hill sales representative for more information about the Instructor's Resource CD-ROM, and visit the Web site at www.mhhe.com/faheyweighttraining6e.

## ACKNOWLEDGMENTS

Any book is the product of more than the person who wrote it. I'm grateful to the people at McGraw-Hill, including Christopher Johnson, sponsoring editor; Kathleen Engelberg, director of development; Julia D. Ersery, technology development editor; Pamela Cooper, executive marketing manager; Michele Borrelli, media producer; Brett Coker, production editor; Preston Thomas, design manager; Ayelet Arbel, art editor; Brian Pecko, photo research manager; and Rich DeVitto, production supervisor. Thanks also to Beth Baugh, developmental editor at Carlisle Publishing Services, and to Bev Kraus and the Carlisle Communications team for their careful composition of the book. I'm indebted to the many professors, athletes, and coaches who taught me the art and science of weight training, including George Brooks, Bob Lualhati, Frank Verducci, Franklin Henry, Art Burns, John Powell, Carl Wallen, Tom Carey, Harmon Brown, Lachsen Akka, Bob Fritz, Richard Marks, Dick Trimmer, Larry Burleson, Rich Schroeder, James Wright, Steve Hendersen, and Steve Blechman.

Finally, I would like to thank the reviewers of both this edition and the previous edition for their insightful comments: James DeWitt, North Carolina State University; Todd Farmer, Texas A&M International University; Lu Sparkman, Laredo Community College; Declan Connolly, University of Vermont; Peter Hastie, Auburn University; Larry Levermann, Texas State University; Elliott Oppenheim, Baltimore City Community College; and Tonia Stubbs, Broward Community College–South.

# 1

# BASIC WEIGHT TRAINING

There are two kinds of people—those who think they can
and those who think they can't. . . . They're both right.

—HENRY FORD

BE HONEST WITH YOURSELF. IF YOU HAD TO APPRAISE THE REAL REASONS YOU EXERCISE,
what would they be? Would preventing coronary artery disease and bone deterioration be
at the top of the list? Unless you're much different from most people, avoiding diseases is
not the reason you lift weights, go to aerobics classes, run, or swim 3 or 4 days a week. Let's
face it, you exercise because you want to look and feel good.

Time is a problem. Few people have enough time to spend the whole day trying to
make the Olympic team. You may have to work, go to school, take care of the family, and
follow other interests. Fortunately, you don't have to devote a lot of time to a fitness program to get fantastic results. The key is to choose the right activities and design a well-
structured program. Weight training can be an important part of your exercise routine.

A few hours of training a week will give you a fit, healthier-looking body as well
as increased strength, which will carry over to other activities. After only a few months
of weight training, you will begin to feel stronger and more confident participating in
other physical activities and sports—skiing, aerobics, tennis, racquetball, volleyball, or
jogging. Now is the time to get started and begin reaping all the benefits that weight training can provide.

There are many ways to begin a weight-training program, ranging from setting up a home gym to joining a posh health spa. It is generally best, however, to train in a health club or class because you can receive expert instruction. Also, you can usually work out on better equipment than you can at home.

Instruction is critical. On your own, you may waste much time and effort doing poor weight-training routines and end up with little to show for it. Worse, you may develop muscle and joint problems, such as kneecap and back pain. A competent instructor or personal trainer can help you avoid these pitfalls. Good health clubs have qualified instructors who can set up a program tailor-made to your needs. Try to join a club that hires instructors who have had formal training in **exercise physiology** and sports sciences and who are certified by professional organizations, such as the **American College of Sports Medicine.**

If you find it difficult to stay with a program, maybe a weight-training class is the place for you. A class makes it easier to start a program—and stay with it. It gives you a place and time to train and someone to teach you about the basics of weight training. A class helps motivate you to train consistently. Because you have made a basic commitment to attend the class, you are likelier to devote the time needed to meet your goal.

If you don't want to join a club or take a class, you can set up a home gym that can substitute for a program at the health club or supplement a weight-training class. Weight training at home is also beneficial if you have difficulty scheduling a class, if attending a spa is inconvenient, or if you don't want to spend the money for a health-club membership. A vast array of inexpensive, high-quality home-fitness products is available and can provide many of the benefits of a well-equipped gymnasium. To sum up, there is a way to fit weight training into almost anyone's program.

# BRIEF HISTORY OF WEIGHT TRAINING

Soldiers, athletes, and common people all practiced weight training in ancient times. Soldiers in the Chou dynasty (3600 B.C.) in China took weight-lifting tests to enter the military. Inscriptions on rocks found in Mesopotamia stand as monuments to the athletic prowess of ancient strongmen. Lifting stones was part of the health program of people in ancient Greece and India.

Milo of Krotona—six-time Olympic champion in wrestling—is called the father of resistance overload. According to legend, he carried a calf on his shoulders every day until it became a full-grown cow. His strength and muscle mass increased as he adapted to the animal's increased weight.

During the Middle Ages, knights increased their strength by lifting rocks and by running and swimming while wearing shirts made from heavy chain mail. In Scotland, men trained by throwing and lifting heavy stones.

After the invention of the printing press, books on weight training appeared in England (Sir Thomas Elyot, 1531; John Paugh, 1728), Germany (Joachim Camerius, 1544), and Scotland (Archibald MacLaren, 1860). In 1863, MacLaren published an article in the popular British magazine *McMillan's* that compared popular exercise programs of the day. Strongmen such as Eugen Sandow were popular performers in circuses and sideshows in the late 19th and early 20th centuries. Their training programs set the stage for the weight-training programs of modern body builders and power athletes.

Dr. Gustav Zander, from Sweden, developed more than 70 exercise machines that were widely used in medical facilities in the late 19th century. Many of these were similar to machines used today. At the same time, German gymnastics systems used kettlebells and Indian clubs to build strength and flexibility. The machines disappeared during the early 1900s as medical authorities came to advocate rest and inactivity to treat disease and promote health. By the 1920s and 1930s, YMCA and college gyms featured hydraulic leg-press and rowing machines. Charles Atlas introduced strength training and **body building** to the masses by selling "physical culture" training programs through magazines and comic books from the 1930s to the 1960s.

Publications such as *Muscular Development, Strength and Health,* and *Muscle and Fitness* described training programs and provided role models for millions of Americans, making body building and strength sports mainstream pursuits. Champion body builders such as Steve Reeves and Arnold Schwarzenegger became movie stars, popularizing weight training further. Body-building magazines and famous body builders influenced athletes to use body-building workouts to build strength and power for sports. The popularity of body building led to the development of sophisticated weight-training equipment developed by Universal Gym and Nautilus. Universal Gym became a fixture in most high-school and college weight rooms for more than 30 years. Nautilus machines—weight machines that isolate individual body parts—revolutionized the fitness industry and led to the development of scores of weight-training machines by other manufacturers. Today these machines are found in health clubs and home gyms around the world.

Weight-training methods developed differently in eastern European countries. In 1885, Vladislav Krayevsky founded the St. Petersburg Amateur Weightlifting Society and introduced whole-body training techniques involving regular workouts, progressive overload, cross-training, sports psychology, and general wellness. While Americans emphasized body building, and later **aerobics,** eastern Europeans gravitated toward **weight lifting** and whole-body training methods. In the 1960s, the USSR had more than a million registered weight lifters, while America had fewer than a thousand. Russian scientists and coaches developed plyometrics (see Chapter 11) and sophisticated workout cycles (periodization of training) that were not introduced in America until the mid 1980s.

Sports scientists in Germany, Great Britain, Russia, and the United States began studying strength training in the late 1800s. The Harvard Fatigue Laboratory tested athletes more than a hundred years ago and attempted to transfer knowledge of sports science to the playing field. Thomas DeLorme and Alan Watkins revolutionized weight training in 1948 when they introduced a progressive overload technique consisting of 3 sets of 10 repetitions (reps) of each exercise—1 set of 10 reps at 50 percent of 10-rep maximum, 1 set of 10 reps at 75 percent of 10-rep maximum, and 1 set of 10 reps at 100 percent of 10-rep maximum. Studies by Robert Berger, Thomas Cureton, and Pat O'Shea helped identify the ideal combination of sets and repetitions for building strength and muscle size. In 1963, Franklin Henry, from UC Berkeley, presented the concept of specificity of training—the idea that changes in the body reflect the nature of the training program.

Health experts deemphasized the importance of weight training for health in the 1970s, when aerobic exercise became popular. They believed that aerobic exercise prevented coronary artery disease and stroke, with weight training and high-intensity exercise providing little more than window dressing. Research on strength and muscle hypertrophy slowed until the mid 1980s, when the importance of strength training was finally recognized. Since then, sophisticated studies by researchers such as George Brooks, William Kraemer, John Faulkner, Phil Gollnick, Alfred Goldberg, Ken Baldwin, Frank Booth, Pavo Komi, Carmelo Bosco, Per Tesch, Digby Sale, and Charles Tipton have revolutionized our knowledge of weight training and muscle physiology. These studies have improved our understanding of the importance of weight training, and exercise in general, for health and have helped athletes develop more effective ways to build muscle mass and strength.

# WEIGHT TRAINING AND YOUR TOTAL PHYSICAL FITNESS PROGRAM

Weight training alone is not enough to develop and maintain optimal health and fitness. You should follow a well-rounded health-promotion program that includes proper nutrition, good health habits, and exercise for endurance, strength, and flexibility.

Proper nutrition will supply enough energy and nutrients to help you avoid or get rid of excess body fat and to prevent diseases such as **osteoporosis** (bone weakness) and **coronary artery disease** (hardening of the arteries). The healthy lifestyle includes not smoking or taking dangerous drugs, handling emotional stress properly, and practicing good personal hygiene.

Endurance exercise is necessary to prevent coronary artery disease; strengthen the heart, lungs, and blood vessels; and improve chemical regulation within cells. Activities such as running, aerobics, cycling, and skiing contribute to endurance fitness and provide an enjoyable recreational outlet while improving other components of fitness, such as muscle strength. Flexibility training helps maintain normal joint movement, which will prevent injury and future disability (particularly as you age). Weight training, which develops muscle strength, is an important part of a general program of developing a healthy lifestyle.

## Benefits of Weight Training

Weight training provides benefits such as a more attractive body, increased strength and power, enhanced metabolism, improved sports performance, enhanced self-image, and a competitive outlet. With weight training, almost all people can achieve rapid gains and self-improvement.

Weight training will help you look healthy and trim. You can lose weight and inches, acquire a more shapely body, and develop strong muscles that are difficult or impossible to achieve by dieting or other forms of exercise. Weight training is the best way to develop muscle size. No other training activity can provide the large arms, big chest, rippled abdominal muscles, and powerful legs that weight training can. See the "Fact or Fiction?" box for more benefits.

Of course, weight training will not do it all. For a fit, defined body you must watch what you eat and expend plenty of calories in endurance exercise. A combination of weight training, endurance exercise, and proper diet will improve your fitness level and tone your body. See the box "Healthy Highlight: Government Says Eat More Vegetables, Fruits, and Whole Grains" on p. 6.

## FACT OR FICTION

*MYTH: WEIGHT TRAINING BUILDS MUSCLE, BUT IT DOES LITTLE TO PREVENT CORONARY ARTERY DISEASE, STROKE, OR DIABETES.*

Weight training builds muscle—the most metabolically active tissue in the body. It improves the way insulin works in the body (which reduces body fat, particularly in the abdomen); lowers blood pressure; decreases blood cholesterol, triglycerides, and insulin; increases insulin sensitivity; and improves the way the blood clots. These changes boost your energy level and reduce the risk of many diseases.

For the past 30 years, exercise experts have emphasized the importance of cardiovascular fitness. Other physical fitness factors, such as muscle strength and flexibility, were mentioned almost as an afterthought. However, as we learned more about how the body responds to exercise, it became obvious that these other factors were vital to health, wellness, and quality of life. Muscles make up about 45 percent of your body mass. You depend on them for movement, and, because of their mass, they are the site of a large portion of the energy reactions (i.e., metabolic reactions) that occur in your body. Strong, well-developed muscles help you perform daily activities better and contribute to a lean, healthy-looking body. Exercises that strengthen muscles also contribute to the health of your bones.

***Improved quality of life*** Strong, powerful muscles are important for the smooth and easy performance of everyday activities, such as carrying groceries, lifting boxes, and climbing stairs, as well as for emergency situations. They help keep the skeleton in proper alignment, preventing back and leg pain and providing the support necessary for good posture. Strength and power mean freedom to the average person. If you lose your balance when taking a shower, you will recover quickly if you're strong and powerful but might fall and risk breaking your hip if your muscles are weak and slow. The stronger person can hike up hills while on vacation, lug groceries easily from the car to the house, and push a car to the side of the road when it runs out of gas. Sedentary people remain on the sidelines while life passes them by.

***Improved muscle and bone health with aging*** (See Chapter 2.) Good muscle strength will help you live a longer and healthier life. Regular, lifelong participation in strength training prevents muscle and nervous system degeneration that can ruin the quality of life and increase the risk of serious injury, such as hip fracture, that can prematurely shorten your life.

After age 30, most men and women lose a little strength and muscle mass every year—a condition called "sarcopenia." By age 75, about 25 percent of men and 75 percent of women can't lift more than 10 pounds. As a person ages, motor nerves become disconnected from the portion of muscle they control. Aging and inactivity also lead to slow

# HEALTHY HIGHLIGHT

## GOVERNMENT SAYS EAT MORE VEGETABLES, FRUITS, AND WHOLE GRAINS

Every 5 years the U.S. Department of Health and Human Services and the U.S. Department of Agriculture jointly issue an update of *Dietary Guidelines for Americans,* which summarizes and synthesizes current scientific information on nutrition, food components, eating patterns, and physical activity. The most recent update, *Dietary Guidelines for Americans 2005,* released in January 2005, emphasizes fruits, vegetables, and whole grains as the basis of a healthy diet. The *Guidelines* also recommend that adults engage in at least 30 minutes of moderate-intensity physical activity every day—60 minutes if they want to manage weight and prevent gradual weight gain, 90 minutes if they want to sustain weight loss. Children should exercise at least 60 minutes a day. In their introduction to the *Guidelines,* Secretary of Health and Human Services Tommy Thompson and Secretary of Agriculture Ann Veneman acknowledge that putting these recommendations into practice is difficult. Doing so, however, will help Americans combat the current epidemic of overweight and obesity and live healthier, longer, more active lives. (For more information on *Dietary Guidelines for Americans 2005,* visit the Web site at www.health.gov/dietaryguidelines.)

muscles, which are less able to perform quick, powerful movements. This occurs because fast-twitch motor units are converted to less powerful slow-twitch motor units. Weight training helps maintain motor nerve connections and muscle quickness.

Strength and muscle losses occur slowly. At first, you'll notice that you can't play sports as well as you could in high school. With years of inactivity and strength loss, you may have trouble performing the simple movements of daily life—getting out of a bathtub or automobile, walking up a flight of stairs, or doing yard work. Poor strength makes it much more likely that you'll be injured during everyday activities. Inactivity—not age—causes most of the loss in strength and muscle mass. Middle-aged and older adults gain strength at the same rate as younger people do.

Bone loss, a condition called osteoporosis, is common in people over age 45 (particularly women after menopause). The condition leads to fractures that can be life-threatening. Although hormonal changes due to aging account for much of the bone loss, lack of bone stress due to inactivity is a contributing factor. Strength training decreases bone loss with aging and may even increase bone density slightly.

***Improved cardiovascular function***    Weight training improves blood pressure regulation. For example, blood pressure increases temporarily during high-intensity upper-body exercise, such as water skiing or snow shoveling. Intense muscle contractions constrict blood vessels, which in turn raises blood pressure. The stronger you are, however, the less your blood pressure will increase. Stronger muscles don't have to work as hard to exert the same force, so they constrict blood vessels less. Every year, many people die from the effects of high blood pressure.

| CAUTION | ♦ High blood pressure is a leading risk factor of coronary artery disease. Do not attempt to treat this problem without medical advice. |
|---------|---|

***Enhanced metabolism***    Problems with insulin metabolism lead to what is called the "Metabolic Syndrome." Insulin resistance is linked to high insulin secretion, high blood pressure, obesity (particularly the more dangerous abdominal obesity), and blood fat abnormalities. Weight training helps combat many of the factors associated with this syndrome. Weight training helps promote a better ratio of "good" HDL to "bad" LDL cholesterol and reduces insulin resistance.

***Weight training and body fat***    Scientists have known for many years that muscle mass determines metabolic rate—the body's energy level. The higher your muscle mass, the more calories you metabolize (burn) every day. Weight training helps you gain muscle, making it easier to control body fat.

While most studies show that exercise alone is insufficient for long-term weight loss, exercise (including weight training) and dietary restriction combined appear to improve both the early and the longer-term outcome of a weight-control program. Weight training helps preserve lean body mass **(fat-free weight),** increases total energy output, and increases fuel utilization. Although not as significant as aerobic exercise, weight training increases energy output by boosting resting metabolic rate. It also increases the calories you burn while digesting food. Most important, it increases the calories you burn during and after exercise—mainly by increasing fat-free mass. Fat-free mass is composed mostly of muscle.

Metabolism includes all the chemical reactions that occur in your body. Every time you exercise, make new proteins, break down foods you eat, or repair injured tissue, your body uses energy that contributes to metabolism. Muscles are a hotbed of metabolism. They make up about 45 percent of your body weight—more than any other tissue. When muscles contract, they use an incredible amount of energy. During exercise, metabolism increases by more than 10 times above resting levels. World-class endurance athletes can increase their metabolism to more than a whopping 20 times above resting levels.

Muscles are highly metabolic tissues. The more muscle you have, the higher your metabolic rate. Weight training builds muscle mass. Greater muscle mass helps stoke metabolism during and after exercise. Increasing metabolism is the key to losing weight.

Weight training also reduces abdominal fat, a particularly dangerous type of fat because it promotes coronary artery disease, diabetes, elevated cholesterol, and high blood pressure. Weight training affects abdominal fat metabolically rather than through **spot reducing.** You can't do hundreds of curl-ups and lose your gut without affecting total body energy balance. Weight training induces subtle changes in metabolism, such as preventing insulin resistance, that help the body avoid storing fat in the abdomen.

*Increased strength and power*    Increased strength and power are advantages in daily life, in tasks ranging from carrying groceries to lifting suitcases at the airport. Everyday activities such as unscrewing jar tops and carrying children are much easier if you are strong.

Strength training also makes muscles, tendons, and ligaments stronger and less susceptible to injury. Although this is of obvious benefit in sports, it may also protect you from injury and disability related to everyday activities. Studies have shown that people with good muscle endurance and strength are much less susceptible to back pain. (Back pain affects over 85 percent of Americans.)

## Improved Sports Performance

Have you ever skied, hiked, or played tennis with someone with poor muscle strength? They tire more easily and are less effective in participating in the activity. People with stronger muscles hit a tennis ball harder, climb more easily to the top of the mountain, and get over the edge of a ski better. Athletes in most sports have known for years that strength training improves performance. In high-power sports, such as track and field, weight training is a cornerstone of the conditioning program.

Weight training can also help you in endurance sports such as distance running and swimming. Weak people use a greater percentage of their strength than strong people do and thus compromise endurance. In endurance sports, people place great emphasis on the fitness of the heart and lungs. However, success in endurance sports requires speed, which depends partially on muscle strength. The best way to build strength for these sports is through weight training and plyometrics (see Chapter 11).

Whether you are an athlete or a person who just likes to play sports, increased strength and power can make you better in the sports you enjoy. Staying in shape through sports is a lot more fun than doing boring exercise routines for the sake of health. Weight training enhances your enjoyment of sports by making you more successful and capable of handling more advanced techniques.

## Emotional and Social Benefits

Everyone likes to feel special and unique. Few things improve self-image more than having a lean, healthy-looking body. Few activities affect the body as quickly and positively as weight training. Weight training provides benefits that everyone can see in a short time.

People who develop fit, attractive bodies naturally feel good about themselves. Many people who take up weight training find it a good form of personal therapy and radiate self-confidence.

Weight training also has social benefits. Many people gain as much from meeting and talking with other people at the health club as they do from the exercises themselves. Work hard when you lift weights, but take time to enjoy the company of the people training with you.

## Competitive Outlet

Weight training can provide people with a competitive outlet. Some people use weight training to give them a competitive edge in their favorite sport. Others compete directly in weight-training activities such as body building and competitive weight lifting. Even people who are only casually interested in weight training can get satisfaction from the competitive aspects of the activity. When you lift weights, you are competing against yourself for PRs (personal records). You are always trying to lift a little more weight, do a few more repetitions, or achieve a fitter-looking body. There is no more important competition than the competition you have against yourself.

### Exercise and Disability

People with disabilities often have poor physical fitness, which limits their quality of life. By building strength and power, weight training increases mobility, improves metabolic capacity, and boosts self-confidence. It is critical for rehabilitating injured joints and muscles. Increasingly, physicians are using weight training to treat diseases ranging from diabetes to neurological disorders.

### Weight Training for Children

Until recently, pediatricians did not recommend weight training for children, fearing that overloading the bones would injure fragile growth centers. More than 30 studies have shown that weight training is safe and effective for children. Children who do the exercises properly and under supervision show little risk of injury. Weight training is particularly good for overweight children, who often are stronger than leaner children. Weight training is an excellent activity that can be continued throughout life.

## LET'S GET STARTED!

Basic information about training and exercise helps you get the most from your fitness program. You need to know basic weight-training terms and understand how weight training affects your muscles, nerves, and joints—and where to train and what clothes to wear. The next few chapters will introduce you to the basics of weight training so you can get started.

## WEB SITES DEALING WITH WEIGHT TRAINING AND FITNESS

ACE; professional organization for personal trainers: www.acefitness.org

American Alliance for Health, Physical Education, Recreation, and Dance; professional organization: www.aahperd.org

American College of Sports Medicine; professional organization for people in sports medicine: www.acsm.org

Centers for Disease Control and Prevention; exercise and health: www.cdc.gov/nccdphp/sgr/ataglan.htm

Dan John; strength training and throwing: danjohn.org/coach.html

ExRx.net; resource page for fitness professionals: www.exrx.net

Information on training principles and ergogenic aids: www.t-nation.com

Information on weight training: www.weightsnet.com

Mayo Clinic; fitness and sports medicine: www.mayoclinic.com/findinformation/
conditioncenters/centers.cfm?objectid=000BDE1A-6219-1B37-8D7E80C8D77A0000

MEDLINEplus; exercise: www.nlm.nih.gov/medlineplus/exerciseandphysicalfitness.html

National Institute for Fitness and Sport; professional organization: www.nifs.org

National Strength and Conditioning Association; professional organization for strength
coaches: www.nsca-lift.org

President's Council on Physical Fitness and Sports: fitness.gov

Shape Up America; fitness organization: www.shapeup.org

Sports Coach; track and field, strength, and fitness: www.brianmac.demon.co.uk

Stretching and flexibility information page:
www.cmcrossroads.com/bradapp/docs/rec/stretching/stretching_toc.html

C H A P T E R

# 2 WEIGHT TRAINING AND YOUR BODY

*It is hard to fail, but it is worse never to have tried to succeed.*

—THEODORE ROOSEVELT

WEIGHT TRAINING AFFECTS MORE THAN YOUR MUSCLES. IT ALSO STRENGTHENS TENDONS and ligaments and improves coordination between the nervous and muscular systems. This chapter is a primer on the effects of weight training on your body.

## YOUR BODY'S RESPONSES TO WEIGHT TRAINING

Skeletal muscle is highly adaptable. Overloaded muscles get stronger, while inactive muscles get weaker. You build strength by increasing the size of your muscles and improving the way your nervous system transmits information to your muscles.

### How Strong Can You Get?

Three factors determine your strength-gaining potential: genetics, gender, and your training program. You can't do much about the first two factors, but you can maximize your potential with a systematic training program.

*Genetic potential*   Your genes determine the number of muscle fibers and fiber types within each muscle, how well your nervous system coordinates muscle function, your body size, and your bone length. Each of these factors helps determine your strength.

The main determinant of strength is muscle size. People with more muscle fibers per muscle can increase strength more easily than others—their more numerous fibers contribute to the greater overall strength of the muscle.

Timing and coordination, partially determined by genetics, are also important aspects of strength. The force produced by the club or racquet determines the velocity of a golf ball or tennis ball. Few "big hitters" in golf or tennis, however, look like competitive weight lifters. Rather, they are able to channel forces effectively through timing and coordination. These factors are often as important as muscle size for developing effective strength (i.e., strength you can use in activities other than weight training). The remarkable athletic feats of professional basketball players, Olympic high jumpers, and world-class ballet dancers are due largely to superior neuromuscular control and faster muscle fiber types.

Body size, which also is genetically determined, governs strength as well. Larger people tend to be stronger than smaller people. However, bone length and frame size are important, too. For example, people with shorter arms and larger chests tend to have an advantage in the bench press. They don't have to push the weight as far as do people with long arms and small chests. Body size can be a disadvantage when you must move your own body weight. For example, pull-ups are more difficult for people with higher body weights.

*Gender differences*    Men and women gain strength at the same rate, but men are considerably stronger than women due to their larger muscle mass. However, when strength is expressed per unit of cross-sectional area of muscle tissue, men are only 1 to 2 percent stronger than women in the upper body and about equal to women in lower-body strength. Because women have a greater proportion of their muscle mass in the lower body, they can gain strength more easily in the legs than in the shoulders. Men, with more muscle in their upper bodies, have much stronger shoulders than women.

Women don't get big muscles from weight training. The extreme muscularity of some top female body builders is due to anabolic steroids and naturally higher levels of the muscle-building hormone **testosterone.** Testosterone promotes the growth of muscle tissue. Testosterone levels in males are about 6 to 10 times higher than those in women, so men tend to have larger muscles. Also, the male nervous system can activate muscles faster, so men tend to have more **power** (the ability to exert force rapidly).

*Training program*    A well-designed weight-training program practiced systematically will increase muscle strength in almost anyone. You are ultimately in control of your training gains—if you have a good program and train regularly, you will get stronger.

## MUSCLES AND THE SKELETON

Muscles move the skeleton. The muscular system includes the skeletal muscles, tendons, and associated connective tissue that make up muscle groups. Muscles almost always appear in pairs (agonists and antagonists) because they can actively cause movement only when they shorten. The **agonist** muscle moves the skeleton in one direction, and the **antagonist** muscle returns it to its original position. For example, the biceps muscle flexes the elbow, while the triceps muscle—the bicep's antagonist—extends the elbow and returns it to its previous state. Antagonist muscles make the smooth coordination of movement possible. As the one muscle contracts, the antagonist muscle relaxes, and vice versa. Terms used to describe the movements of the musculoskeletal system are listed in Table 2–1.

Muscles move the skeleton by contracting and pulling on bones. Muscles and bones are arranged in a system of levers that increase either the force or the velocity of movement. You can run, throw, or jump because muscles pull on the bones using the corresponding lever system.

Understanding the role of muscles in movement—and training them effectively through weight training—can be complicated because a single muscle often can cause more than one movement. For example, the hamstring muscles cause knee flexion and hip extension. Hamstring injuries usually occur during hip extension rather than knee flexion, but most people rehabilitate them by doing leg curls, a knee flexion exercise. Also, to cause movement muscles get help from other muscles. The main muscles causing movement are called **prime movers.** Muscle groups that produce the movement are called agonists, and their helper muscles are called **synergists.** Synergist muscles increase precision by preventing unwanted secondary movement. Muscles in the legs, shoulders, and **core** (trunk muscles) often provide stabilization during movement of the hands or feet.

**TABLE 2–1**
**Movement of Joints**

Use these terms when describing motions used in exercise or movement skills.

| | |
|---|---|
| **Flexion** | Movement of a joint that results in a decreased angle between two adjacent segments (bones) |
| **Extension** | Return from flexion; movement of a joint that results in an increased angle between two adjacent segments |
| **Abduction** | Lateral movement of a body segment away from the midline of the body |
| **Adduction** | Lateral movement of a body segment toward the midline of the body |
| **Circumduction** | Movement of a body segment around a point so that the free end traces a circle and the segment traces a cone |
| **Rotation** | Movement of a body segment around its longitudinal axis |
| **Dorsiflexion** | Movement of the foot toward its dorsal (upper) surface |
| **Plantar flexion** | Movement of the foot toward its plantar (lower) surface |
| **Eversion** | Rotation of the foot that lifts the lateral border of the foot upward |
| **Inversion** | Rotation of the foot that lifts the medial border of the foot upward |
| **Pronation** | Inward rotation of the forearm |
| **Supination** | Outward rotation of the forearm |

Every muscle has an **origin** (where it begins on one bone) and an **insertion** (where it connects to another bone). Muscles move the bone from the insertion toward the origin. The attachment to the stationary bone is the origin, while the attachment to the movable bone is the insertion.

## Skeletal-Muscle Structure

Muscles consist of individual muscle cells, or **muscle fibers,** connected in bundles called **fasciculi** (singular, fasciculus) and subdivided into **myofibrils** and **myofilaments** (Figure 2–1). A single muscle is made up of many bundles of muscle fibers covered by layers of connective tissue. Connective tissue gives the muscle form, strength, and elasticity. It runs from end to end in a muscle, from the tendon of origin to the tendon of insertion.

Muscle fibers are made up of smaller units called myofibrils. When your muscles are given the signal from the nervous system to contract, protein filaments within the myofibrils slide across one another, causing the muscle fiber to shorten. Weight training increases the size of individual muscle fibers by increasing the number of myofibrils. Larger muscle fibers mean a larger and stronger muscle. The development of large muscle fibers is called **hypertrophy.**

Under a magnifying glass or a light microscope, skeletal muscle fibers have a **striated** (striped) appearance (Figure 2–2, p. 16). These striations are due to the presence of **actin** and **myosin,** the two main proteins of contraction and the principal components of the myofibrils. The sarcomere—made up of the contractile proteins lying between two **Z lines**—is the basic functional unit of the muscle. Figure 2–2 shows how the thin actin filaments are attached to the Z line, which forms the foundation for shortening in muscle.

Muscle contraction occurs when actin (A) combines with myosin (M) and **adenosine triphosphate (ATP)** to produce actomyosin, force, **adenosine diphosphate (ADP),** and **inorganic phosphate (Pi).** ATP is the most important energy-supplying chemical in the body, while ADP and Pi are breakdown products of ATP. A nerve impulse (a message sent from the brain and spine) causes the release of calcium in the muscle, triggering muscle contraction. The reaction leading to muscle contraction is shown in this equation:

$$\textbf{actin} + \textbf{myosin} + \textbf{ATP} \rightarrow \textbf{actomyosin} + \textbf{ADP} + \textbf{Pi} + \textbf{force}$$

The muscle relaxes as calcium is withdrawn.

Does strength training enlarge the muscle fibers, or increase their number? The bulk of evidence suggests that strength training makes muscle fibers larger (hypertrophy), not more numerous (**hyperplasia**). However, there is some proof that muscle fibers can increase in number under certain circumstances (animal studies only). Also, some extremely strong people may be born with or develop more muscle fibers. Generally, though, it is muscle hypertrophy that makes muscles stronger.

## The Motor Unit

Muscle fibers receive the signal to contract from nerves connected to the spinal column. A motor nerve (a nerve connected to muscle fibers) links as few as 1 or 2 muscle fibers up to

**Figure 2–1** Components of skeletal muscle tissue: fasciculi, muscle fibers, myofibrils, and myofilaments

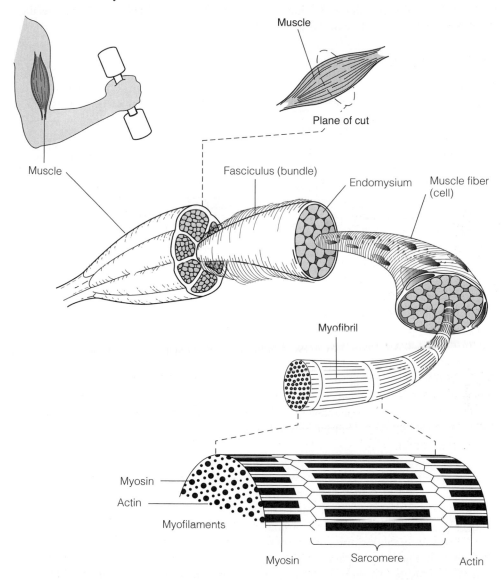

more than 150 muscle fibers. Nerve–muscle combinations are called **motor units** (Figure 2–3, p. 17). Powerful muscles, such as the quadriceps in the legs, have large motor units—each motor nerve connects to many muscle fibers. Smaller muscles, such as those around the eye, have much smaller motor units.

**Figure 2–2**  The sliding-filament theory of muscle contraction. The myosin filaments pull on the actin filaments, causing the muscle fiber to shorten. The basic contractile unit of the muscle fiber is the sarcomere. The Z line serves as the outer boundary of the sarcomere.

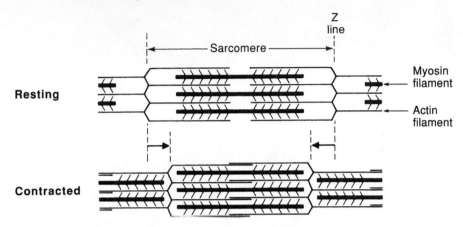

The three types of motor units are fast glycolytic (FG), fast oxidative glycolytic (FOG), and slow oxidative (SO). They are subdivided according to their strength and speed of contraction, speed of nerve conduction, and resistance to fatigue. The type of motor unit chosen by the body depends on the requirements of the muscle contraction. The body chooses FG fibers for lifting heavy weights or sprinting because they are fast and powerful. For prolonged standing or slow walking, SO fibers are chosen because they are more resistant to fatigue. New fiber-typing methods subdivide fibers according to the speed of the proteins that cause the muscle fibers to contract (scientists call these proteins *myosin isoforms*).

The body exerts force by calling on one or more motor units to contract, a process known as **motor unit recruitment.** When picking up a small weight, for example, you use few motor units to perform the task. However, when picking up a large weight, you use many motor units. When a motor unit calls on its fibers to contract, all the fibers contract to their maximum capacity (the all-or-none principle).

Strength increases through improved motor unit recruitment: Training with weights improves your nervous system's ability to coordinate the recruitment of muscle fibers. It is a kind of "muscle learning" and is an important way of increasing strength. Most of the changes in strength during the first weeks of weight training are due to neurological adaptations. The nervous system adapts by improving the way it stimulates motor units—it learns to call on larger motor units and better coordinates motor unit activation. Table 2–2 on p. 18 summarizes some ways your body improves its function through weight training.

In summary, weight training increases muscle strength by increasing the size of your muscle fibers and improving the body's ability to call on motor units to exert force. The first process is muscle hypertrophy, and the second process is motor unit recruitment.

**Figure 2–3** The motor unit. The motor unit is composed of a motor nerve and a number of muscle fibers.

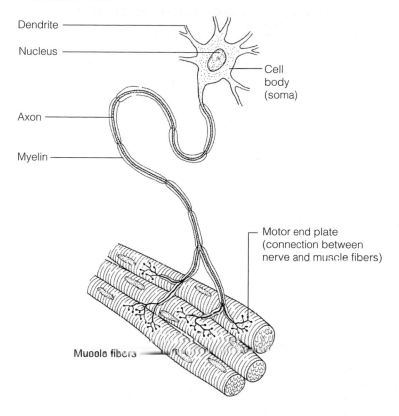

Dendrite

Nucleus

Cell body (soma)

Axon

Myelin

Motor end plate (connection between nerve and muscle fibers)

Muscle fibers

# WEIGHT TRAINING AND YOUR HEALTH

Weight training generally has a positive effect on health. It strengthens muscles, bones, and soft tissues, improving the quality of life. It significantly reduces the effects of risk factors that lead to coronary artery disease.

## Weight Training and the Strength of Ligaments, Tendons, Bones, and Joint Surfaces

**Tendons** connect muscle to bone, and **ligaments** connect bones to other bones. Cells called chondrocytes cover **joint** surfaces. These tissues have little or no blood supply, so they have a very low energy level and they heal slowly when injured. Weight training helps strengthen the tendons, ligaments, and joint surfaces so that you're less likely to injure these structures when you perform physical activities.

| TABLE 2-2 | |
|---|---|
| **Changes to the Body from Weight Training** | |
| CHANGE | EFFECT |
| Increased muscle mass | Tighter, firmer-looking body and stronger muscles |
| Increased size of fast- and slow-twitch muscle fibers | Increased muscle strength and power |
| Increased blood supply (high-repetition program) | Increased delivery of oxygen and nutrients to the cells and increased elimination of wastes from the cells |
| Increased fuel storage in muscles | Increased resistance of muscles to fatigue |
| Ability to use more motor units during muscle contraction | Increased strength and power |
| Improved coordination of motor units | Increased strength and power |
| Increased strength of tendons, ligaments, and bone | Lower risk of injury to these tissues |

Most people suffer from back pain at some time in their lives. The causes of back pain are complex. In many cases, weak, inflexible muscles in the back, legs, and abdomen cause back pain. Poor posture can also cause back pain. Weight training develops stronger, more flexible muscles. If you receive proper instruction, weight training can improve your posture by teaching you proper lifting techniques and by strengthening muscles that can take the stress off sensitive spinal nerves.

## Weight Training, Weight Control, and Coronary Artery Disease

Weight training can be an important tool in a long-term weight-management program. Dieting without exercise causes decreased lean body mass (fat-free weight), negative nitrogen balance (i.e., the body loses protein), and diminished muscle strength. Weight training during dieting increases or maintains lean body mass and maintains nitrogen balance. Researchers reported improvements in strength of between 17 and 22 percent in people who weight-trained during weight-loss dieting. Lean mass is the most important determinant of resting metabolic rate.

Like endurance exercise, weight training has no effect on regional fat deposition (i.e., spot reducing is ineffective). Although the improved muscle tone that results from training will usually make a particular area of the body look better, the subcutaneous adipose layer that lies over the muscles is unaffected (except as it is affected by any negative caloric balance). People who have a problem processing blood sugar store more fat in their abdomen. Weight training improves the way the cells handle blood sugar, which helps prevent fat accumulation around your middle.

Weight training may reduce the risk of coronary artery disease by helping people maintain a healthy weight, lowering blood fats, enhancing insulin resistance, and decreasing blood pressure in hypertensive patients (people with high blood pressure). However, *weight training alone is not enough to prevent coronary artery disease.* It must be integrated into a healthy lifestyle program that includes endurance exercise, proper nutrition, and not smoking.

Weight training can result in explosive increases in blood pressure, so be cautious. Hypertensive patients should work with low-intensity, high-repetition training programs. They should avoid performing the Valsalva maneuver during the exercises. (The Valsalva maneuver is expiration against a closed glottis, that is, straining.)

## Gastrointestinal Transit Time

Weight training speeds the passage of food through your stomach and intestines. This aids digestion and may decrease the risk of colon cancer.

## Osteoporosis

Decreased bone density, a condition known as osteoporosis, is a serious health problem because it can lead to brittle, easily broken bones that don't heal quickly. Although the problem usually is most common in women who have reached menopause, recent evidence suggests that even active women in their 20s are susceptible. The causes of decreased bone density involve an interaction of hormonal controls, diet, and mechanical stress.

---

CAUTION   ♦  If you have reached menopause, exercise alone may not be the most appropriate treatment for preventing osteoporosis. See your doctor for proper medical advice.

---

Bone density is, in part, proportional to the stresses placed on the bones. Many studies show that the bones of active people are denser than those of sedentary people. If a woman's estrogen levels are normal and her dietary intake of calcium is adequate, then weight training will help maintain bone density. If estrogen levels and dietary calcium are low, then weight training will be less effective in maintaining bone density. This appears to be true for adult women of any age. Once the bones' growth center closes, mineral content doesn't increase. Some studies show that women can increase bone density slightly through intense weight training. The best women can do is attempt to maintain bone mineral content through weight-bearing exercise, proper nutrition, and, after menopause, possibly estrogen therapy.

---

### COMMON QUESTIONS ABOUT WEIGHT TRAINING AND YOUR BODY

**1.  How long before I see changes in my body from weight training?**
You will increase strength very rapidly during the early stages of a weight-training program. Most of the changes during the first 6 weeks of training
*(Continued)*

*(Continued)*

are caused by learning—your nervous system improves its ability to use muscle fibers (motor units) to exert force. Changes in muscle size take longer. You will begin to see significant changes in the way your muscles look after 6 to 8 weeks of training. Early measurable changes in strength as a result of training occur in the nervous system; changes to muscle cells occur after the first workout but are not visible until later.

**2.  Will weight training make my body look better?**

Weight training will increase the size of your muscles, which will tend to make your body look fitter and firmer. Most people must also reduce body fat to improve the appearance of their bodies. Increasing muscle size will do little to improve appearance if you have a large layer of fat over your muscles. There is no such thing as spot reducing (exercising a body part to reduce body fat in the area). To reduce body fat, you must eat less and burn more calories through endurance exercise. Body fat must be lost gradually. If you try to lose weight rapidly, you will lose some of the muscle you worked so hard to get.

**3.  What is overtraining? Is it possible to train too hard?**

Although improving any type of fitness requires hard work, it is possible to exercise too much. Overtraining is an imbalance between training and recovery. It may occur if training sessions are too frequent, intense, or prolonged, with insufficient rest and recovery. Depending on its severity, symptoms of overtraining last anywhere from a few days to many months. A mild case is accompanied by fatigue, depressed performance, and muscle stiffness. A more serious case may involve impaired immune function (making you more susceptible to illness), depression, stress fractures, and suppression of reproductive hormones. The latter symptom is particularly distressing in women because it can lead to loss of bone density.

The symptoms of overtraining are often subtle and difficult to detect. Suspect this condition if you fail to recover adequately from a weight-training workout after several days' rest. If you find that you are training hard but not improving, perhaps you are training too hard. Try changing your program or taking a couple of extra days off. Adaptation to exercise is highly individual. A program that works well for one person may be excessive for another. The best advice for selecting the optimal training program is to start with a basic workout, then modify it gradually. If you have trouble recovering from a training program, back off a little. However, if the program seems too easy, increase the intensity or the number of exercises.

## Are Body-Building and Strength-Building Programs the Same?

While there is some overlap—body builders can increase strength, and strength trainers can develop big muscles—the training programs are different. Do 8 to 20 reps for 3 to 10 sets per exercise if your goal is to build large muscles. Do 1 to 6 reps for 1 to 6 sets per exercise if strength building is your goal. You can develop high levels of strength with only minimal increases in muscle size. Conversely, people with large muscles aren't necessarily strong.

## Weight Training and Aging

After age 30, people start to lose muscle mass. At first, you notice that you can't play sports as well as you could in high school. However, years of inactivity and loss of strength may leave you having trouble performing even the simple movements required in everyday life. Some people eventually have trouble getting out of a tub or automobile, walking up a flight of stairs, or working in the yard. When your strength is poor, it's easy to slip in the tub or hurt your back when you try to get up from a chair. See the box "Healthy Highlight: Women Lose Strength with Age Faster Than Men in Masters Weight Lifting."

As you age, motor nerves (the nerves that turn on muscle fibers) become disconnected from individual muscle fibers. In other words, as you get older, you develop loose connections between your nerves and your muscles. Muscle physiologists estimate that for most people, 15 percent of the motor nerves become disconnected from their muscle fibers by age 70. Doing strength exercises can prevent much of this loss.

Your muscles have fast and slow motor units. Fast motor units are used to perform quick, powerful movements, while slow motor units are used for slower movements, such as maintaining posture. In older muscles, the slower motor units start to take over, which makes powerful movements more difficult. Muscles become slower due to inactivity. Doing strength exercises prevents this. See the "Fact or Fiction?" box.

Weight training improves muscle metabolism in older adults, which helps prevent fat gain, coronary artery disease, and stroke. As they age, many people have problems processing sugar, leading to increased fat deposition in the abdomen, elevated blood cholesterol and triglycerides, high blood pressure, and blood clotting problems. Increasing muscle mass through weight training alleviates these metabolic problems and reduces the risk of many degenerative diseases that often accompany aging.

Strength also improves joint health and performance. Joints become stiff and lose their range of motion with disuse. Weight training loads the cartilage cells that line joints, keeping them lubricated and healthy. You can promote increased range of motion by doing the exercises through the full ranges of joint motion. A progressive weight-training program helps maintain joint health.

## Kneecap Pain

Women are particularly susceptible to kneecap pain because their wider pelvis tends to draw the kneecap laterally (to the outside of the joint) (Figure 2–4, p. 23). This tends to put increased pressure on the underside of the kneecap and causes pain. However, this condition is not uncommon in men. If your kneecaps ever hurt while you are sitting down, be careful not to make the problem worse by putting excess pressure on the joint.

Some weight-training exercises can lessen kneecap pain by building up the muscle on the inside of the thigh (vastus medialis). Appropriate exercises are described in Chapter 10. Also, keeping the hamstring muscles (those on the back of your thigh) as flexible as possible reduces pressure on the kneecap.

# FACT OR FICTION?

*MYTH: MUSCLE TURNS INTO FAT WHEN YOU QUIT TRAINING.*

Muscles don't turn into fat, but you may gain fat when you stop weight training. Muscle and fat are different tissues. Weight training builds muscle and may help you lose fat. When you stop weight training, your muscles atrophy—shrink in size—because they are no longer being stressed. You gain fat when you take in more calories than you burn. You may gain fat when you stop weight training because you lose muscle mass—a high-energy tissue that burns a lot of calories—and you are burning fewer calories during the day because you're less active.

# HEALTHY HIGHLIGHT

## WOMEN LOSE STRENGTH WITH AGE FASTER THAN MEN IN MASTERS WEIGHT LIFTING

Masters track and field, swimming, softball, weight lifting, and power lifting are growing in leaps and bounds. Men and women as old as age 100 years or older train and compete at high levels, providing scientists the opportunity to study how aging affects physical performance. University of Texas researchers found that strength decreased with age in power lifters, and decreased faster in women than in men. The decline with age was slower in weight-lifting performance (Olympic lifting) than in power lifting, but women's strength again declined faster than men's. Weight lifting requires more skill and finesse than power lifting, suggesting that older athletes can maintain performance levels longer in technique events. In both sports, performances declined substantially between young and middle age. Studying masters athletes to evaluate the effects of aging and gender on performance has its limitations. Top Olympic and professional athletes rarely compete seriously after retiring, so the quality of athlete is not the same in all age groups in cross-sectional studies. Also, masters women athletes did not have the same opportunity to learn their sport when they were young as do women athletes today, so their performances can't be compared. Anabolic steroid and growth hormone use is probably greater in younger athletes than in masters athletes, further obscuring true changes in performance with age. Men and women can maintain remarkable levels of strength and skill as they age if they continue training.

(*Medicine and Science in Sports and Exercise* 36: 143–147, 2004)

**Figure 2–4** The Q angle is formed by the axis of the femur and the axis of the patellar ligament. A wide Q angle causes the kneecap to be pulled outward. This may irritate the underside of the kneecap and cause knee pain.

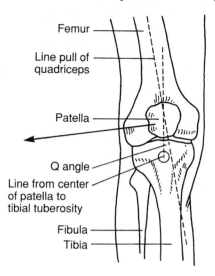

CAUTION ◆ Some weight-training exercises, such as knee extensions and full squats, may make kneecap pain worse. Check with a sports orthopedic physician or physical therapist if you are unsure which exercises are appropriate for you.

## Muscle Soreness

Delayed-onset muscle soreness is an overuse injury common in people who weight-train and typically occurs after eccentric exercise (the muscle exerts force as it lengthens). It usually appears 24 to 48 hours after strenuous exercise and results from tissue injury caused by muscle overload (Figure 2–5). High forces damage parts of the muscle cell responsible for contraction. Damage also causes release of calcium into the muscle. Excessive calcium is toxic to muscle. Substances released in response to the calcium further break down muscle tissue. The result is muscle soreness that peaks 24 to 72 hours after exercise. Gradually, the muscle fibers repair themselves and form proteins that protect the muscles from further damage. These protective proteins are fortified with further training but begin to disappear when you stop exercising. That's why if you stop training for 2 to 3 weeks, you are more susceptible to muscle soreness. Avoid excessive muscle soreness by increasing the volume and intensity of your workout *gradually.* And, to prevent protective proteins from dissipating, avoid long layoffs from training. Some studies show that taking nonsteroidal anti-inflammatory drugs, such as ibuprofen and aspirin, and applying ice packs may lessen muscle soreness.

**Figure 2–5** Delayed-onset muscle soreness. Damage to the muscle results in tissue inflammation. Substances are formed that break down muscle tissue. Muscle soreness results. With time, the cells regenerate.

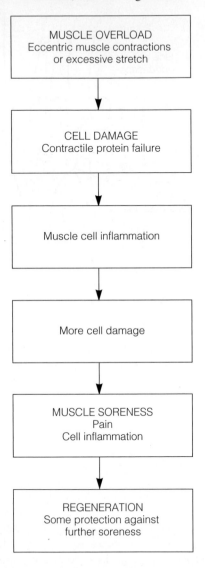

C H A P T E R

# 3 WEIGHT TRAINING GUIDELINES

Your opponent, in the end, is never really the player on the other side of the net, or the swimmer in the next lane, or the team on the other side of the field, or even the bar you must high jump. Your opponent is yourself, your negative internal voices, your level of determination.

—GRACE LICHTENSTEIN

THE HUMAN BODY IS A REMARKABLE ORGANISM BECAUSE IT ADAPTS TO THE PHYSICAL requirements of daily life. If you lift heavy objects regularly, then your muscles get stronger. If you seldom exercise, then your muscles will be small, reflecting your sedentary lifestyle.

Weight training works best when you have a plan. The plan helps you make progress in small steps that bring you closer and closer to your eventual goal. The training principles presented in this chapter are very simple but are guaranteed to bring results if followed faithfully.

When you train, you are acting very much like a doctor who works to cure a disease. You administer a treatment (e.g., a workout involving weight training, swimming, or running) to change the body's functioning (to improve fitness). When you train with weights, you're stimulating your body to improve communications between nerves and muscles and you're getting the muscles to make more protein, which makes them stronger and improves their tone. Through training, you are compelling your body to adapt to increased demands and to improve its ability to function.

Design your training program to increase fitness and prevent injury (see discussion of stress adaptation in Chapter 4 and Figure 4–1). Every time you plan a workout, ask yourself whether this exercise session is going to help your body improve its functioning. The answer won't always be yes. Sometimes rest is more appropriate than exercise, or a less intense workout is better than an exhausting one. The basic purpose of a workout is to introduce a stress you can adapt to, but not one so severe that you break down.

To get the most from your weight-training program, I recommend following 14 training guidelines. These guidelines will lead to gradual and long-lasting fitness development and to improved performance with the smallest risk of injury.

1. *Train the way you want your body to change.* If your main interest is general fitness, choose a well-rounded program that concentrates on the major muscle groups. Besides your weight-training routine, your program should include endurance and flexibility exercises. Weight training alone will not develop all-around physical fitness.

    Work on your weaknesses. For example, if you are a skier, having strong, flexible lower-body muscles is more important than having strong arms and shoulders. Analyze what you're doing. A well-designed program will be more effective and less time-consuming.

2. *Do the exercises properly.* Maintain good posture and a neutral position of your spine when doing weight-training exercises. Train intensely, but don't use so much weight that you can't maintain the correct technique.

3. *Eat a well-balanced, high-performance diet.* During the past 20 years, sports scientists have shown that the right diet can improve performance and keep off unwanted pounds of fat. Eat a sensible, nutritious diet (one containing plenty of fruits, vegetables, whole grains, nonfat dairy foods, lean meats, fish, poultry, and healthy fats such as omega-3 fatty acids) that supplies enough calories to meet your energy needs but still allows you to control your weight. If you want to lose weight, do so gradually—lose no more than 2½ pounds per week. If you are training hard, eat more carbohydrates and fewer fats.

4. *Train year-round.* If you take too much time off from your exercise program, you will lose the gains you've made and be more susceptible to injury if you then try to get back in shape rapidly. Establish a year-round program with specific goals and procedures for each period of the year—and stick to it.

    Make sure you have alternative training plans for times when the weather is bad or when you don't have access to a weight room. For example, if you are on a trip, substitute calisthenic exercises—such as push-ups and sit-ups—for your regular routine. Set aside a certain part of the day for your exercise routine to ensure you will get that workout. Your exercise time is the part of the day that belongs to you alone. Don't let anyone take it away.

5. *Get in shape gradually.* Training is a stress the body must overcome, so give your body time to adapt to the stress of exercise. Muscles are more susceptible to injury during the early phases of conditioning. Overzealous training, or intense conditioning when you aren't prepared for it, will lead to injury and delay progress.

    Staying in good shape all year is much easier than trying to achieve fitness in a few months. It's much easier to apply a little pressure rather than going on a crash conditioning program.

6. *Don't train when you're ill or seriously injured.* The body has problems trying to fight more than one stressor simultaneously. Training when you are sick or injured may seriously hinder your progress or even be dangerous. It is particularly important not to train when you have a fever. After an injury, you can return to intense workouts if you can answer yes to these questions:

   ◆ Can you move the injured area (joint, muscle, etc.) normally?
   ◆ Do you have normal strength and power?
   ◆ Are normal movement patterns restored (more than 90 percent recovered)?
   ◆ Are you relatively pain free?

   If the answer to any of these questions is no, then let the injury heal (through a combination of **rehabilitation** and rest) or modify your program before resuming your normal workout. Dealing effectively with injuries is just as important as having a well-designed training program.

7. *Train first for **volume** (more repetitions) and only later for **intensity** (more weight or resistance).* Soft tissues, such as muscle, tendons, and ligaments, take a long time to adjust to the rigors of training. If your goal is to get as strong as possible, begin your program by doing more repetitions, not by adding weight. This will prevent injury, strengthen your body gradually, and prepare it for heavy training. See the box "Healthy Highlight: *Dietary Guidelines for Americans 2005* Recommend 60 to 90 Minutes of Exercise per Day."

 **HEALTHY HIGHLIGHT**

*DIETARY GUIDELINES FOR AMERICANS 2005* RECOMMEND 60 TO 90 MINUTES OF EXERCISE PER DAY

Fifty percent of Americans do not exercise moderately 30 minutes a day, and only 12 percent exercise vigorously—defined as training 3 to 5 days per week for at least 20 minutes above 50 percent of maximum effort. Twenty-five percent of Americans do not exercise at all. The new exercise recommendations from the U.S. Department of Agriculture and the U.S. Department of Health and Human Services will be a challenge to most Americans. They advise at least 30 minutes of moderate-intensity physical activity on most days of the week if the goal is greater health and the prevention of chronic disease. People should exercise moderately to vigorously for 60 minutes per day to prevent weight gain, and 60 to 90 minutes a day to maintain weight loss. Physical activity should include aerobics, strength training, and flexibility exercises. Physical fitness should be achieved through cardiovascular conditioning, stretching exercises for flexibility, and resistance exercises or calisthenics for muscle strength and endurance. Children should exercise for at least 60 minutes every day.

(www.healthierus.gov/dietaryguidelines, January 2005)

During later training sessions, when you're in shape, you can use more weight and fewer repetitions to increase strength at a faster rate. If your goal is to have good muscle tone and muscular endurance, continue to do more repetitions instead of using more weight.

8. *Listen to your body.* Don't stick to your planned program too rigidly if it doesn't feel right. Sometimes your body needs rest more than it needs exercise. However, if your body always tells you to rest, you won't make any progress. Most studies show that intense workouts are essential for improving fitness. If you never feel like training hard, it may be that you have a medical problem or lack motivation.

9. *Vary the volume and intensity of your workouts.* **Cycle training,** or **periodization of training,** is a technique that allows the body to recover more fully and to train hard when intense training is required. The principle is simple: You do a particular exercise more intensely in one workout than in another rather than training at maximum intensity for every exercise during every weight-training session.

   Although sophisticated workout cycles are most suitable to athletes, anyone can benefit from them because they help increase strength more rapidly. If your goal is to improve muscle tone and body composition (the proportion of fat to fat-free weight), you can also benefit from cycle training. Try varying the exercises in your workouts. For example, instead of doing bench presses 3 days a week, substitute incline presses on 1 day. Cycle training makes working out with weights more interesting and helps you progress faster.

10. *Don't overtrain.* This principle is difficult to stick to because it opposes the work ethic ingrained in so many of us. Think of conditioning as a long-term process. Adaptations to training happen gradually. Too much training tends to lead to overtraining and overuse injuries, not faster development of fitness. Signs of **overtraining** include fatigue, decreased performance, irritability, and sometimes depression. Typically, an overtrained person has not recovered enough to train hard; a few days' rest is sometimes necessary to provide enough recovery to allow for more intense training.

11. *Train systematically.* Plan a proper workout schedule for the coming months, but don't be so rigid that you can't change the program to fit unforeseen circumstances. The important thing is that you have a plan that allows you to comfortably and consistently improve fitness.

   A coach, training partner, and training diary will help make your workouts more systematic. A good coach or instructor can keep you from making common mistakes and will help motivate you to meet your fitness goals. People who need more motivation may make rapid gains with a personal trainer who works with them during their workout.

   A training partner is important for motivation and safety. This person can encourage you and **spot** (assist) you during the exercise. He or she will share the agony and ecstasy that accompany training.

   Writing down what you hope to achieve in a training diary or on a workout card will help you attain your fitness goals. Use your diary to keep track of which training techniques work for you and which don't. A sample workout card is attached to the back cover of this book.

12. *Train your mind.* One of the most difficult skills to acquire—but one critical for attaining high levels of physical fitness—is mind control. To become physically fit or to succeed as an athlete, you must believe in yourself and in your potential, have goals, and know how to achieve these goals. This requires discipline and is an ongoing process.

13. *Learn all you can about exercise.* If you know why the various components of training are important, you are much more likely to plan an intelligent, effective program. You will be less likely to jump into every training fad that comes along, and you will always be in control of your own training program. If you are informed, you'll buy better and more economical sports equipment, be able to manage many of your own athletic injuries, and have a more efficient training routine.

14. *Keep the exercise program in its proper perspective.* Too often, the exercise program acquires an unequal emphasis in a person's life. Some people think of themselves almost solely as football players, body builders, aerobic dancers, runners, triathletes, or swimmers rather than as human beings who participate in those activities. Although exercise is important, you must also have time for other aspects of your life. Leading a well-rounded life will not diminish your chances of achieving your exercise goals and will make your training program more enjoyable.

These 14 weight training guidelines are summarized in Table 3–1.

---

### TABLE 3–1
### Weight Training Guidelines

- Train the way you want your body to change.
- Do the exercises properly.
- Eat a well-balanced, high-performance diet.
- Train year-round.
- Get in shape gradually.
- Don't train when you're ill or seriously injured.
- Train first for volume (more repetitions) and only later for intensity (more weight or resistance).
- Listen to your body.
- Vary the volume and intensity of your workouts.
- Don't overtrain.
- Train systematically.
- Train your mind.
- Learn all you can about exercise.
- Keep the exercise program in its proper perspective.

---

# WEIGHT TRAINING AS PART OF THE TOTAL FITNESS PROGRAM

Exercise training is an attempt to mold your body in order to improve it. Your body changes according to the way you stress it. If you work your muscles to exert more force than normal, the muscles get stronger. If you exercise for extended periods, your endurance improves. You can tailor your program to develop the kind of fitness you want.

## Determining Your Goals

There are many weight-training exercises and programs. The right one for you depends on your goals. For example, if your goal is to have a lean, fit body, your program will be different from that of someone trying to improve fitness for sports. Whatever your ultimate goal, it is best to begin the program by doing 10 to 15 repetitions before trying heavy loads. Specific programs for a variety of goals appear in Appendix 3.

## Developing an Attractive, Healthy-Looking Body

Developing a slim, shapely body is no easy task. Much of the problem stems from bad information and unrealistic expectations about the methods and benefits of weight training. Several principles apply to people interested in developing an attractive, healthy-looking body.

The first principle is to *reduce body fat.* Weight training alone won't do it! Energy balance, discussed in detail in Chapter 12, determines the control of body fat: If you consume more energy than you expend through metabolism (body chemistry) and exercise, then you gain fat; conversely, you lose fat when you expend more energy than you take in. Control body fat by eating a well-balanced diet containing adequate but not excessive calories (energy) and by doing aerobic exercise in addition to weight training.

---

**CAUTION** ♦ Don't try to improve the appearance of your body through weight training alone. Weight training should be part of a general program that includes a sensible diet and aerobic exercise.

---

Weight training affects mainly your muscles, which are covered by a layer of fat and skin. Increasing strength and muscle tone will do nothing if the muscles are covered by a lot of fat. Weight training *will* improve the appearance of your body if you lose fat gradually, don't develop too much loose skin, and gain muscle mass. Then the increased size of the muscles gives your body a leaner, more attractive shape. (See the "Fact or Fiction?" box.)

Weight-training exercises trigger metabolic changes in the cells that decrease fat accumulation, particularly in the abdomen. They can also improve the appearance of certain parts of the body, particularly the abdomen, to some degree. The exercises increase muscle tone, which makes the body part look tighter—but the fat will stay unless you shift the general energy balance. There is no such thing as spot reducing: You cannot lose fat in one area of the body by exercising nearby muscles.

## FACT OR FICTION?

*MYTH: WEIGHT TRAINING MAKES YOU "MUSCLE-BOUND."*

Many people think that weight training makes people lose flexibility and joint range of motion. Building extremely large muscles and not doing exercises through a full range of motion will decrease joint range of motion, but you will increase joint flexibility and range of motion if you do the exercises properly.

The second principle is to build muscle size through high-intensity, high-volume exercise. Combined with reduced fat, this will help tone and firm up your body. Muscles get bigger when they are subjected to heavy loads (i.e., high muscle tension).

People who don't want to increase muscle bulk should not do very much high-repetition weight training to the point of muscle failure. Instead, they should do more repetitions and use less weight or do just a few repetitions using heavy weights. Such programs will help tone your muscles, but they develop strength more slowly than more intense programs.

**CAUTION**    ♦  If you want to prevent excessive muscle bulk and tend to put on a lot of muscle tissue when you weight-train, avoid doing sets to failure. Instead, do more repetitions and use less weight, or do only a few repetitions and use more weight.

The third principle involved in developing a great-looking body is to develop muscle definition. **Muscle definition** is the elusive property of muscles that allows their structure to be defined and seen more clearly. For example, legs look a lot better when defined muscle gives them more shape. The way to achieve muscle definition is through high-set, high-repetition workouts. However, high numbers of repetitions and sets are of limited value in improving muscle definition if you have too much body fat.

## Improving Strength for Other Activities

Physical stress is necessary for improved fitness. Each sport or physical activity has specific physical demands. Skiers need strong leg muscles with plenty of endurance. Golfers need strong forearm, back, and leg muscles. Structure the weight-training routine to meet the needs of the sport.

It is also important to focus on muscles and joints that commonly are injured in sports. For example, many swimmers and tennis players get shoulder ("rotator-cuff") injuries. Unfortunately, loosely structured weight-training programs seldom condition these muscles—

until you injure them. It makes a lot more sense to precondition vulnerable joints and muscles to prevent injury.

Three major weight-training principles to practice for increasing strength for sports and daily physical activities are:

- ◆ Identify and train muscles and joints particularly important in the activity.
- ◆ Identify and train muscles and joints prone to injury in the activity.
- ◆ Maintain a good level of fitness in the major muscle groups of the body.

## Developing Strength and Power for Sports

More and more people are interested in building strength for its own sake. There are weight-lifting competitions for men and women in power lifting and weight lifting (popularly known as Olympic weight lifting). Power lifting involves **maximum lifts** in the bench press, squat, and dead lift. Weight lifting (Olympic weight lifting) consists of the clean and jerk and snatch.

Many people want to improve strength and fitness for high power sports, such as track and field. The weight-training programs for such people center on three types of weight-lifting exercises: presses, pulls, and multijoint lower-body exercises. Presses include the bench press, incline press, military press, seated press, push-press, jerks, and dumbbell press. Pulls include cleans, snatches, high pulls, and dead lifts. Multijoint lower-body exercises include squats, leg presses, hack squats, and rack squats.

Generally, use heavy loads (70 to 100 percent of your maximum) and a moderate number of repetitions (1 to 8 reps) to gain maximum strength and power. Do supporting exercises to develop arm, back, abdominal, calf, and neck muscle strength (depending on the sport). However, presses, pulls, and multijoint lower-body exercises form the core of the program.

High-power athletes have many training philosophies. Traditional programs often involved 3 days of training per week using as much weight as possible for each lift, and each workout was alike. Today, new ideas have hit the scene. Athletes and coaches have found that doing all three types of strength–speed exercises during each workout hinders recovery, leads to overtraining, and delays progress. Cycle training, in which the volume and intensity of exercises vary from workout to workout and at different times of the year, speeds up progress (Chapter 5 describes cycle training in greater detail).

## WEIGHT TRAINING AS PART OF A GENERAL CONDITIONING AND WELLNESS PROGRAM

Strength training is an essential part of your physical fitness program, particularly as you get older. Fitness has many components, including cardiorespiratory endurance, muscular strength and endurance, flexibility, healthy body composition, and sports-related fitness. Each component is developed in a particular way in each sport or physical activity. For example, a person may have excellent endurance on a ski slope but poor endurance on the running track or in the swimming pool. To be fit for a variety of activities, you have to practice all of those activities. Regular participation in weight, flexibility, and endurance training will carry over into most of the activities of daily life and will improve your performance.

Despite the many benefits of an active lifestyle, levels of physical activity have declined in recent years and remain low for all populations of Americans. More than 60 percent of U.S. adults do not engage in recommended amounts of physical activity; 25 percent are not active at all. In the summer of 1996, the U.S. Surgeon General published *Physical Activity and Health,* a landmark report designed to reverse these trends and get Americans moving. The report summarized current knowledge about the relationship between physical activity and health; its major findings include these:

- ◆ People of all ages benefit from regular physical activity.

- ◆ People can obtain significant health benefits by including a moderate amount of physical activity on most if not all days of the week. Through a modest increase in daily activity, most Americans can improve their health and quality of life.

- ◆ Additional health benefits can be gained through greater amounts of physical activity. People who maintain a regular regimen of more vigorous or longer-duration activity are likely to obtain even greater benefits.

- ◆ Evidence is growing that simply becoming more physically active may be the single most important lifestyle change for promoting health and well-being.

The U.S. Department of Agriculture (USDA) and the Department of Health and Human Services (DHHS) recently issued new dietary guidelines to reflect new knowledge in nutrition and health. The new guidelines—issued in January 2005—include recommendations about exercise that mark a new chapter in the war against America's bulging waistlines. The USDA and DHHS increased the recommended amount of exercise from 30 to 60 minutes per day. The average person expends about 480 calories an hour during exercise, enough to lose a pound of fat when done 7 days a week. Exercising any less can cause a downward spiral of small monthly weight gains. The message from the USDA and DHHS reflects the hard truth—if you want to be lean, you have to work for it. (See the box "Healthy Highlight" on p. 27.)

## Choosing Activities for a Balanced Physical Fitness Program

An ideal fitness program combines a physically active lifestyle with a systematic exercise program designed to develop and maintain physical fitness. This overall program is illustrated in the physical activity pyramid in Figure 3–1. If you are currently sedentary, your goal is to start at the bottom of the pyramid and gradually increase the amount of moderate-intensity physical activity in your daily life. Appropriate activities include brisk walking, climbing stairs, working in the yard, and washing your car. You don't have to exercise vigorously, but you should experience a moderate increase in your heart and breathing rates. Your activity time can be broken up into small blocks over the course of a day. The time it takes to walk to the library, climb a flight of stairs five times, and clean the house can quickly add up to 30 or more minutes of moderate activity.

The next two levels of the pyramid illustrate parts of a formal exercise program. The American College of Sports Medicine has established guidelines for creating an exercise

**Figure 3–1** Physical activity pyramid. This physical activity pyramid is designed to help people become more active. If you are currently sedentary, begin at the bottom of the pyramid and gradually increase the amount of moderate-intensity physical activity in your life. If you are already moderately active, begin a formal exercise program that includes cardiorespiratory endurance exercise, flexibility training, and strength training to help you develop all the health-related components of fitness.

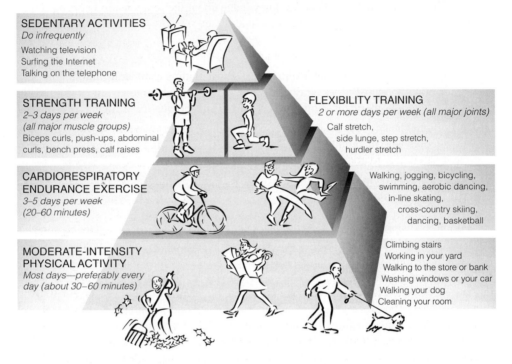

SEDENTARY ACTIVITIES
*Do infrequently*
Watching television
Surfing the Internet
Talking on the telephone

STRENGTH TRAINING
*2–3 days per week*
*(all major muscle groups)*
Biceps curls, push-ups, abdominal
curls, bench press, calf raises

FLEXIBILITY TRAINING
*2 or more days per week (all major joints)*
Calf stretch,
    side lunge, step stretch,
    hurdler stretch

CARDIORESPIRATORY
ENDURANCE EXERCISE
*3–5 days per week*
*(20–60 minutes)*

Walking, jogging, bicycling,
swimming, aerobic dancing,
in-line skating,
    cross-country skiing,
    dancing, basketball

MODERATE-INTENSITY
PHYSICAL ACTIVITY
*Most days—preferably every
day (about 30–60 minutes)*

Climbing stairs
Working in your yard
Walking to the store or bank
Washing windows or your car
Walking your dog
Cleaning your room

program that will develop physical fitness (Table 3–2). A balanced program includes activities for developing all the health-related components of fitness.

♦ *Cardiorespiratory endurance* is developed by activities that involve continuous rhythmic movements of large-muscle groups. Walking, jogging, cycling, swimming, and aerobic dancing (also referred to as "group exercise") are all good activities for developing cardiorespiratory endurance. Choose activities that you enjoy and that are convenient. Many popular leisure activities can develop endurance, including in-line skating, dancing, and backpacking. Start-and-stop activities such as tennis, racquetball, and soccer can also develop endurance if your skill level is sufficient to enable periods of continuous play.

**TABLE 3–2**
**Exercise Recommendations for Healthy Adults**

*Exercise to Develop and Maintain*
*Cardiorespiratory Endurance and Body Composition*

| | |
|---|---|
| Mode of activity | Any activity that uses large-muscle groups, can be maintained continuously, and is rhythmic and aerobic in nature; for example, walking-hiking, running-jogging, cycling-bicycling, cross-country skiing, group exercise (aerobic dancing), rope skipping, rowing, stair climbing, swimming, skating, and endurance game activities. |
| Frequency of training | 3–5 days per week. |
| Intensity of training | 55/65–90 percent of maximum heart rate or 40/50–85 percent of maximum oxygen uptake reserve. The lower-intensity values (55–64 percent of maximum heart rate and 40–49 percent of maximum oxygen uptake reserve) are most applicable to individuals who are quite unfit. |
| Duration of training | 20–60 total minutes of continuous or intermittent (in sessions lasting 10 or more minutes) aerobic activity. Duration is dependent on the intensity of activity; thus, lower-intensity activity should be conducted over a longer period of time (30 minutes or more). Lower- to moderate-intensity activity of longer duration is recommended for the nonathletic adult. |

*Exercise to Develop and Maintain Muscular*
*Strength and Endurance, Flexibility, and Body Composition*

| | |
|---|---|
| Resistance training | One set of 8–10 exercises that condition the major muscle groups should be performed 2–3 days per week. Most people should complete 8–12 repetitions of each exercise; for older and frailer people (approximately 50–60 years of age and above), 10–15 repetitions with a lighter weight may be more appropriate. Multiple-set regimens may provide greater benefits if time allows. |
| Flexibility training | Stretches for the major muscle groups should be performed a minimum of 2–3 days per week; at least 4 repetitions, held for 10–30 seconds, should be completed. |

*Source:* American College of Sports Medicine, 1998. Position Stand: The Recommended Quantity and Quality of Exercise for Developing and Maintaining Cardiorespiratory and Muscular Fitness, and Flexibility in Healthy Adults. *Medicine and Science in Sports and Exercise* 30(6): 975–991.

- *Muscular strength and endurance,* the primary focus of this book, can be developed through resistance training—training with weights or performing calisthenic exercises such as push-ups and sit-ups.

- *Flexibility* is developed by stretching the major muscle groups regularly and with proper technique.

- *Healthy body composition* can be developed by combining a sensible diet and a program of regular exercise. Endurance exercise is best for reducing body fat; resistance training builds muscle mass, which helps increase metabolism (the rate of energy expenditure).

- *Sports-related fitness* is developed by practicing the sport. Many sports, particularly the strength–speed sports, such as tennis, football, basketball, and soccer, require power and speed for optimal performance. In addition to practicing sports skills, include speed exercises and plyometric (i.e., muscle "bouncing") exercises in your program to improve performance in your sport (see Chapter 11).

Participate in as many activities as time allows, but don't get stuck in a rut or overemphasize one component of fitness. Too many people either weight-train or run—they forget the other areas of fitness. If your goal is to develop a healthy, attractive body capable of doing many activities, you are better off participating in several types of exercise (endurance, strength, and flexibility) than concentrating on only one.

CHAPTER

# 4

# HOW WEIGHT TRAINING IMPROVES YOUR BODY

To exercise at or near capacity is the best way I know of reaching a true introspective state. If you do it right, it can open all kinds of inner doors.

AL OERTER, FOUR-TIME OLYMPIC GOLD MEDAL WINNER IN THE DISCUS

WEIGHT TRAINING IS MUCH LIKE A SAVINGS ACCOUNT TO WHICH YOU ADD A SMALL AMOUNT of money each week. The money from any weekly deposit will not make you rich, but the accumulated small deposits can add up to a lot of money. A single weight-training session will not improve fitness very much, but if you add up the effects of months of training, improvements will be substantial.

## STRESS ADAPTATION

When you subject your body to a **stress** such as exercise, the result is either **adaptation** or breakdown. You get injured when your body can't handle the stress (see Figure 4–1). The purpose of a training program is to subject the body to a physical stress to which it can adapt—not a stress so severe it causes injury. Every time you walk into the weight room, ask yourself how the workout is helping your body adapt and become stronger. Sometimes you will have to train harder to accelerate the rate of adaptation. At other times you will need to rest to get the most from your program. See the "Fact or Fiction?" box on p. 39.

**Figure 4–1**  Stress adaptation. Reasonable exercise stress causes improved fitness, but excessive stress causes injury.

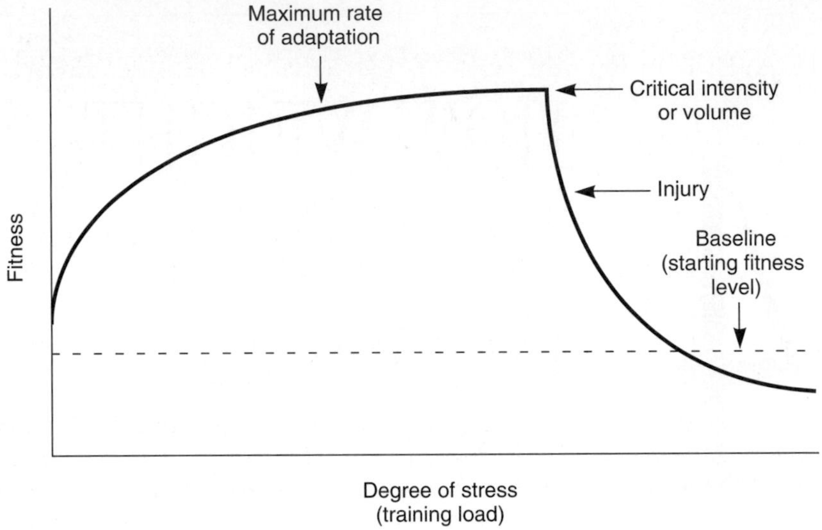

## Overload

The basis of stress adaptation is **overload,** which exposes the body to more stress than is normal. The components of overload are load, repetition, rest, and frequency. Each factor affects the others. For example, if load is high, then repetitions are usually lower and rest is longer.

**Load** is the intensity of exercise, the amount of **resistance,** or weight, used during the movement. Generally, the greater the load, the faster you fatigue and the longer it takes to recover. Of all the components of overload, load is probably the most important for gaining strength. High loads lead to the fastest improvements in strength and muscle size. If you are gaining more muscle mass than you want, keep the resistance down and increase repetitions.

A **repetition** is one performance of an exercise. A **set** is a group of repetitions followed by rest. Adaptation tends to happen more quickly when you do an exercise more than once. Beginners should initially use 10 to 12 repetitions and 1 to 3 sets per exercise. After 2 to 3 weeks of training, do 3 sets per exercise, with the same number of repetitions, but use more weight. Advanced routines will include between 1 and 15 repetitions, depending on the purpose of the training program. Many fitness experts currently recommend doing only 1 set of 8 to 10 exercises. They contend that the vast majority of studies show that doing 1 set of an exercise is just as effective for gaining strength as doing 2 or more sets. Studies with this finding were conducted for as long as 6 months and included trained and untrained people as test participants. However, other researchers and strength experts scoff at this idea and feel that you get additional benefits by including 3 or more sets of each exercise in your program. Given this controversy, start with 1 set of each exercise and add more sets if you find your progress slowing.

FACT OR FICTION?

*MYTH: YOU SHOULD LIFT AS MUCH WEIGHT AS POSSIBLE AND TRAIN AS HARD AS YOU CAN EVERY TIME YOU LIFT WEIGHTS.*

High-tension training is best for increasing strength and muscle size. You must be adequately recovered in order to train intensely. You won't recover adequately if you are training maximally every time you exercise. Plan for high-intensity workouts. That means resting or training with less weight before target workouts during which you plan to train intensely. Rest prepares you for intense workouts.

**Rest,** the time between sets, is vitally important for adaptation and should be applied according to the desired result. For example, a weight lifter who wants maximum strength is most concerned with load and therefore needs considerable rest between exercises. A runner is more concerned with muscular **endurance** (the ability to sustain prolonged muscular exercise), so shorter rest intervals between sets are more appropriate.

**Frequency** is the number of training sessions per week. Most people who train with weights do so three times per week, but frequency may vary between two and five times per week. People who train with weights four or five times per week typically emphasize specific muscle groups during a workout. For example, they might exercise lower-body muscle groups on Monday and Thursday and upper-body muscles on Tuesday and Saturday.

Determine your frequency of training according to the desired result. Although intense training programs can improve performance in many sports, you should allow for proper recovery periods to avoid injury. More is not always better. Excessive training programs may also lead to overtraining, which will stall progress and cause injury. See the box "Healthy Highlight: Are You Overtrained?"

Consistency in training is also critical. You make large gains in small steps. Although overtraining is a critical problem for many people, inconsistency is the main problem the average person faces. You have to do your exercise routine regularly to improve fitness.

## Specificity of Training

The body adapts specifically to the stress of exercise. In other words, the adaptation to endurance exercise (e.g., distance running or swimming) is different from the adaptation to strength exercise (e.g., weight training) or power exercise (e.g., sprinting). Your training program and the exercises you choose should reflect the desired adaptation. The closer the training is to the requirements of the sport, the more valuable will be the result. If you are weight-training to get in shape for skiing, for example, then concentrate on lower-body exercises. If you're interested in improving your appearance, then do more varied exercises, concentrating on those parts of the body that need work.

## HEALTHY HIGHLIGHT

### ARE YOU OVERTRAINED?

Are you sick and tired of waking up sick and tired? Maybe you're overtrained. The consequences include decreased performance, injury, depressed immunity, and psychological depression. There is no single marker of overtraining, but signs include decreased performance, low energy level, the perception of fatigue, and an inability to improve from training. Other, more precise measures—such as hormone, fuel, and enzyme concentrations—often provide valuable information. Unfortunately, the usefulness of these measures is compromised by our lack of knowledge of the physiology of overtraining. Active people must carefully balance training intensity and volume with adequate rest, using simple measures such as experience, daily body weight, perception of effort and feelings of well-being, frequency of illness, and improvement in performance.

(*Sports Medicine* 34: 967–981, 2004)

## Individual Differences

Differences in body shape, strength, physical skill, and endurance determine how quickly we learn sports skills, how our body looks, and how we respond to an exercise program. Our ability to respond to any type of exercise program depends on genetics as well as on the intensity of training.

Even people with naturally well-defined bodies and good health will fail to get in top shape if they don't devote enough time and effort to training. However, people without genetic gifts of fitness may find it difficult to achieve superior levels of strength and body composition, even if they "kill" themselves in the weight room.

Most of us fall somewhere in the middle between Olympic champion and total klutz. A good training program helps us develop what gifts we have and overcome our weaknesses. Even the weakest among us can get strong if the training program is intense enough and if we're patient and train consistently and correctly.

## Reversibility

"If you don't use it, you'll lose it." That's an old maxim of exercise training. The purpose of weight training, or any other type of exercise, is to stress the muscles more than usual so that they will become stronger and larger. If you place less than normal stress on the muscles, your muscles will **atrophy** (shrink) and get weaker. In other words, gains made by training are subject to **reversibility.**

It is important to stay fit year-round. Maintaining fitness is much easier than regaining a level of conditioning you have lost. High levels of fitness and a great body call for many years of training and involve small stages of progression. Attempting to force the body to adapt rapidly will only cause injury.

# TYPES OF WEIGHT-TRAINING EXERCISES

People who weight-train want at least one of three of its main effects on the body: (1) an increase in muscular strength, (2) an increase in muscular power, and (3) a change in the muscular shape. **Strength** is the ability to exert force. **Power** is work divided by time—in other words, the ability to exert force rapidly. In most sports, power is more important than strength. Fortunately, exercises that develop strength also tend to develop power. Specific exercises to develop muscular power are discussed in Chapter 11.

Many people spend long hours developing strength in the weight room in order to increase power in sports. Tennis players, for example, often do bench presses or lat pulls so that they can serve and hit the ball harder. You lift weights more slowly than you raise your racket during a tennis match, yet the strength gained during the relatively slow weight-training exercises increases power in the faster tennis movements.

There are two kinds of strength exercises: isometric (static) and isotonic (dynamic). **Isometric** exercise involves applying force without movement; **dynamic** exercise is exerting force with movement. You can do these exercises concentrically or eccentrically. A **concentric muscle action** occurs when the muscle applies force as it shortens. This happens during the active phase of a weight-training exercise. In an **eccentric muscle action,** you exert force as the muscle lengthens, as, for example, when you lower the weight to begin the pushing phase of the exercise.

## Isometric Exercise

Isometric exercise is a static muscle contraction involving no movement. Immovable objects, such as a fixed bar or wall, provide resistance.

Although isometric exercise received considerable attention in the late 1950s, it is now less popular as a primary means of gaining strength. Isometric exercise does not increase strength through a joint's range of motion (unless practiced at various points in the range of motion); strength gains from isometrics occur only at or near the joint angle involved in practicing the exercise. Research studies have shown that isometric training will increase isometric force by 14 to 44 percent in 16 weeks. Hold isometric contractions for 3 to 5 seconds. Also, isometric training does not improve power. Too much isometric training may lead to injury.

Weight trainers occasionally use isometrics to overcome "sticking points" in an exercise's range of motion. For example, people who have difficulty pushing weights from the chest during the bench press may do the exercise isometrically at the point where they are having the most difficulty. They may use a **power rack** or **Smith machine** for this type of isometric training.

You can also do isometric exercise without using anything for resistance. For example, you can simply tighten and release the abdominal muscles, a good way to tone and strengthen them. This type of exercise is particularly valuable when you are recovering from an injury. Examples of isometric exercises useful for strengthening the lower back and abdomen appear in Chapters 8 and 9, respectively.

**Electrical muscle stimulation** (EMS) is a form of isometric exercise used by some people as a substitute for active movement. The EMS machine introduces a small electrical charge into the muscle, causing it to contract. EMS can build muscle strength and is particularly valuable for injured people who are not capable of active movement (e.g., following surgery). Beware of false claims that EMS is equal or superior to weight training or aerobic exercise. It has its place in the rehabilitation of injuries but is not suitable as a primary form of physical activity.

| CAUTION | ♦ Electrical muscle stimulation can cause injury if applied incorrectly. It is not an effective way for healthy people to gain strength or muscle size. |
|---|---|

## Dynamic Exercise

Dynamic exercise involves muscle contractions that result in movement. The most common and popular type of weight training, dynamic exercise may utilize weight machines, barbells, dumbbells, or the body's own weight (e.g., push-ups). Dynamic techniques include constant resistance, variable resistance, eccentric loading, plyometrics, speed loading, and isokinetic exercise.

*Dynamic constant resistance*   The most common form of weight-training exercise, **dynamic constant resistance** uses a constant load, such as a barbell or dumbbell, throughout the range of motion. Despite the fact that you are using a constant load (the same barbell or dumbbell) throughout the exercise, the *relative* resistance of the load varies with the angle of the joint, so it is usually easier to move the weight at the end of the movement, where you have better leverage, than at the beginning. Maximum loading therefore occurs at the weakest point in the range of motion.

*Dynamic variable resistance*   **Dynamic-variable-resistance** exercise involves special weight machines that change the load throughout the range of motion to put a more consistent stress on the muscles. Compared to dynamic-constant-resistance loads, dynamic-variable-resistance machines place more stress on the muscles at the end of the range of motion, where you have better leverage and are capable of exerting more force.

Many dynamic-variable-resistance machines are on the market, including those made by Ariel, Hammer, Universal, Nautilus, Eagle, Marcy, and Kaiser. Sports scientists have not yet determined whether this form of training is superior to dynamic-constant-resistance exercise. However, the machines are safe and easy to use, and they are extremely popular with many people.

*Eccentric loading*   As discussed earlier, **eccentric loading** occurs when the muscle lengthens while exerting force. Muscles contract eccentrically whenever you lower a weight into position prior to lifting it. This type of contraction is vital in training because it allows you to control the weight.

The active phase of most weight-training exercises (lifting the weight) is concentric. However, you can also do exercises solely eccentrically, a type of training popularly called "negatives." Eccentric loading is an effective way to gain strength and a useful supplement to concentric exercises.

Eccentric and concentric training improve both concentric and eccentric muscle strength. However, concentric training is more effective at improving concentric strength, while eccentric training is better for improving eccentric strength. This simple and obvious finding has important implications for training and rehabilitation. For example, hamstring strains in sprinters often occur when the hamstrings are contracting eccentrically. Optimal rehabilitation or preventive strengthening of the hamstrings is probably better accomplished through eccentric exercise than through concentric exercise. It is important to *train the body for the stresses you will encounter in your favorite sports.*

**CAUTION**    ♦ Eccentric exercise can cause extreme muscle soreness.

One drawback of eccentric loading is that it seems to cause more muscle soreness than other methods. The high tensions generated by this technique cause injury in the muscle that results in muscle soreness 1 to 2 days after the workout (see Chapter 2). Increase the volume and intensity of eccentric loading very gradually.

***Plyometrics***    **Plyometrics** involves sudden eccentric loading and stretching of muscles followed by forceful concentric contraction. The sudden stretch stimulates receptors in the muscles to react, and the muscles' own elasticity causes a stronger contraction when they shorten.

Plyometrics is an effective way to develop power and speed. This form of exercise is particularly effective in improving communication between the muscles and the nervous system (see "Skeletal Muscle Structure" in Chapter 2). Exercises to improve power and speed, including plyometrics, are discussed in Chapter 11.

**CAUTION**    ♦ Plyometrics can cause injury if practiced excessively. Begin with only a few repetitions of these exercises and increase the volume and intensity very gradually. Begin with ground exercises before progressing to box jumping. Don't attempt box jumping until your legs are strong enough to handle the load.

***Speed loading***    **Speed loading** (see Chapter 11) involves moving a weight as rapidly as possible in an attempt to approach the speeds used in movements such as throwing a softball or sprinting. This type of exercise may be effective in improving power (the ability to exert force rapidly). For gaining strength, weight training at ordinary speeds is superior to speed loading because speed loading prevents the muscles from creating sufficient tension to cause a training effect.

***Isokinetic exercise***    Also called "accommodating resistance exercise," **isokinetic** exercise involves muscle contraction at a constant speed. The exerted force is resisted by an equal force from the isokinetic machine. Because you feel resistance only when you're applying force, therapists consider isokinetics safer than other forms of strength training. Isokinetic devices are used for strength training and measurement at fast speeds of movement.

Promoters of isokinetic strength-training equipment claim that the machines improve power, the type of strength needed in most sports. Physical therapists use them for rehabilitating muscle and joint injuries. These machines are considerably more expensive than traditional weight-training equipment, and thus are not as widely available.

CHAPTER

# 5 GETTING STARTED: THE BASICS

Far better is it to dare mighty things, to win glorious triumphs, even though checkered by failure, than to take rank with these poor spirits who neither enjoy much nor suffer much. Be wise, they live in the gray twilight that know not of victory, nor defeat. Nor true sorrow nor true love.

—THEODORE ROOSEVELT

STARTING A NEW TYPE OF EXERCISE PROGRAM IS A LOT LIKE MOVING TO A NEW TOWN— you feel awkward, and everything is new and strange. To begin weight training, you must first make some decisions: what clothes to wear, which exercises to do, and where to train. When you know the basics, you'll feel more at ease, your program will be safer and more enjoyable, and you'll be on the path to becoming an informed fitness consumer.

## MEDICAL CHECKUP

Before beginning a program, you should determine if weight training is suitable for you. Most people can exercise safely if they are in good health and follow basic training principles. However, exercise may pose a risk to health and well-being for people with pre-existing medical conditions, such as coronary artery disease. People who die suddenly from heart attacks—some of them during exercise—usually have risk factors of coronary artery disease, such as high blood pressure or cigarette smoking, that predispose them to the disease. Medical screening can help identify people who should not exercise or who should exercise only on a modified program. For most people, it is safer to exercise than to remain sedentary. To paraphrase exercise scientist Per Olaf Åstrand: If you don't want to exercise, you should see a physician to determine if you can withstand the physical deterioration that occurs with the sedentary lifestyle.

Men 40 years and older and women 50 years and older, or any person with significant health problems, should get a medical examination before beginning a vigorous exercise program. If you are younger than that and in good health, there is nothing preventing you from entering a weight-training program. Health problems that need medical evaluation include high blood pressure, coronary artery disease, stroke, obesity, and musculoskeletal disorders.

It is best to choose a physician who is knowledgeable about exercise and, ideally, has training in exercise physiology or **sports medicine,** which deals with the medical problems of athletes. Local health clubs, college exercise-physiology departments, and medical societies are often good sources for referrals to physicians with knowledge of sports medicine.

If you are over 40 to 50 (depending on your gender) or have significant health problems, beware of health clubs or fitness classes that offer fitness screening without proper medical supervision. Fitness evaluations by nonphysicians are not substitutes for a pre-training medical examination, and relying on them could be dangerous. Organizations such as the American College of Sports Medicine and the American Heart Association have established guidelines for fitness testing of adults and children (see the References section at the end of this book). Make sure your club follows these guidelines.

## WHAT TO WEAR

Sports clothing has come a long way since the old high-school gym suit. Modern exercise clothing is attractive, comfortable, and functional. Shorts made of elastic material, such as spandex, hug the body, supplying support. If you prefer, you can wear running shorts and a T-shirt. The main requirement for workout clothes is that they let you move easily but are not so loose that they get caught in the exercise machines. Don't wear street clothes in a weight room, because sweat, oil, and dirt can ruin them.

### Shoes

Wear shoes that provide good lateral support, such as tennis shoes, aerobics shoes, or cross-training shoes. It is important that you wear shoes at all times to protect your feet against falling weights and being stepped on.

If competitive weight lifting interests you, consider buying a pair of weight-lifting shoes. They provide excellent lateral support and raise your heels slightly to give you better balance during your lifts. These shoes are available through weight-lifting and fitness magazines, such as *Powerlifting USA* or *Muscular Development,* or from leading sports shoe companies, such as Adidas, Nike, and Puma. Hiking boots, which have a low heel, are a good substitute.

## Weight-Lifting Belt

Many experts urge weight trainers to wear a **weight-lifting belt** when doing whole body exercises, such as squats, dead lifts, Olympic lifts, and bench presses. They believe that the belts prevent injuries by stabilizing the spine. However, most studies show that back belts do not prevent on-the-job injuries in people who do manual labor. Some researchers think that back braces give people a sense of invincibility, leading them to lift beyond their capacity and get injured.

Belts will enable you to lift more weight during squats, cleans, snatches, and bench presses, but you won't condition the stabilizing muscles of the trunk. Don't use a belt when training. Do your lifts strictly and lift within your capacity. Use a belt only when you are attempting maximum lifts and want to achieve maximum performance. When using a belt, cinch it tightly to get the maximum benefit. See the "Fact or Fiction?" box.

| CAUTION | ♦ Don't rely solely on a belt to protect your back. Good lifting technique and strong, flexible muscles with good endurance are critical for preventing back injury. |
|---|---|

Belts come in a variety of colors that complement exercise clothing and look fashionable and attractive. You can buy them through exercise equipment stores or fitness magazines.

## Lifting Shirts and Suits

Serious power lifters often use special clothing, such as bench shirts or stiff lifting suits, to help them lift more weight. This clothing is made of very stiff material that provides a "rebound effect" as you do bench presses or squats. While lifting shirts and suits are effective, they should not be used consistently during workouts. They may decondition stabilizing muscles that normally would be trained if you weren't wearing the special clothing.

## Wraps

**Wraps** support injured joints or provide extra support. They can be made of elastic bandages, athletic tape, leather, or neoprene. Although many advanced weight trainers use wraps to support their knees, wrists, or elbows, wraps are unnecessary for the recreational weight trainer.

Some people use wraps to counteract knee pain during and after weight-training sessions. Knee pain has many causes, and one cause is that the kneecap puts too much pressure on the bone underneath. Knee wraps may increase this pressure and make the pain worse. One solution is to buy a knee wrap with a hole built in for the kneecap. The wrap provides support, while the hole reduces pressure on the kneecap.

## FACT OR FICTION?

*MYTH: YOU SHOULD WEAR A WEIGHT-LIFTING BELT WHENEVER YOU TRAIN WITH HEAVY WEIGHTS.*

Until recently, most experts recommended that almost everyone wear a weight-lifting belt when lifting weights intensely. Belts were thought to stabilize the spine and reduce the risk of injury. Scientific studies show that while belts will help you lift more weight, they will not protect your back against injury. Also, wearing a belt weakens the stabilizing muscles of the trunk—important for whole body strength—because the muscles no longer are stressed during training. Train using good technique, and you will build these important trunk muscles. Wear a belt if you're trying to do a heavy single or double (1 or 2 repetitions using heavy weights). When wearing a belt, make sure that it is tightened securely.

Grip wraps are strips of cotton webbing (such as the webbing used in karate belts) wrapped around the wrist and the weight bar; they take stress from the forearm muscles during lifts such as cleans and lat pulls. The grip is often the limiting factor in these lifts. Grip wraps allow you to use more weight during workouts so you can make faster progress.

## Breast Support for Women

Although breast support is not as important in weight training as it is in running or volley-ball, it is a good idea to wear a good sports bra whenever you exercise. The breasts can be injured if barbells press too firmly against them when you are weight-training or if they aren't properly supported when you run. If weight training is combined with aerobics, the need for a good sports bra becomes obvious.

A good sports bra should support the breasts in all directions, contain little elastic material, absorb moisture freely, and be easily laundered. Seams, hooks, and catches should not irritate the skin. You might consider buying a bra with an underwire for added support and a pocket in which to insert padding if you do exercises that could cause injury.

## Gloves

Gloves are not recommended for weight trainers. It's best to condition the hands for the activity by training without gloves. However, weight training can severely roughen your hands if you don't protect them. Barbells, dumbbells, and some weight machines are knurled (contain small ridges to aid in gripping), and the knurls are abrasive. Gloves may prevent your hands from becoming rough and callused. Buy gloves that fit snugly and follow the contours of your hands enough so that you don't lose too much of your sense of touch. Using hand lotion after a workout protects the hands against roughening.

# WEIGHTS AND OTHER RESISTIVE EXERCISE EQUIPMENT

Use of free weights is the most common form of resistive exercise. Other forms of resistive exercise employ weight machines, rubber tubing, water, immovable objects, or gravity (your own body weight). It is beyond the scope of this book to present exercises for all of these.

## Free Weights

Free weights include barbells and dumbbells. Barbells are usually 5 to 7 feet long, with weights placed at both ends and secured by collars. The two most common types of barbells are standard and Olympic. Specialized barbells are available for doing curls (see Chapter 7), squats, and rotator-cuff exercises.

Standard barbells vary in length and weight. To get the total weight you're lifting, you must know the weight of the bar as well as that of the weight plates at the ends. In general, standard barbells weigh 15 to 30 pounds.

Olympic barbells are 7 feet long, weigh 45 pounds (20 kg), and have a rotating sleeve at each end. The finest bars are made of spring steel; these bend and recoil during heavy lifts but remain straight after the lift. Poor-quality bars often become permanently bent when loaded with a lot of weight.

The holes in Olympic weight plates are larger than those in standard plates, so Olympic plates can be used only with Olympic barbells. The most common weight plate denominations are 20, 15, 10, 5, and 2.5 kilograms per plate. Common nonmetric plates include weights of 45, 35, 25, 10, 5, 2½, and 1¼ pounds. Heavier or lighter plates are available for weight-lifting contests or leg-press machines. Rubberized plates, called "bumper plates," are used to protect the floor in Olympic weight lifting because the plates are often dropped during training or competition.

Olympic bars have special markings to help you get an even grip. The middle of the bar typically is smooth, but most of the bar is knurled (roughened) to provide a good grip. Markers are also found toward the end of the bar and help you get an even handhold for wide-grip exercises, such as the snatch (an Olympic lift).

Collars are used to prevent the weights from falling off the bar. Collars weigh 2.5 kilograms apiece. A relatively new innovation is the clip collar, which weighs very little, secures the weights tightly, and easily slides on and off the bar.

Dumbbells are much shorter than barbells and generally are held in each hand. They are either constructed from various combinations of weight plates or molded into a particular weight. Most well-equipped gyms have large racks of dumbbells, ranging in weight from 2½ pounds to well over 100 pounds.

## Weight Machines

The weight room has gone high tech. It is amazing to go to a commercial fitness show and see the incredible array of computerized exercise machines, rowing machines that allow you to compete against a computerized rower, and machines that "remember" your last workout and automatically provide the right resistance for you. Are these technological marvels going to make you twice as strong in half the time, with less work than traditional free weights? No!

Muscles get stronger if you make them work against resistance. You can increase strength by pushing against free weights (barbells and dumbbells), your own body weight, or sophisticated exercise machines. Table 5–1 summarizes the advantages and disadvantages of free weights and exercise machines.

Exercise machines are the preferred method of weight training for many nonathletes because they are safe, convenient, and technologically advanced. All you need to do is set the resistance (usually done by placing a pin in the weight stack), sit down on the machine, and start exercising. You don't have to bother anyone for a spot (assistance) or worry about a weight crashing down on you. Many people can work out in a small area. Also, free weights tend to twist in your hands when you try to balance them, which can cause blisters and calluses, whereas weight machines require little or no balancing, so beginners find the machines easier to use.

Weight machines also provide different amounts of resistance as you do the exercise—the weight is heavier as the exercise progresses. The theory behind this feature is that the stress on the muscle is more uniform as it contracts through its range of motion.

---

### TABLE 5–1
### A Comparison of Free Weights and Exercise Machines

#### EXERCISE MACHINES

| *Advantages* | *Disadvantages* |
|---|---|
| • Safe | • Expensive to buy |
| • Convenient | • Expensive to maintain |
| • Don't require spotters | • Inappropriate for performing dynamic movements |
| • Provide variable resistance | • Offer only limited number of exercises |
| • Have high-tech appeal | • Do not develop stabilizing muscles |
| • Require less skill | |
| • Make it easy to move from one exercise to the next | |

#### FREE WEIGHTS

| *Advantages* | *Disadvantages* |
|---|---|
| • Allow dynamic movements | • Not as safe |
| • Develop control of weight | • Require spotters |
| • Help overcome strength differences between the two sides of the body | • Require more skill |
| • Allow greater variety of exercises | • Can cause equipment clutter |
| • Less expensive to buy and maintain | • Cause more blisters and calluses |
| • Develop stabilizing muscles | |

It is not known whether this type of resistance is superior to the resistance supplied by free weights.

Few skilled strength–speed athletes train on machines. Their programs center on three main exercises: presses (bench press, incline press, etc.), pulls (cleans, snatches, etc.), and squats. Explosive lifts, such as pulls, are difficult or impossible to mimic on machines. Machines restrict you to a few movements, whereas many exercises are possible with free weights. Free-weight exercises, such as cleans, squats, and standing press, require coordinated use of many joints and muscles. Many coaches believe that increased power for sports movements is better achieved by doing large-muscle, multijoint free-weight exercises rather than machine exercises that isolate specific muscles.

Popular weight machines are expensive to buy and maintain. You can buy an elementary free-weight set at a fraction of the cost. However, to equip a gym with a full array of free-weight equipment, including Olympic weights, dumbbells, barbells, and **racks** to support them, is also very expensive. So don't base the choice between weight machines and free weights on cost alone.

Many coaches and athletes feel free-weight exercises are essential to developing explosive strength for sports. Because free weights are not on a controlled track as machine weights are, you must control them, which probably helps you increase strength. Free weights help you overcome asymmetrical strength and let you do a greater variety of exercises. So which is better? Because you can increase strength either way, it really boils down to personal preference.

# OTHER FORMS OF RESISTIVE EXERCISE

You don't need expensive weight machines or even free weights to get a weight workout. Anything that provides resistance to your muscles can help you increase strength.

## Gravity

Your own body weight provides excellent resistance for your muscles. Traditional, reliable exercises (sometimes called "calisthenics") such as pull-ups, push-ups, sit-ups, and dips use gravity as the resistance and require little or no equipment. The most popular calisthenic exercises are described throughout this book.

## Exercise Balls

Training on unstable surfaces, such as Swiss balls (which resemble large beach balls) or bosu balls (half-balls on a platform), is extremely popular in health clubs across the country. Unstable surfaces force lifters to stabilize the trunk muscles—the core, composed of the abdominal, back, and side trunk muscles—during the exercise. Doing squats on bosu balls, for example, activates core muscles more than doing normal free-weight squats or Smith-machine squats. Squatting on unstable surfaces decreases the load on the quads and glutes. While exercising on unstable surfaces helps build muscle strength in the trunk **stabilizers** (muscles that contract with no significant movement), it does not overload the prime movers as well as does performing lifts on stable surfaces.

## Rubber (Surgical) Tubing

Rubber tubing is an excellent inexpensive source of resistance. You can simulate the movements of many popular free-weight and weight-machine exercises using a few dollars' worth of surgical tubing. If you need more resistance, use thicker tubing.

## Medicine Balls and Lifting Stones

Performing exercises with medicine balls or lifting stones is excellent for developing whole body functional fitness. **Medicine balls** resemble overweight basketballs; examples of exercises include plyometric chest passes, overhead squats, and overhead throws. **Lifting stones** vary in weight from about 16 pounds to more than 200 pounds.

## Water

Water has become a popular resistance medium because the risk of injury is low and this type of exercise is less threatening to beginning exercisers. Water is much more viscous than air, so almost any movement becomes more difficult. Using fins on the hands and feet increases the resistance and thus the intensity of the exercise.

## Other Devices

Weight-equipment manufacturers show considerable ingenuity in designing resistive exercise devices. Devices range in complexity from friction placed on a rope that is wrapped around a cylinder to complicated instruments that use variable-speed motors. The important thing to remember is that almost any equipment or technique that provides resistance to muscle contraction will increase strength—if you train systematically with it.

# RESISTIVE EXERCISE WITHOUT WEIGHTS

You can increase strength without weights, using your body weight and gravity as resistance. Although these exercises will not build strength as well as weight training does, they are convenient. People interested mainly in aerobic exercise can do these exercises to help increase muscle mass without having to join a gym or take a class.

Table 5–2 describes a basic program you can follow in your home that doesn't require any equipment (other than a door frame pull-up bar). Because your body weight is constant, increase the intensity of the exercise by doing more repetitions. For some exercises, you can increase resistance by changing body position or using household items to add weight to your body. For example, push-ups become more difficult if you elevate your feet by putting them on a chair. For pull-ups, add body weight by putting sandbags in your pocket. You can make sandbags by filling old socks with sand. With a little imagination, you can create a "home gym" without any special equipment.

**TABLE 5–2**
**Resistive Exercise Program without Equipment**

| Muscles | Exercise | Sets | Reps |
|---|---|---|---|
| Neck | Manual neck exercise | 1–3 | 1 (10–20 sec) |
| Trapezius ("traps") | Isometric shoulder shrugs using low bar or doorknob for resistance | 1–3 | 1 (10–20 sec) |
| Pectoralis major, deltoids | Push-ups | 1–3 | 25 |
| Latissimus dorsi ("lats") | Pull-ups | 1–3 | 5 |
| Abdominals (rectus abdominis, obliques) | Hip flexors Leg raises Crunches Sit-ups Side-bends Twists Reverse beetles | 1–3 | 10–25 |
| | Isometric tighteners | 1–3 | 1 (10–40 sec) |
| Spinal extensors | Spine extensions Pelvic tilts | 1–3 | 1 (10–40 sec) |
| Quadriceps, gluteus maximus, hamstrings | Squats | 1–3 | 10–20 |
| | Wall squats (Phantom chair) | 1–3 | 1 (10–40 sec) |
| Calf (gastrocnemius, soleus) | Heel raises | 1–3 | 10–20 |

## STRUCTURE OF THE WEIGHT-TRAINING PROGRAM

The structure of your weight-training program depends on your goals. Serious body builders may train 4 to 6 hours per day, 5 or 6 days per week, while "fitness addicts" incorporate weight training into programs involving other activities—such as aerobics, running, cycling, yoga, and swimming. Most people do not have that much time to devote to fitness training, and a commitment of a few hours a week will suit some people perfectly.

### Number of Training Sessions per Week

Most people should train between 2 and 4 days per week. Two days per week is the minimum necessary to improve strength. After the early phases of training, 2 days per week tends only to maintain strength rather than improve it. Training fewer than 2 days per week leads to muscle soreness and injury and is not recommended.

Excessive training often leads to overtraining and delayed progress. Studies show that heavy-training days invariably lead to tissue damage. Damaged tissue needs time to recover before the next intense session. Also, more training is not necessarily better training. Training intensity is the primary factor determining increased strength. A person who trains too often and too hard never recovers enough to train intensely. Sometimes it is better to rest than to train.

**CAUTION** ♦ Training too many days per week can lead to overtraining and injury. The body needs time to adapt. Sometimes it is better to train less often but more intensely. Most experts recommend training 3 or 4 days per week.

Four-day-a-week programs are popular with some athletes trying to get into peak condition. Typically, they work the upper body 2 days per week and the lower body the other 2 days. For example, Monday and Thursday might be devoted to training the upper body, and Tuesday and Friday the lower body. For most people, a 3-day-a-week schedule is optimal.

## Warm-Up

Most experts agree that **warm-up** is essential before exercise, and empirical evidence suggests that warm-up improves performance and prevents injury. Warm-up raises body temperature so that the muscles respond better. It increases tissue blood flow and elasticity, making tissues less prone to injury. Warm-up also promotes joint lubrication. Intense exercise without warm-up may place the heart at risk.

**CAUTION** ♦ Always warm up before exercise. Adequate warm-up may enhance performance and prevent injury.

Warm-up can be either general or specific. General warm-up involves the whole body—large-muscle exercises such as jumping jacks, running in place, or stationary cycling. Specific warm-up involves doing the same lift you intend to do to begin your program, but using a lighter weight. For example, a person who plans to do 3 sets of 10 repetitions of 160-pound bench presses might do 1 set of 10 repetitions with 90 pounds as a warm-up. Do similar warm-up exercises for each major lift that forms your program.

## Cool-Down

**Cool-down** returns muscle temperatures and metabolic rate to normal levels. Cool-down after weight training usually consists of relaxing. After endurance exercise, in contrast, it is important to gradually wind down the tempo of activity. Because weight training is not a continuous activity, winding down is unnecessary—unless you drastically increase your heart rate during the workout. In that case, do an active cool-down during recovery, such as riding a stationary bicycle at a slow cadence and with no friction on the flywheel.

Many experts recommend stretching after a workout to help prevent muscle soreness. This is also a particularly good time to work on flexibility because the muscles and joints are warmed up.

*Don't take a shower or whirlpool bath immediately after a vigorous weight-training workout.* During intense training, blood is shunted to the skin and muscles, and hormones mobilize to help you exercise. Taking a hot shower immediately after exercise places stress on the heart that some people may not be able to tolerate. Give yourself at least 5 to 10 minutes to relax first.

---

**CAUTION**   ♦  Cool down after a workout before taking a hot shower or whirlpool bath. Exercise redirects blood to the skin for cooling and to the muscles for exercise metabolism. The combination of inadequate cool-down and exposure to a hot shower or whirlpool after exercise could result in fainting or other problems.

---

## Choosing the Correct Weight

Don't use too much weight when you begin your program. For the first set, choose a weight that you can move easily for at least 10 repetitions. (Again, a repetition is one execution of the exercise, and a set is a group of repetitions followed by a rest.) If you aren't sure about a good starting weight, use only the barbell or the lowest weight on the exercise machine. You can always add weight later.

Do only 1 set of each exercise during the first workout. The exercises may feel very easy to do, but you must be careful not to overexert yourself. As discussed in Chapter 2, tissue damage causes muscle soreness 1 to 2 days after a workout. Some delayed-onset muscle soreness is common, and perhaps necessary for improved strength, but excessive soreness suggests that you trained too hard.

Devote the first weeks of weight training to learning the exercises. Not only do you need to understand how to do the exercises, but your nervous system has to learn to communicate with the muscles so you can exert the necessary force. This takes time. Gradually add sets to your program. By the end of the second week of training, you should be doing a complete workout.

During later training sessions, gradually add weight until you are bearing a significant load and the 10-repetition set becomes difficult. The time to add weight is when you can finish each set with relative ease. If you feel as though you can do 11 or 12 repetitions with a particular weight, it's time to add more resistance. If, after adding weight, you can do only 8 or 9 repetitions, stay with that weight until you can again complete the 10 repetitions per set. If, after adding weight, you can do only 4 to 6 repetitions, then you have added too much weight and must remove some.

Experienced weight trainers should avoid using too much weight after a layoff to prevent soreness or injury. As described in Chapter 3, getting in shape gradually is a basic principle of training. Excessive training loads do not encourage the body to adapt faster but instead cause injury and delay progress.

| CAUTION | ♦ Don't use too much weight after a layoff from training because you may get sore or injured. |

## Order of Exercises and Development of Antagonistic Muscle Groups

During weight training, smaller-muscle groups fatigue more easily than larger ones. Therefore, do exercises that use more than one joint at a time (e.g., bench presses, squats, or power cleans) before those using only one joint (e.g., biceps curls, leg extensions, and wrist curls).

Most experienced weight trainers work one body part at a time. For example, they do all the leg exercises before doing upper-body exercises. Some even work lower-body and upper-body muscle groups on separate days. Intensity (the amount of weight used during the exercise) is the most important factor in increasing strength. If you mix exercises for large- and small-muscle groups and those for the upper and lower parts of your body, you decrease the amount of weight you can use—and slow your progress. See the box "Healthy Highlight: Train Large Muscles First, Then Small Muscles."

Circuit training (performing a number of exercises rapidly in series) often purposely mixes exercises. This type of training is very effective for developing muscular endurance but is less effective for gaining strength.

# HEALTHY HIGHLIGHT

### TRAIN LARGE MUSCLES FIRST, THEN SMALL MUSCLES

A basic principle of weight training is to do large-muscle exercises, such as bench presses and squats, before small-muscle exercises, such as biceps curls and knee extensions. Small-muscle exercises fatigue the target muscles rapidly, limiting their ability to contract during large-muscle exercises. Fatigued small muscles limit the ability to build larger muscles during large-muscle exercises. Brazilian and American scientists affirmed this training principle. They compared performance in a five-exercise program progressing from large-muscle exercises (bench press, lat pull, shoulder press, biceps curls, triceps extensions) to small with performance in the same program progressing from small-muscle exercises to large (the same exercises in reverse order). Predictably, performance on large-muscle exercises suffered when preceded by small-muscle exercises. In general, performance on a specific exercise suffers whenever it is performed last in a program. You may choose to do curls first in your program if you're trying to increase arm size. In summary, do large-muscle exercises before small-muscle exercises unless you want to emphasize and build the smaller muscles.

(*Journal of Strength and Conditioning Research* 19: 152–156, 2005)

Include in your program exercises for antagonistic muscle groups. Muscles work much like a seesaw: Every movement initiated by a muscle group is opposed by an antagonistic muscle group (see Chapter 2). For example, the quadriceps muscles cause the knee to extend (straighten), while its antagonistic muscles, the hamstrings, cause it to flex (bend). If you develop the quadriceps muscles without working on the hamstrings, you create a muscular imbalance that can lead to injury and faulty movement patterns.

## Sets and Repetitions

Your goals determine the ideal number of repetitions and sets. Generally, if you want increased endurance, do more repetitions (10 or more) and more sets (3 or more). If increased strength is your primary goal, do fewer repetitions and use more weight.

Doing 4 to 6 repetitions per set for 1 to 5 sets is best for developing strength. People interested in doing single maximum lifts must occasionally do 1 to 3 sets so they can adjust to the heavier weights. Experienced weight trainers use a variety of combinations of sets and repetitions. (The next section, on cycling techniques, discusses some of these programs.)

Beginners should start off with more repetitions and lighter weights, which gives the tissues a chance to adjust to increased muscular loading and minimizes the chances of injury. Start with 1 set of 8 to 10 repetitions of about 8 to 10 exercises. Practice this program, gradually increasing the weight, for at least 2 months before decreasing repetitions in each set. If you want to progress more rapidly, try increasing the number of sets per exercise to 2 or 3. If rapid increases in strength are not too important to you, stay with 10 repetitions per set. An example of a beginning weight-training program appears in Table 5–3. You can do these exercises with free weights or with weight machines.

Several training systems use a technique called **pyramiding,** which contains built-in warm-up. In pyramiding, you practice an exercise for 3 or more sets, increasing the weight during each set. This technique was first introduced by T. L. DeLorme in the 1950s.

**TABLE 5–3**
**Example of a Beginning Weight-Training Program**

| Exercise | Sets | Repetitions |
|---|---|---|
| Bench press | 1–3 | 10 |
| Lat pull | 1–3 | 10 |
| Lateral raise | 1–3 | 10 |
| Biceps curl | 1–3 | 10 |
| Triceps extension | 1–3 | 10 |
| Abdominal curl | 1–3 | 10 |
| Back extension | 1–3 | 10 |
| Leg press | 1–3 | 10 |
| Calf raise | 1–3 | 10 |

DeLorme recommended 3 sets of 10 repetitions of each exercise. The resistance should progressively increase from 50 to 75 to 100 percent of maximum capacity.

There are many other systems for regulating loads, including the **constant set method, the failure method, circuit training, super sets, giant sets,** drop sets, and **paused reps** (see Table 5–4 for examples of selected programs). Some of these techniques reduce the weight during later sets after you reach the maximum weight. Any technique you choose should allow you to warm up before significantly loading your muscles.

---

### TABLE 5–4
### Selected Weight-Set-Repetition Methods

#### CIRCUIT TRAINING

Uses 6 to 20 exercise stations set up in a circuit (i.e., in series). The person progresses from one station to the next, either performing a given number of repetitions or doing as many repetitions as possible during a given time period (e.g., 20 sec) at each station.

#### CONSTANT SET METHOD

Uses the same weight and number of sets and repetitions for each exercise. Example: Bench-press 5 sets of 5 repetitions at 80 lb.

#### PYRAMID METHOD

Uses multiple progressive sets, either ascending or ascending–descending, for each exercise. Variations: Increase weight while decreasing repetitions, or decrease weight while increasing repetitions.

*Ascending Pyramid*

| | | |
|---|---|---|
| Set 1 | 5 repetitions | 75 lb |
| Set 2 | 5 repetitions | 100 lb |
| Set 3 | 5 repetitions | 120 lb |

*Ascending–Descending Pyramid*

| | | |
|---|---|---|
| Set 1 | 5 repetitions | 75 lb |
| Set 2 | 5 repetitions | 100 lb |
| Set 3 | 5 repetitions | 120 lb |
| Set 4 | 5 repetitions | 100 lb |
| Set 5 | 5 repetitions | 75 lb |

*(continued)*

## TABLE 5–4
## Selected Weight-Set-Repetition Methods—*continued*

### DeLORME METHOD

Three sets of 10 repetitions at 50, 75, and 100 percent of maximum. Example for a person who can do 10 repetitions at 100 lb:

| | | | |
|---|---|---|---|
| Set 1 | 10 repetitions | 50 lb | (50 percent) |
| Set 2 | 10 repetitions | 75 lb | (75 percent) |
| Set 3 | 10 repetitions | 100 lb | (100 percent) |

### SUPER SETS

Usually uses two exercises, typically with opposing muscle groups, in rapid succession.

| | | | |
|---|---|---|---|
| Set 1 | 10 repetitions | 30 lb | Knee extensions |
| Set 1 | 10 repetitions | 15 lb | Knee flexion |
| Rest | | | |
| Set 2 | 10 repetitions | 30 lb | Knee extensions |
| Set 2 | 10 repetitions | 15 lb | Knee flexion |
| Rest | | | |
| Repeat | | | |

### GIANT SETS

Uses multiple exercises in succession for the same muscle group.

| | | | |
|---|---|---|---|
| Set 1 | 10 repetitions | 75 lb | Bench press |
| Set 1 | 10 repetitions | 5 lb | Dumbbell fly |
| Rest | | | |
| Set 1 | 10 repetitions | 75 lb | Bench press |
| Set 1 | 10 repetitions | 5 lb | Dumbbell fly |
| Rest | | | |
| Repeat | | | |

### DROP SETS

The drop set technique is terrific for pushing your muscles to their absolute maximum. Use this technique during the last set of an exercise. Do as many

*(continued)*

---

**TABLE 5–4**
**Selected Weight-Set-Repetition Methods—*continued***

---

reps as you can. Then immediately drop the weight by 10 to 15 percent and try to squeeze out a few more reps. Continue to use even less weight and do as many reps as you can. Keep going until you can't do any more repetitions. This technique is very difficult but a great way to overload muscles.

A similar high-tension training method is called "training down the rack." Use this technique with any dumbbell exercise, such as curls or inclines. Choose dumbbells heavy enough so that you can complete only 5 reps of the exercise. Take a 30-second rest and then move to the next-lightest set of dumbbells and do as many reps as you can. Rest 30 seconds and move to the next set of dumbbells. Continue down the rack until you can't complete any more repetitions or you run out of dumbbells.

### PAUSED REPS

You can do more reps in your workout if you pause regularly in the middle of sets. Pause in the unloaded part of the motion—the **lockout** (fully extended) position when doing the bench, incline, or dip, and with the machine unloaded during the overhead press exercise. Intense muscle contractions require energy from the high-energy chemicals adenosine triphosphate (ATP) and creatine phosphate (CP). ATP and CP, whose maximum capacity is about 3 seconds, are used rapidly during intense weight training, which is the main reason the last few reps of an exercise are so difficult. Pausing for 5 to 15 seconds in the middle of a set allows your muscles to recover quickly by replenishing ATP and CP in the muscles, enabling you to do more repetitions and to work harder. Muscles grow in response to tension and to the amount of time they are under tension.

## Basic Cycling Techniques

As mentioned in Chapter 3, many elite athletes use cycle training, or periodization of training, a powerful technique that allows the body to adapt rapidly without overtraining and prepares it to accept and benefit from intense workouts.

In cycle training, the type, volume, and intensity of training are varied throughout the year. In athletics, the year is divided into off-season, preseason, early season, and peak season. The weight-training program is different during each part of the year.

During the off-season, athletes do general conditioning exercises. The program maintains fitness and provides mental and physical rest from the rigors of training. A tennis or field hockey player might run, play volleyball, swim, and do some circuit training. Light training in the sport maintains skill.

During the preseason and early season (sometimes called the "load phase"), if the goal is to develop maximum power for a strength–speed sport such as track and field, the program develops base fitness—strength that serves as the basis for maximum lifts later in the season. The weight-training program involves high volume (5 sets of 5 to 8 repetitions for the major exercises, at moderately high intensities). This phase typically is very exhausting.

The peak phase (competitive phase) helps the athlete achieve peak performance. The weight-training program involves high-intensity workouts with much less volume than in the preseason and early season. The athlete gets plenty of rest between intense workouts, a technique that allows peak performance, or "peaking." If you time workouts and rest correctly, you can predict top performances.

Each major cycle contains microcycles in which volume, intensity, and rest vary from workout to workout or from week to week. The purpose of microcycles is to allow muscle systems adequate recovery time. According to several studies, intensity is the chief factor in enhancing fitness. In traditional training programs, athletes train hard every session, which may lead to overtraining. Microcycles prepare people for intense training days by giving them time to recover.

In this way, cycle training encourages your body to adapt steadily with a minimum risk of injury. You make small, consistent gains over a long period of time. The system improves fitness, and peak performance happens at a predetermined time in the season. One basis for this method is that people adapt better to changing stimuli than to a constant program—partly because learning progresses fastest when a new activity is introduced and partly because change is psychologically stimulating.

Considerable muscle and connective-tissue damage occurs during and after intense endurance or strength training. Although scientists don't completely understand the relationship between tissue healing rate and the structure of the training program, common sense tells us there is a relationship. Muscle fibers need to heal to some extent before you can safely stress them again.

Cycle techniques are ideal for people participating in general conditioning programs. It is unnecessary to do the same exercises every session using the same weights. Vary your program. Do some exercises intensely during one workout and other exercises intensely during the next. A basic 3-day-per-week conditioning program using the cycle-training technique appears in Table 5–5.

## Making Progress

Initially, gains seem to come easily, but eventually you will reach a plateau where progress comes more slowly. Because the body adapts rapidly at first, many gains are due as much to learning new exercises as to actual changes in the muscles. The best thing to do when you're no longer improving is to examine your program. The cause is usually too much work, not enough work, or a bad program.

If you're working very hard every session and never miss a workout but still are not making any progress, then maybe you're doing too much. Try cycling your workouts, or take a week or two off. Rest can do amazing things—often you can expect to return to personal records in the weight room if you just take a brief rest.

Sometimes you may not work hard enough. Are you only going through the motions when you train, not putting much effort into the exercises? Try adding more weight for at

### TABLE 5–5
### An Example of Cycle Training for General Conditioning

#### MONDAY

| Exercise | Sets | Repetitions | Weight (lb) |
|---|---|---|---|
| Bench press | 4 | 10 | 60 |
| Lat pulls | 3 | 10 | 30 |
| Squats | 4 | 10 | 80 |
| Abdominal curls | 3 | 20 | — |
| Back extensions | 3 | 15 | — |
| Arm curls | 3 | 10 | 25 |
| Triceps extensions | 3 | 10 | 15 |

#### WEDNESDAY

| Exercise | Sets | Repetitions | Weight (lb) |
|---|---|---|---|
| Incline press | 3 | 10 | 40 |
| Modified pull-ups | 5 | 5 | — |
| Pull-overs | 3 | 10 | 20 |
| Leg presses | 3 | 10 | 150 (machine) |
| Calf raises | 4 | 20 | 150 (machine) |
| Abdominal curls | 3 | 40 | — |
| "Good mornings" | 3 | 10 | 15 |

#### FRIDAY

| Exercise | Sets | Repetitions | Weight (lb) |
|---|---|---|---|
| Bench press | 3 | 10 | 50 |
| Lat pulls | 3 | 10 | 40 |
| Squats | 3 | 10 | 70 |
| Abdominal curls | 3 | 20 | — |
| Back extensions | 3 | 15 | — |
| Arm curls | 4 | 10 | 30 |
| Triceps extensions | 4 | 10 | 20 |

*Note:* Exercises can be done on weight machines or with free weights. Notice that the exercises, the amount of weight used in an exercise, and the number of sets and repetitions vary from one workout to the next. Exercises are described in Chapters 6–11.

least 1 set of each exercise, even if that makes you do fewer repetitions. Make sure you complete each workout—cutting a few exercises out of the program each session can amount to a lot of work *not* being accomplished over a few weeks.

If you get enough rest and complete your workouts but still don't make progress, you can often begin to make progress again by changing your program. Do exercises that are slightly different from the ones you usually do. For example, if you do bench presses on a machine or with barbells, try switching your program to include the incline press. Changing the way you do a lift sometimes helps you make progress. Having a spotter assist you so you can use more weight may also get you over the hump. If you are doing normal-grip bench presses, change your grip and do the exercise with a narrower or wider grip.

Another effective technique is to add exercises that strengthen muscles needed for the primary exercises. For example, doing bar dips is effective in improving the bench press. If you have trouble doing dips, have a spotter put his or her hands around your waist and help you with the movement. Knee extensions will improve the squat. Change the exercise, and your body will again adapt more quickly.

## Training for Body Building, Strength, and Power

Body builders have different goals than people training primarily to gain strength and power. Body builders strive to isolate and build muscles. They attempt to minimize surface fat and optimize symmetrical, proportional muscle development. Strength and power trainers also seek to build muscle size, but they best achieve their goals by doing functional exercises that use many joints at the same time. In addition to weight training, people interested in building strength and power for sport should do plyometrics and fast, explosive exercises.

# COMBINING WEIGHT TRAINING WITH OTHER SPORTS AND EXERCISES

Intense weight training is exhausting, interfering with performance in other activities. After a vigorous weight-training session, you may be more susceptible to injury if you immediately do another sport. If possible, get plenty of rest after an intense workout before participating in a sport in which you might get injured. If most of your program consists of general conditioning exercises, schedule strength and endurance workouts on different days. At least schedule intense weight training on light endurance-training days. If you weight-train and have an aerobics class on the same day, go to the class first.

Weight-training exercises improve power in sports skills best when the exercise uses the same muscles and resembles the movements required for the skill. If you want to transfer power to motor skills (e.g., jumping), multijoint, large-muscle exercises such as squats or power cleans are better than those that develop isolated muscle groups, such as knee extensions or leg curls. Exercises done on many popular exercise machines usually develop isolated muscle groups, while free-weight exercises such as squats, cleans, and snatches more closely resemble the movements involved in many sports.

# PREVENTING ACCIDENTS

Accidents and injuries do happen in weight training. Maximum physical effort, elaborate machinery, rapid movements, and heavy weights can combine to make the weight room a dangerous place if you don't take proper precautions. Table 5–6 presents the basic principles of preventing accidents in the weight room.

## Spotting

Spotters help the lifter during a failed repetition, help move the weight into position to begin a lift, actively help with the lift, and help during an unsuccessful repetition (Table 5–7). Helping with the weight after a failed repetition is the critical job of the spotter, who must be quick to go to the lifter's aid if necessary. You will need one or two spotters. During a bench press or an incline press, one spotter is sometimes preferable because coordination is easier between one spotter and a lifter than between two spotters and a lifter. During a squat, you will need two spotters, one to stand on each side of the weight and help if the lift cannot be finished.

| CAUTION | ♦ Use spotters whenever you might be in danger of missing a lift and being caught under the fallen weight. |

---

**TABLE 5–6**
**Safety Rules for Weight Training**

Weight training can be dangerous if safety guidelines are not followed. These are basic principles for preventing injuries in the weight room:

- Lift weights from a stabilized body position.
- Be aware of what is going on around you.
- Stay away from other people when they are doing exercises. Bumping into them could result in injury.
- Always use collars on barbells and dumbbells.
- Remain clear of the weight stack when someone else is using a weight machine.
- Don't use defective equipment. Report malfunctions immediately.
- Protect your back by maintaining control of your spine (protect your spine from dangerous positions). Observe proper lifting techniques, and use a weight-lifting belt for heavy single or double lifts.
- Don't hold your breath. Avoid the Valsalva maneuver (holding your breath and straining). This results in greatly reduced blood flow from the heart and could cause fainting.
- Always warm up before training.
- Don't exercise if you're ill.

---

### TABLE 5–7
### Skills and Responsibilities of the Spotter

- Be strong enough to assist with the weight being lifted.
- Know the proper form of the exercise and the spot.
- Know the number of repetitions being attempted.
- Establish signals for beginning and ending the exercise with the lifter.
- Pay constant attention during the lift, but don't interfere unless necessary or requested.
- Pay particular attention to collars or weight plates that are sliding and to whether the weight trainer is using asymmetrical lifting techniques (i.e., moving one arm at a different speed than the other). These situations may require immediate intervention.
- When spotting people doing dumbbell exercises, keep your hands as close to the weight as possible (at the wrists).

---

The lifter must indicate when he or she wants the weight removed. A spotter who removes the weight too soon may deprive the lifter of the chance to make a maximum effort and complete the lift. If there is too much delay in removing the weight, the lifter may get injured. Spotters must position themselves so as to be ready to help the lifter if needed, and they must use proper lifting techniques themselves: Bend the knees, maintain a straight back, and keep the weight close to the body (see Figure 6–1 in Chapter 6). During the lift, spotters should be attentive but should not disrupt the lifter's concentration.

**CAUTION**    ♦ Spotters must be wary of injuring themselves. Use proper lifting techniques when spotting for someone.

When you use spotters to help move a weight into position to begin an exercise, co-ordination between the spotters and you, the lifter, is important. Work out signals before the lift so that everyone understands when to raise the weight from the rack. For example, the lifter may count "one, two, three," with the weight being lifted into position on "three." It's best to work with the same spotters regularly because you'll learn what to expect from each other after a while.

**CAUTION**    ♦ Spotters must take great care to keep their head away from the bar; they can be seriously injured if the lifter suddenly lets go of the bar.

You will sometimes want a spotter to actively help with the exercise, with either free weights or weight machines. When doing negative exercises (eccentrics), the spotter may do most of the work for you during the active phase of the lift. The spotter can also provide the extra amount of force needed to finish an exercise. Lifters sometimes call this "the magic fingers" because the spotter may be able to help complete the lift by lifting with just a couple of fingers.

## Collars

**Collars** secure weights to a barbell or dumbbell. Lifting weights without collars is dangerous. It is easy to lose your balance or to raise one side of the weight faster than the other. Without collars, the weights on one side of the bar will slip off, resulting in the weights on the opposite side crashing to the floor. Obviously this can knock you off balance and lead to injury. Clip collars, which weigh very little, are a good safety compromise for lifters who don't like to use standard collars.

<table>
<tr><td>CAUTION</td><td>♦</td><td>Always use collars when lifting weights, and be sure they are secured properly.</td></tr>
</table>

## Preventing Accidents on Weight Machines

One of the attractions of weight machines is their safety. But weight machines are not totally harmless, so be cautious around them. Keep away from moving weight stacks. It's very easy for someone to jump on the machine ahead of you and begin an exercise while your fingers are close to the weight stack. Be particularly attentive when changing weights.

Don't do exercises near moving parts or weight plates. Also, don't walk near a machine when someone else is on it—you may break the person's concentration or collide with the moving machine.

Many weight machines can be adjusted to accommodate people of different sizes. Make sure the machine is properly adjusted and locked in place before beginning an exercise. It can be dangerous to begin an exercise and have the machine move suddenly.

Beware of broken machines. Broken bolts, frayed cables, broken chains, and loose cushions can give way and cause serious injury. If you notice that a machine is broken or damaged, tell an instructor immediately.

Make sure the machines are clean. Equipment upholstery should be cleaned daily. Dirty vinyl is a breeding ground for germs that can cause skin diseases. A good practice is to carry a towel around with you and place it on the machine where you will sit or lie down. If you're sweating a lot, wipe down the upholstery with a towel after you finish the exercise.

## Behavior in the Weight Room

Weight trainers should always have the utmost respect for the equipment because misuse can lead to serious injury. Fooling around in the weight room can cause injury. Be attentive to what's happening around you.

Be courteous to others. When you are doing more than 1 set and other people are waiting to use the machine, let them do a set of the exercise while you are resting. Likewise, don't use exercise machines as resting stations. This disturbs other people's workouts and slows the flow in the gym. Sign up for equipment that requires reservations—people tend to feel uncomfortable asking someone to get off a machine they have reserved. Get off the machine when your time is up. The next person's workout is probably just as important to her or him as your workout is to you.

## Medical Concerns

Report any obvious injury to muscles or joints to the instructor or a physician. Don't keep working out in the hope that the injury will go away. Training with an injured joint or muscle usually leads to more serious injury.

Be careful not to overdo. It's easy to strain or cramp a muscle by doing too many sets or repetitions. If you do injure yourself, either work on another body part or take the rest of the day off. Make sure you get the necessary first aid. Even minor injuries heal faster if you follow the RICE principle for treating injuries: Rest, Ice, Compression, Elevation.

Weight training tends to increase blood pressure, which in some people can cause serious medical problems. In people with coronary artery disease, weight training can cause symptoms such as arm or chest pain. Consult a physician if you are having any unusual symptoms during exercise or if you are not sure that weight training is a proper activity for you.

 **CAUTION** ◆ Immediately report to the instructor any headaches; chest, neck, or arm pain; dizziness, labored breathing; numbness; or visual disturbances.

# PROPER MECHANICS OF EXERCISE

Each exercise has a proper technique. These techniques will be discussed in Chapters 6–11. Several principles, however, are common to all exercises. These principles will help you prevent injury and derive the maximum benefit from your weight-training program.

## Lifting Techniques

Back injuries are among the most serious injuries that can happen in the weight room. You can prevent them by following some basic principles of lifting:

◆ Keep the weight as close to your body as possible (Figure 5–1). The farther out you hold a weight from your body, the more strain on your back.

◆ Do most of your lifting with your legs. The large muscles of the thighs and buttocks are much stronger than those of the back, which are better suited to maintaining an erect posture. Keep your hips and buttocks tucked in.

◆ When picking up a weight from the ground, keep your back straight and your head level or up. Bending at your waist with your legs straight places tremendous strain on the muscles and spinal disks of the lower back.

**Figure 5–1** Proper lifting technique: Keep the bar close to the body; place your feet a shoulder-width apart; keep your arms straight, back flat, and head in neutral position.

- Don't twist your body while lifting. Twisting places an uneven load on back muscles, causing strain.

- Lift the weight smoothly, not with a jerking, rapid motion. Sudden motions place more stress on the spinal muscles and disks.

- Lift through a full pain-free range of motion without forcefully locking out the joints.

- Allow for adequate rest between lifts. Fatigue is a prime cause of back strain.

- Lift within your capacity. Don't lift beyond the limits of your strength.

- When training on a weight machine, make sure it is properly adjusted to your body. Uncomfortable, twisted positions may place unnecessary stress on vulnerable spinal muscles and nerves.

## Breathing

Never hold your breath when lifting. Exhale when exerting the greatest force, and inhale when moving the weight into position for the active phase of the lift. Holding your breath while straining to perform a lift (the Valsalva maneuver) causes a decrease in the amount of blood returning to the heart, which means that blood cannot be pumped as easily to the brain. This can cause dizziness and fainting.

## Exercise Movements

Exercises should be done smoothly and in good form. With practice, you will "groove" your lift so that the weight is moved in the same general way every time you do the exercise.

Generally, move the weight into position for the active phase of the exercise slowly and with control. Lift or push the weight forcefully during the active phase of the lift. Obviously, if you are using enough resistance, these powered movements will be slow—but you should still try to do the movements explosively. Remember the old weight-lifting saying "Go down slow and up fast."

Do not "bounce" the weight against your body during the exercise. Bouncing means that you make an explosive transition between the pushing and recovery phases of the lift. Advanced weight trainers sometimes do this so that they can practice an exercise using heavier weight. This practice is not recommended, however, because it can cause serious injury.

---

| **CAUTION** | ♦ Never bounce a weight against the body. |

---

Do all lifts through the full pain-free range of motion. Limiting the range of motion increases strength only in the part of the range you are exercising. Practiced correctly, weight training improves flexibility. "Muscle-boundness"—the inflexibility sometimes developed from weight training—happens only when exercises aren't done through a full range of motion.

## Grips

Use the correct grip for each lift. There are three basic types of grip: **pronated grip** (palms away from you), **supinated grip** (palms toward you), and **mixed grips** (one palm toward you, one away). The pronated grip is used in most presses, pulls, and squats. The supinated grip is used in exercises such as biceps curls and chin-ups. The mixed grip is used in the dead-lift exercise to increase grip strength during the lift. (See Figure 5–2.)

The thumbless grip and thumblock grip are not recommended. The thumbless grip, as the name implies, involves placing the thumb in the same plane as the fingers. This grip places the thumb under less stress, but it is dangerous. For example, in a bench press you could easily lose control of the weight, which then could fall on you. The thumblock grip, in which the thumb is wedged between the index and middle fingers, places the thumb at increased risk of injury.

# Choosing a Health Club or Weight-Training Class

Good health-club or college weight rooms typically have expensive and specialized weight machines that help you get the most from your program. These machines help you safely isolate and develop specific muscle groups in the chest, arms, hips, buttocks, and legs. You don't have to worry about a mountain of weights falling on your head when you miss a

**Figure 5–2** Basic barbell grips: (a) pronated grip, (b) supinated grip, (c) mixed grip

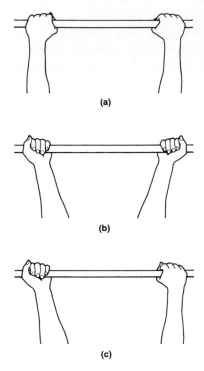

repetition of an exercise. Instead, if a weight is too much or not enough for you, you simply move the weight pin from one place to another in the weight stack.

Some clubs cater to athletes, weight lifters, body builders, or people interested in lifting free weights. Typically, these clubs have well-designed platforms for doing whole body lifts (i.e., cleans, snatches, clean and jerk, etc.), extensive dumbbell racks, and high-quality barbells, benches, and racks. If you are interested in lifting free weights, join a gym that caters to your needs.

Joining a health club allows you to get in some aerobic exercise, saving you a trip to the track or pool. Most clubs have aerobics classes going almost constantly. It's easy to catch a class for 40 or 50 minutes and then go to the weight room to finish your workout. If aerobics classes aren't for you, you can ride a stationary bike or train on a stair-climbing machine. Well-equipped clubs often have a running track, a swimming pool, racquetball courts, or computerized rowing machines.

A club is also a great place to socialize. Many have juice bars, where you can meet new friends. Socializing helps take the drudgery out of working out.

The following guidelines can help you choose the right club. Making the wrong choice will lead to a frustrating and possibly very expensive experience.

1. *Get value for your money.*

   ◆ Be wary of signing up for a health club that does not yet exist. There have been many instances of clubs collecting money from potential members for facilities that are being built; then the club never opens or delays opening for many months. Research the company thoroughly before signing a "pre-opening" contract.

---

| CAUTION |

◆ Don't get cheated by unscrupulous health-club owners. Although most club owners are honest, the industry is plagued by fly-by-night operators. Check with your local Better Business Bureau or Consumer Affairs office if you think you are being treated unfairly.

---

   ◆ Initiation fees and monthly dues are often negotiable. Talk to club members to get an idea of the range of possible financial arrangements. Often, initiation fees are transferable; ask about people who might want to sell their membership or check the local newspaper for this information.

   ◆ Try the club for a few months before signing a long-term contract. Health clubs make their money from people who don't use the facilities. Be particularly wary of "lifetime" memberships. The club may go out of business long before you die!

   ◆ Join a club you can afford. Many clubs charge a "prestige" fee. A club that is more modest and less expensive than the $150-a-month "Beverly Hills Health Club" may provide you with the equipment and activities you need. Shop around!

   ◆ Don't be pressured into signing a contract on your first visit. Go home and think about the offer. Return only after all your questions have been answered and you are sure the deal is right for you.

   ◆ Make sure the contract extends your membership if you have a prolonged illness or go on vacation.

2. *The club should be convenient.*

   ◆ You probably will not attend a club very often if the club is in an inconvenient location.

   ◆ Beware of memberships that offer reduced dues if you train during "non-prime-time hours." If you can train only at 6 A.M., then a discounted early-morning membership may be advantageous. If you want to train immediately after work or school at 5:00 P.M., then pay the extra money for an unrestricted membership.

   ◆ Check out the club during the time you want to train. Verify that you will have easy access to the equipment and exercise classes.

3. *The club should have a well-trained staff.*

   ◆ A recent study from UCLA showed that less than 50 percent of personal trainers could pass a basic test on knowledge of anatomy, exercise physiology, nutrition, exercise prescription, and the prevention and care of athletic injuries. A university degree in exercise physiology or sports science or certification by a leading organization was the best predictor of competence. Many universities offer degrees in exercise physiology that call for extensive study in chemistry, physiology, anatomy, nutrition, exercise physiology, sports injuries, kinesiology (study of movement), mathematics, and psychology. The best health clubs have staff members with this training. National groups, such as the National Strength and Conditioning Association and the American College of Sports Medicine, certify exercise leaders after they have shown adequate training and knowledge. It is no longer acceptable for health clubs to rely solely on poorly trained ex-athletes or former body builders for their exercise leaders. Don't join a club with a poorly trained staff!

◆ The club should consider your medical history before putting you on a program. This is especially important if you are over 40 to 50 (depending on your sex) or have any health problems.

◆ Beware of clubs that do exercise-tolerance tests without adequate medical supervision. Organizations such as the American Heart Association and the American College of Sports Medicine have strict guidelines regarding exercise stress tests. A physician should supervise the test if you are over 40 or have significant health problems. Some clubs try to get around these regulations by doing submaximal tests. If your fitness is low, however, it is very easy for such a test to stress you maximally. Don't let clubs cut corners with your health.

◆ The club should have established emergency procedures.

◆ Choose a club that puts its members on systematic programs. Many different weight-training programs will improve strength and fitness if practiced systematically. The club should have some way of monitoring your program. Some modern health clubs are so technologically advanced that a central computer keeps track of your workout as you move from one machine to another. The next time you work out, the computer remembers what you did the time before. Although such a high-tech approach is not necessary for most people, you should make some effort to chart your progress.

4. *The club should offer amenities besides weight training.*

◆ If you have children, ask if the club offers reliable and reasonable child care. Some clubs offer fitness activities for children.

◆ Is there a chance to develop other types of fitness besides strength and power? Well-equipped clubs have equipment such as stationary bikes, rowing machines, and stair machines, and facilities such as swimming pools; racquetball, volleyball, basketball, and tennis courts; and rooms for aerobics classes.

◆ Are you socially compatible with the membership? Different clubs attract different types of people. If you are down-to-earth, you may be better off avoiding a posh, pretentious health club. Some clubs cater to hard-core body builders, who sometimes can seem overbearing to the more casual weight trainer. The best way to determine the social environment is to observe the club on several occasions and talk to the members. Find a club where you will fit in.

◆ Many clubs have a restaurant or snack bar and a shop that sells exercise accessories, such as exercise clothing and weight belts. Although the products may be overpriced, such a shop is convenient and could be an important selling point for the club.

# EXERCISING AT HOME

Home gyms currently are very popular in the United States, with exercise equipment selling at an all-time high. Weight training is a very safe activity compared to football, skiing, or basketball, but weight training injuries have increased 38 percent since 1998. About 25 percent of injuries occur because of abuse or misuse of equipment, and injuries occur twice as often in home gyms as in health clubs. Nearly 75 percent of injuries occur in people younger than age 24. The greatest increase in the injury rate has been among the very young (younger than 5 years) and older adults. Soft-tissue injuries, particularly to the hands and neck, are most common. However, there have also been an alarming number of fractures and dislocations. Injury rates can decrease with proper supervision and instruction as well as consistent equipment maintenance. Home gyms are particularly dangerous—almost all the deaths associated with weight training have occurred in home gyms. Most people undertaking an exercise program, particularly teenagers, should join a gym. Health clubs are safer, provide a better environment for training, and usually offer expert instruction. Home gyms are convenient, however. If you decide to set up a home gym, buy the best equipment you can afford.

C H A P T E R

# 6 DEVELOPING THE CHEST AND SHOULDERS

Let us run the risk of wearing out rather than rusting out.

—THEODORE ROOSEVELT

CHEST AND SHOULDER EXERCISES ARE BY FAR THE MOST POPULAR WITH PEOPLE WHO train with weights. For women, these exercises improve the form of the chest and shoulders. For men, chest and shoulder exercises give them the T-shaped look of a powerful dynamo. Many sports require a strong upper body. Strong shoulder and chest muscles are an advantage when serving a tennis ball, for example, or rock climbing or wind surfing. Chest and shoulder exercises build strength and power that help both men and women excel in the activities they enjoy.

The chest and shoulders are more difficult to develop in women than in men because women carry less muscle mass in that part of the body. Also, there is no exercise that will increase the size of women's breasts. Breast tissue is made largely of fat. If the size of the chest muscles is increased, the breasts may look a little larger. But because women have a limited ability to increase muscle size through weight training, the increase in breast size can be only minimal.

The major muscles of the chest and shoulders are **multipennate muscles.** Multipennate means the muscle fibers are aligned in several directions. Because of this, you should do several exercises to develop chest and shoulder muscles. For example, the pectoralis major muscle (the principal muscle of the chest) can be divided into upper, middle, and lower parts according to how the fibers are aligned. To completely train and develop this muscle, you must do exercises that build each of the muscle's three segments. Likewise, the deltoid

74

# HEALTHY HIGHLIGHT

HAND POSITION AFFECTS CHEST AND ARM LOAD
DURING PUSH-UPS

How many push-ups can you do? That depends on how you do them. According to scientists from the University of Athens in Greece, arm and foot position during the exercise affects both performance and the load on chest and arm muscles. They compared standard push-ups (hands forward, a shoulder-width apart; leg support on toes) with modified push-ups (women's push-ups, leg support on knees) for hands spread beyond shoulder-width, hands together, hands forward of the chest, and hands behind the chest. Modified push-ups decreased the muscle load by about 15 percent. The pecs were activated more with a wide-arm position, while triceps were stressed more with the narrow-arm position. Perform push-ups according to instructions when you take or administer push-up tests, because altering arm or foot placement affects performance.

(*Journal of Strength and Conditioning Research* 19 :146–151, 2005)

(the principal muscle of the shoulder) is a three-part muscle that requires three or more exercises to develop fully

It is extremely difficult to present exercises that functionally isolate specific muscle groups. For example, exercises for the chest, such as the bench press, also train the muscles of the arms, back, abdomen, and, to a limited extent, legs (the legs stabilize the upper body in some chest and shoulder exercises). Throughout Chapters 6–10, exercises are grouped according to the body part they work the best.

Also, it would be difficult and cumbersome to list exercises for every type of machine. The book presents exercises that can be done using free weights and many types of weight machines. This is not an endorsement of these machines. Rather, exercises using them are presented because these machines are commonly found in schools and gyms in the United States and Canada and are popular with many recreational weight trainers. See the table "Weight-Training Exercises for Selected Machines and Free Weights" in Appendix 3. When using other machines, follow the basic guidelines for the machine exercises described in the text. They usually will be appropriate. See the box "Healthy Highlight: Hand Position Affects Chest and Arm Load During Push-Ups."

## THE CHEST MUSCLES AND HOW TO TRAIN THEM

Building a powerful, round-looking chest is the Holy Grail of a toned body. If you follow the principles outlined in this chapter, you will be well on your way to developing strong, shapely chest muscles. If you haven't been training, it will take about 6 weeks to see noticeable improvement in the size, shape, and strength of your muscles.

The pectoralis major and the pectoralis minor make up the chest muscles. The pectoralis major is a large, fan-shaped muscle that originates on the collarbone and breastbone and attaches to the upper arm. The pectoralis minor lies beneath the pectoralis major and assists it in moving the shoulder. The chest muscles move the arm across the chest and lower it when it is overhead. They are particularly important in any pushing movement, such as blocking in football or making a chest pass in basketball. You use these muscles when you hit a forehand in tennis or racquetball, throw a ball or discus, or do the free-style in swimming.

Muscles work by shortening and pulling on the bone to which they're attached. The pectoralis major is divided into upper, middle, and lower parts that you can build with specific exercises. Work the upper chest muscles with incline presses or incline flys. Do dumbbell or barbell bench presses to work the middle chest, and decline presses to work the lower chest. Emphasize the upper chest if you want to develop a full, round chest.

Muscles grow best when you load them—the heavier the stress, the more muscles grow. You can load and build the chest muscles better when you do multijoint exercises, such as bench presses and incline presses. These exercises allow you to use heavy weights and overload the chest muscles to the maximum. They also build accessory muscles, such as the triceps and deltoids, that allow you to work the chest muscles harder. Complete your chest-building program by doing exercises that isolate the chest muscles, such as incline dumbbell flys and machine flys.

## EXERCISES FOR THE CHEST MUSCLES

You will build your chest muscles best by training them twice a week. If you do more than that, you will develop sore shoulders and suffer from overtraining. If you train less than that, you won't progress very quickly. Examples of good chest-building exercises include these:

- Bench press
- Barbell incline press
- Dumbbell incline press
- Push-ups and modified push-ups
- Dumbbell flys
- Machine flys
- Cable crossovers
- Pullovers
- Decline-bench press

### Bench Press

The bench press is probably the most popular weight-training exercise. Many people gauge strength by the amount of weight a person can "bench." Although the exercise is often overemphasized, it provides strength and power that can be carried over to many sports and develops well-shaped muscles that look good. This exercise develops primarily the chest, the front of the shoulders, and the back of the arms. See the "Fact or Fiction?" box.

## FACT OR FICTION?

*MYTH: BENCH SHIRTS HELP YOU BENCH-PRESS MORE WEIGHT.*

A bench shirt is a stiff shirt that gives you support and recoil while you are bench-pressing. The "myth" statement is true and false: Yes, you can bench-press more weight when you use a bench shirt, but you do not train the supporting muscles while wearing the shirt. Consequently, you will be weaker if you try to bench-press without the shirt and less powerful when you play sports requiring upper-body strength.

♦ **THE TECHNIQUE** Lie on the bench with your feet flat on the floor. Grasp the bar slightly more than shoulder-width apart (Figure 6–1). Have the spotter help you move the bar from the rack to a point over your chest. Lower the bar in a straight line slightly below your nipples (end of the breastbone). Push the weight straight up to the starting position. Most equipment manufacturers make chest- or bench-press machines. The instructions are similar to those for the free-weight bench press. Figure 6–2 shows a seated chest-press machine.

Most people use poor technique when doing the bench press. Use the major muscles in your body to assist with this lift. Tighten the muscles in your legs, abs, and back and squeeze your shoulder blades together. While lowering the bar to your chest, inhale and expand your chest and belly to help generate more power during the lift. Keep your elbows in so that your upper arms are at 45-degree angles to the sides of your body. Bench-pressing with your elbows out places too much strain on your shoulders and reduces power. As you push the bar upward contract your glutes, press your feet into the floor, and drive the bar upward explosively, exhaling during the lift.

If you are using the free-weight bench press, it is best to use a bench with a built-in rack constructed so that the weight can be taken on and off with little danger of

**Figure 6–1** Bench press. Major muscles developed: pectoralis major, triceps, deltoids

**Figure 6–2** Seated chest press. Major
muscles developed: pectoralis major,
triceps, deltoids

**CAUTION**  ♦  During the motion, be careful not to arch your neck or back, because
this could injure the spinal disks. Never bounce the weight off your
chest, because this could injure the ribs, sternum (breastbone), or internal organs.

pinching your hands. The rack and bench should be sturdy enough to support large
weights safely. The bench should allow your arms and shoulders to travel freely during
the exercise.

Emphasize different muscle groups by varying the width of your grip. Narrow your
grip to increase the stress on the triceps muscle (the muscle on the back of your upper arm);
use a wider grip to stress the pectoralis major muscle (chest).

### Power-rack bench press

♦  THE TECHNIQUE    This exercise is used to help overcome sticking points you may
experience during the bench press. The power rack allows you to place pegs, or stops, at
various points within the vertical range of motion.

Place a bench inside the power rack and select three positions along the range of motion used during the exercise. The pegs should first be placed so the bar can rest close to
your chest. Lying in the basic bench-press position with the bar resting on the first pegs,
push the weight from your chest. After you have completed your workout at the first pegs,
move the pegs so that the bar rests in the middle of the range of motion. Repeat the exercise sequence. Finally, move the pegs so that the bar travels only a few inches during the
exercise. At this level, you will be capable of handling much more weight than you normally can bench press. It's a safe way of getting used to increased weight.

### Smith and Hammer machines
The Smith and the Hammer Strength machines have be-
come popular in many gyms. Smith machines include an Olympic-type bar attached to a

**Figure 6–3** Barbell incline press. Major muscles developed: upper pectoralis major, triceps, deltoids

track. The bar has hooks on its ends to protect the lifter in the event the exercise can't be completed. Smith machines are particularly effective for doing bench presses, seated presses, and squats. The bar on the Smith machine is counterbalanced, so it weighs only 10 pounds. Remember that fact when determining the training load.

Hammer machines are a cross between free weights and traditional weight machines. Hammer press machines are very good for symmetrically developing the muscles on each side of the body because the machines are constructed so that each arm works independently. Instructions for doing exercises on the Smith and the Hammer Strength machines are similar to those for free weights and various other weight machines.

A number of auxiliary exercises can be included in the training program to help improve your bench press. Incline presses, push-ups, and flys are described in the following sections; see Chapter 7 for parallel-bar dips.

## Incline Press

The incline press may be done with a barbell or with dumbbells. Special skill is required to lift dumbbells to the starting position of the exercise.

***Barbell incline press***    This is an excellent exercise for developing mass in the upper chest. Do it on an incline bench with a built-in rack. Use a spotter—even when lifting a light weight—because when you set up for the exercise you grasp the bar with your shoulders externally rotated, a vulnerable position. The spotter will protect your shoulders against injury.

◆    THE TECHNIQUE    Lie or sit on the incline bench and grasp the bar slightly more than shoulder-width apart (Figure 6–3). Have the spotter assist you in moving the bar directly over your upper chest. It is important to keep the bar moving perpendicular to the floor in a straight path upward from the chest, never toward the feet. Lower the bar to your upper chest and press the bar to the starting position. To increase power during the lift, use the same techniques described for the bench press.

**Figure 6–4** Dumbbell incline press. Major muscles developed: upper pectoralis major, triceps, deltoids

CAUTION   ♦   Pushing the weight too far in front of you will make the exercise more difficult to perform and may result in back, shoulder, or elbow injury.

***Dumbbell incline press***   This exercise is excellent for isolating and balancing the muscles of the upper chest.

♦   THE TECHNIQUE   Grasp the dumbbells and sit or lie on the incline bench (Figure 6–4). Place the right-hand dumbbell on your lower quad and boost it to chest level using your thigh. Do the same with the left-hand dumbbell. Keeping the dumbbells high on the chest, press them overhead, then return to the starting position. Try this exercise on an exercise ball to build chest and shoulder strength and core (abdomen and back) strength at the same time.

## Push-Ups and Modified Push-Ups

Push-ups build up the chest, shoulder, and arm muscles. The prime movers (main muscles used) include the pectoralis major, deltoids, and triceps brachii. Many people lack sufficient strength to perform even a single push-up using standard push-up technique. The modified push-up, in which you support yourself with your knees, is less difficult than the standard

**Figure 6–5** Push-ups, modified push-ups. Major muscles developed: pectoralis major, triceps, deltoids

push-up. Use the modified technique if you can't do more than 8 standard push-ups; when you can do more than 30 modified push-ups, switch to the standard technique.

♦   THE TECHNIQUE

1.  Starting position:
    a.  Standard push-ups: Start in the push-up position with your body supported by your hands and feet.
    b.  Modified push-ups. Start in the modified push up position, with your body supported by your hands and knees.
2.  Lower your chest to the floor with your back straight, and then return to the starting position (Figure 6–5).

## Dumbbell Flys

Flys develop the chest and the front part of the shoulders (anterior deltoids). They are done with dumbbells or with machines that simulate the use of dumbbells. This is a good exercise for developing the appearance of fullness of the chest.

♦   THE TECHNIQUE    Lie on an incline or flat bench with a dumbbell in each hand, palms facing inward and arms extended straight above your chest. Keep your elbows bent slightly to prevent hyperextension (Figure 6–6). Slowly lower the weights to the side until they reach shoulder level; then return to the starting position. As you get stronger, lower the weight below shoulder level. Do this exercise with arms bent. Avoid straight-arm flys because of danger to the elbows. Flys can also be done on a decline bench. Incline flys tend to work the upper part of the chest, whereas decline flys work the lower part of the chest.

CAUTION   ♦   Don't use too much weight when you first start doing this exercise because there is a possibility of injuring your elbows. For the same reason, don't do straight-arm flys.

**Figure 6–6** Dumbbell flys. Major muscles developed: pectoralis major, anterior deltoids

## Machine Flys

Many equipment manufacturers make machines that simulate dumbbell flys. They may be superior to using free weights because they allow better isolation of the chest and shoulder muscles.

♦  THE TECHNIQUE    Sit on the machine with your back flat against the seat (Figure 6–7). Adjust the wings (the arms of the machine) at a 90-degree angle. Grasp the handles and draw the wings toward the middle until they almost touch. Return to the starting position.

## Cable Crossovers

This is a good exercise for building the upper-body muscles. It also builds the core muscles—the abdominal, back, and side muscles—because these muscles must stabilize your spine when you do the exercise.

♦  THE TECHNIQUE    Grasp the handles of the upper pulleys and extend your arms upward in a V with palms facing downward. Bend your arms slightly, and bend at the waist. Pull the handles down until your hands touch each other at about waist level; slowly return to the starting position.

**Figure 6–7** Machine flys. Major muscles developed: pectoralis major, anterior deltoids

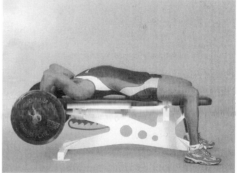

**Figure 6–8** Barbell pullover. Major muscles developed: pectoralis major, latissimus dorsi

## Pullovers

Pullovers are good for developing the pectoralis major, rib muscles, and latissimus dorsi (lats, a large muscle of the back). Pullovers can be done with either weights or machines.

◆    THE TECHNIQUE    Lie on your back on a bench; your head should extend slightly past the end of the bench (Figure 6–8). Grasp a barbell with your hands about 8 inches apart. With arms bent slightly, lower the bar behind your head and reach toward the floor. Return to the starting position. As a variation on bent-arm pullovers, you can work with straight arms, but you should use less weight to prevent elbow injury.

You can also do these exercises on the low pulley station of the crossover pulley machine. The exercises are identical to those described for free weights except that they are done on the floor. A single dumbbell can be used in place of the barbell. Generally, this exercise is accomplished with the bench perpendicular to the weight trainer. Dumbbell pullovers are described in Chapter 8.

## Pullover Machines

♦   THE TECHNIQUE   Adjust the seat so that your shoulders are aligned with the cams. Push down on the foot pads with your feet so you can place your elbows on the pads. Rest your hands lightly on the bar. To get into the starting position, let your arms go back as far as possible. Then pull your elbows forward until the bar almost touches your abdomen.

## Decline-Bench Press

The decline press is not usually part of the typical weight-training routine. Body builders use it to develop the lower part of the pectoralis major muscle. It also builds the front part of the shoulders and the backs of the arms.

Doing decline presses with free weights requires a specialized piece of equipment called a "decline bench." A decline bench can be made by placing blocks under one end of a flat bench. When using free weights, make sure the bench is steady, and use spotters during the exercise. If you fail to complete this exercise, the weight could fall on your neck or face.

♦   THE TECHNIQUE   Lie on a decline bench, face up and head down. Grasp the weight at shoulder-width, bring it to your chest, and then press it upward until your elbows are extended. This exercise can also be done with dumbbells.

## Other Exercises for the Chest

Many other exercises develop the chest muscles to some extent, including lat pulls and catching and throwing medicine balls. Horizontal push presses also develop the chest—in a standing position, push a weight horizontally as rapidly as possible.

## Tips on Building the Chest Muscles

Get plenty of rest and don't overtrain. Muscles grow during recovery, and exercising before muscles have fully recovered interrupts muscle growth processes. Work hard, but give your muscles a chance to recover.

Make sure to work the upper-back muscles, including the traps, lats, rhomboids, and posterior deltoids. Many people do lots of chest exercises but neglect the back muscles, creating muscle imbalances and increasing the risk of overuse injuries to the shoulder and upper back.

Finally, chest muscles—like any muscle group—look best when they are not covered by excess fat. Don't neglect your diet and aerobic exercise. You need adequate calories for muscle growth, but don't use your intense exercise program as an excuse to overeat. If you manage your body fat and work hard, you will soon develop shapely, fit-looking chest muscles.

# EXERCISES TO DEVELOP THE SHOULDERS

The shoulder is one of the most complex joints of the body, composed of four specific joints and more than twelve different muscles. The rest of this chapter focuses on the principal exercises that develop the shoulder's major muscle groups.

## The Deltoid and Rotator-Cuff Muscles

The deltoid has three heads: the anterior (front), middle, and posterior (rear) deltoids. It is a large muscle that works on several planes on the shoulder, so it involves several sometimes opposing actions. The deltoid elevates the arm. The anterior deltoid raises the arm to the front (shoulder flexion) and across the front (horizontal flexion), the middle deltoid raises the arm to the side (abduction), and the rear deltoid hyperextends the shoulder (moves the arm to the rear) and horizontally extends the shoulder. Because the pecs and lats don't operate once the arms are extended to the side, the posterior deltoid is the main muscle that hyperextends the shoulder. You build the posterior deltoids when you do backward raises and rowing exercises.

Shoulder rotator-cuff exercises are also described. The rotator-cuff group is important because injuries to this muscle group are often suffered by swimmers; by baseball, volleyball, softball, and tennis players; and by carpenters and artists.

Although all the exercises described in the previous section ("Exercises for the Chest Muscles") train the shoulder muscles as well, the following exercises are generally recognized as the best for developing the major muscles of the shoulder:

- Overhead press (shoulder press)
- Behind-the-neck press
- Shoulder raises
- Incline reverse dumbbell laterals
- Incline reverse dumbbell rows
- Upright rowing

## Overhead Press

The overhead press, also called the "military press," can be done standing or seated and with a barbell or dumbbells. Many equipment manufacturers make shoulder-press machines, and most health clubs have at least one. This exercise develops the deltoids (the large three-part muscle covering the shoulder joint), upper chest, and back of the arms. Trunk and lower-body muscles stabilize the body during this exercise.

**CAUTION** ♦ When standing, be careful not to arch your back excessively, or you may injure the spinal muscles, vertebrae (bones of the spine), or disks. Using a staggered foot position may help you avoid excessive back lean. This exercise may increase the severity of rotator-cuff injuries.

♦ THE TECHNIQUE    The overhead press with a barbell begins with the weight at your chest, preferably on racks (Figure 6–9). If you are a more advanced weight trainer, you can "clean" the weight to your chest, but attempt this only after receiving instruction from a knowledgeable coach (see Figure 10–10 in Chapter 10). This is one of the best exercises for transferring strength from the weight room to sports, because you must use your legs and core muscles to stabilize your upper body as you do the lift.

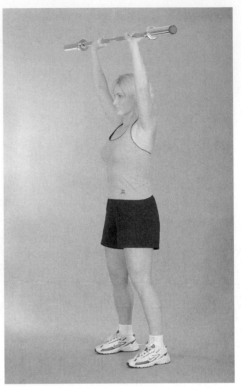

**Figure 6–9** Overhead press. Major muscles developed: deltoids, triceps brachii, trapezius

CAUTION ♦ Do not attempt the clean unless you have some weight-training experience and receive proper instruction from a knowledgeable coach.

## Behind-the-Neck Press

A variation of the standing press is the behind-the-neck press. This exercise develops the shoulders, back of the arms, and upper-back muscles. Avoid this exercise if you have a rotator-cuff injury, because it can pinch sensitive tissues in the upper shoulder and make the condition worse.

♦ THE TECHNIQUE   This exercise can be done standing or seated and requires the use of a barbell. Use a rack to place the weight in the starting position. With a fairly wide grip, place the weight behind your head and rest it on your shoulders. Push the weight above your head until your elbows are extended, and then return to the starting position. This becomes an excellent whole-body exercise in the standing position if you also push with your legs to help complete the repetition.

**Figure 6-10** Behind-the-neck push-press. Major muscles developed: deltoids, triceps brachii, trapezius, quadriceps, gluteus maximus, hamstrings

The behind-the-neck push-press, a variation of this lift, is an excellent whole-body exercise because you also push with your legs to help complete the repetition (Figure 6–10). Do this exercise on a lifting platform using rubber bumper plates so you can let the weight hit the floor if you can't complete the repetition. Also consider wrapping the bar with a pad to protect your upper back. The behind-the-neck push-press is an advanced lift that should not be attempted by beginners. Some, but not all, weight-training experts consider this exercise dangerous.

## Overhead-Press Machines

Most equipment manufacturers make overhead-press machines. These machines usually require that you do the exercise from a seated position with your back supported and feet firmly on the ground. The pressing movement will be either in front of or behind the neck. Beware of behind-the-neck press machines if you have rotator-cuff problems, because the movement could make your problem worse.

## Shoulder Raises

Shoulder raises develop the deltoid muscle, the three-part, round muscle making up the most prominent part of the shoulder. This exercise must be done to the front, side, and rear

**Figure 6–11** Lateral dumbbell raises. Major muscles developed: middle deltoids

**Figure 6–12** Front dumbbell raises. Major muscles developed: anterior deltoids

in order to develop the deltoid fully. Shoulder raises are usually done with dumbbells, although they can be done with wall pulleys or on specialized exercise machines.

♦    THE TECHNIQUE    Lateral dumbbell raises (Figure 6–11): From a standing position, with a dumbbell in each hand and arms straight, lift the weights on both sides until they reach shoulder level, and then return to the starting position. Bend your arms slightly if your elbows hurt. Some people continue the exercise until the weights meet overhead, but this is inadvisable as it may injure the shoulders. Lateral shoulder raises develop the middle section of the deltoid muscle.

♦    THE TECHNIQUE    Front dumbbell raises (Figure 6–12): In a standing position, using dumbbells or a barbell and with arms straight, lift the bar in front of you to shoulder level, and then return to the starting position. This exercise develops the front part of the deltoid muscle.

♦    THE TECHNIQUE    Rear (bent-over) dumbbell raises (Figure 6–13): In a standing or seated position, with a dumbbell in each hand and knees bent slightly, bend at the waist. Lift the weights to the side until they reach shoulder level, and then return to the starting position. Bent-over dumbbell raises develop the back portion of the deltoids.

**Figure 6–13**  Rear dumbbell raises. Major
muscles developed: posterior deltoids

## Lateral-Raise Machines

♦    THE TECHNIQUE    Adjust the seat so that the pads rest just above your elbows when
your arms are at your sides and your hands are forward. Lightly grasp the handles and push
the pads to shoulder level with your arms. Return to the starting position. Lead the movement with your elbows rather than trying to lift the bars with your hands.

## Incline Reverse Dumbbell Laterals

♦    THE TECHNIQUE    Lie facedown on a standing incline bench set at 45 degrees (Figure 6–14). Stay high, with your head down. Keeping your elbows straight, hyperextend your
shoulder and raise the weights as high as you can. You can do this exercise unilaterally—
one arm at a time—for better effect. Also, some "pec-deck" machines (machine version of
free-weight fly) allow you to reverse directions and do reverse laterals.

## Incline Reverse Dumbbell Rows

♦    THE TECHNIQUE    Lie facedown on a standing incline bench set at 45 degrees (Figure 6–15). Grasp a dumbbell in each hand and let your arms hang in front of you. Keeping

**Figure 6–14** Incline reverse dumbbell laterals. Major muscles developed: posterior deltoids, rhomboids, trapezius

**Figure 6–15** Incline reverse dumbbell rows. Major muscles developed: posterior deltoids, rhomboids, trapezius, biceps brachii ·

your head down and the dumbbells high, pull the dumbbells toward your chest in a rowing motion. As with reverse dumbbell laterals, you can do this exercise unilaterally for better effect.

## Upright Rowing

Upright rowing develops the shoulders, the front of the arms, the neck, and the upper back. Because it affects so many large-muscle groups at the same time, it is an excellent upper-body exercise. Rowing exercises (upright and front) help strengthen and balance the muscles of the shoulder joint. They are good complements to the bench press, the shoulder press, and shoulder raises.

♦    THE TECHNIQUE    Using a pronated grip, grasp a barbell with your hands close together and stand with the weight at thigh level (Figure 6–16). Pull the weight to the upper part of your chest; then return to the starting position. Don't initiate the exercise with a forward lean from the waist, avoid leaning back during the lift, and keep your elbows higher than your hands throughout the exercise.

**Figure 6–16** Upright rowing. Major muscles developed: posterior deltoids, trapezius, biceps brachii.

## Rotator-Cuff Exercises

The **rotator cuff** is a group of four muscles that hold the head of the humerus in the glenoid fossa of the scapula and cause internal and external rotation of the shoulder. The muscles of the rotator cuff are the supraspinatus, teres major, infraspinatus, and subscapularis. This muscle group is often injured during activities that require the arm to go above shoulder level, such as swimming, tennis, and throwing. The best way to prevent injuries is to make the muscles strong and flexible. Exercises to strengthen the rotator-cuff muscle group include these:

- Dumbbell external rotation
- Dumbbell internal rotation
- Empty-can exercise

***Dumbbell external rotation***    This exercise strengthens muscles that cause the arm to rotate outward (infraspinatus and teres minor).

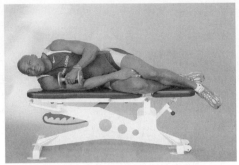

**Figure 6–17** Dumbbell external rotation. Major muscles developed: infraspinatus, teres minor

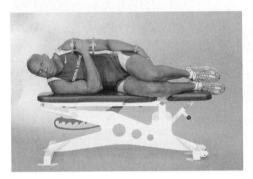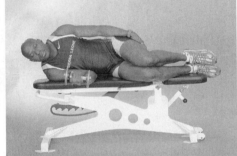

**Figure 6–18** Dumbbell internal rotation. Major muscles developed: subscapularis

◆    THE TECHNIQUE    Lic on your side on a bench (Figure 6–17). Grasping a dumbbell, bend your elbow halfway (90 degrees), keeping the elbow tight against your rib cage. Slowly lower the weight and then lift it back to the starting position.

***Dumbbell internal rotation***    This exercise develops the muscles that cause the shoulder to rotate inward (subscapularis).

◆    THE TECHNIQUE    Lie on your side on a bench with your elbow bent halfway (90 degrees) and held tightly against your side and with your hand extended over your chest (Figure 6–18). Slowly lower the weight to your side, and then slowly lift it back to the starting position.

***Empty-can exercise***    This is an important rotator-cuff exercise because it strengthens the supraspinatus muscle, the muscle of the rotator-cuff group that is most often injured in sports.

◆    THE TECHNIQUE    Stand upright and hold a dumbbell in each hand (Figure 6–19). Keeping your arms straight, raise your arms to shoulder height, move them horizontally about 30 degrees, and rotate them inward as much as possible so that the palms are facing the floor. Slowly lower and raise the weights through a 45-degree arc.

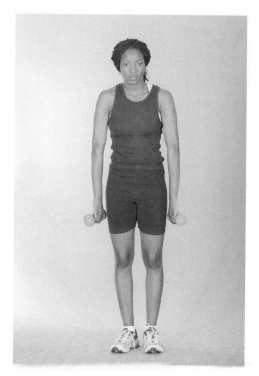 

**Figure 6–19** Empty-can exercise. Major muscles developed: deltoids, supraspinatus

It should look as if you are emptying liquid from two cans—that's how the exercise got its name.

## Preventing Rotator-Cuff Injuries

The shoulder is an extremely complex joint that can easily become unbalanced if you work some muscles around the joint more than others. Build the shoulder muscles by exercising muscles in all the joint's motions. For example, balance a bench press with a rowing exercise, and do raises to strengthen the shoulder flexors and lat pulls to strengthen the shoulder extensors. Poor technique and overtraining are more frequent causes of rotator-cuff injury than muscle weakness.

CHAPTER

# 7
# DEVELOPING THE ARMS

My 90 percent athlete going 100 percent will beat your
100 percent athlete going 90 percent every time.

—BEAR BRYANT

WE USE OUR ARMS FOR ALMOST EVERY ACTIVITY IN WORK AND PLAY. IT HELPS TO HAVE strong arms for a wide variety of tasks—gardening, opening jars, throwing a ball, playing tennis. Strong, attractive arms are within reach of anyone who is willing to devote a little time to developing them. This chapter presents basic arm and forearm exercises as well as specialized arm exercises for preventing "tennis elbow" and increasing grip strength. The table "Weight-Training Exercises for Selected Machines and Free Weights" in Appendix 3 lists some examples. For the sake of this discussion, exercises for the arm will be divided into three categories: the front of the arm, the back of the arm, and the forearm. See the "Fact or Fiction?" box and the box "Healthy Highlight: Body Builders Out of Balance in Upper Body" on p. 96.

## EXERCISES FOR THE FRONT OF THE ARM

Curls are the best exercises for developing the muscles of the front of the arm. The principal muscles of this area include the biceps brachii and the brachialis. Curls can be done using a barbell, dumbbells, special curl bars, or curl machines. Curl bars are useful because

## FACT OR FICTION?

*MYTH: ARMS ARE THE MOST IMPORTANT BODY PARTS FOR POWER SPORTS.*

Most weight trainers are enthusiastic about doing arm exercises because they love the look of toned, defined arm muscles. People interested in power sports—such as golf, tennis, football, skiing, volleyball, basketball, and soccer—should concentrate on the strength of the lower body, trunk, and shoulder muscles. If you are interested primarily in body building, then by all means do plenty of arm exercises.

they reduce stress on the forearm muscles. They allow you to use more weight and prevent injury to your forearms. Among the many variations of curl exercises are these:

- Standing barbell curls
- Dumbbell curls
- Preacher curls
- Reverse curls
- Pole curls (poleates)
- Curls, exercise machines
- Double-arm curls, low pulley

## Standing Barbell Curls

This is the old standby for developing biceps strength. Be sure not to bend your back when doing this exercise or you may hurt yourself. If your forearms get sore after a few weeks, you probably are straining the muscles. Switch from a straight bar to a curl bar.

◆    THE TECHNIQUE    From a standing position, grasp the bar using a supinated grip (palms up), your hands shoulder-width apart (Figure 7–1). Keeping your upper body rigid, bend (flex) your elbows until the bar reaches a level slightly below the collarbone. Return the bar to the starting position.

CAUTION    ◆ To avoid injury, keep your back in a neutral position and bend your knees slightly during this exercise. Standing with your back against the wall will help keep your back straight. If you are lifting heavy weights, use a weight-lifting belt.

# HEALTHY HIGHLIGHT

## BODY BUILDERS OUT OF BALANCE IN UPPER BODY

Most body builders—particularly beginners—spend more time working pecs and delts than any other upper-body muscle. Upper-body movements are incredibly complex. Proper development takes a lot more than bench presses, flys, and raises. Slippery Rock University scientists found that body builders were stronger than controls but showed muscle imbalances and restricted flexibility during a variety of upper-body movements. Do exercises for all upper-body motions—not just the exercises you like.

(*Journal of Strength and Conditioning Research* August 2002)

**Figure 7–1** Standing barbell curl. Major muscles developed: biceps brachii, brachialis, forearm flexors.

## Dumbbell Curls

There are many ways to do dumbbell curls. You may be seated on a flat bench or on an incline bench, alternate between arms, do both arms at the same time, or do all the repetitions with one arm before doing them with the other arm. Although there is little difference between these lifts, each lift stresses the arm in a slightly different way. You can change your routine with these variations to add interest to your program.

♦     THE TECHNIQUE     Standing: Stand with feet shoulder-width apart (Figure 7–2). Grasp the dumbbells using a supinated grip. Begin with arms extended, and bend one arm at a time until the weight approaches your shoulders. Return to the starting position and repeat with the other arm.

♦     THE TECHNIQUE     Seated: While seated on a flat or incline bench, grasp the dumbbells using a supinated grip. Begin with arms extended, and bend your arms until the weights approach your shoulders; then return to the starting position (Figure 7–3). Swinging the weights or bending your back while doing dumbbell curls will make the exercise less effective.

**Figure 7–2** Dumbbell curl. Major muscles developed: biceps brachii, brachialis, forearm flexors.

**Figure 7–3** Incline dumbbell curl. Major muscles developed: biceps brachii, brachialis, forearm flexors.

## Preacher Curls

Preacher curls effectively isolate the biceps, the muscles of the front of the arm. This lift is particularly effective because it is difficult to cheat while doing it. It requires a special apparatus called a "preacher stand" or "seated preacher bench," so named because it resembles a pulpit. If a preacher stand is not available, you can substitute an incline bench.

♦   THE TECHNIQUE   This lift can be done using a barbell, dumbbells, or a curl bar. Use a supinated grip to hold the weight, place your elbows on the preacher stand, and fully extend your elbows. Bend your arms ("curl" the weight) until they almost reach your collarbone; then return to the starting position (Figure 7–4). With dumbbells, this exercise can be done one arm at a time (Figure 7–5).

## Reverse Curls

Reverse curls have an effect similar to that of preacher curls, except that they place a different stress on the forearm muscles. You can do this exercise with a barbell, dumbbells, or a curl bar and in a seated or standing position.

 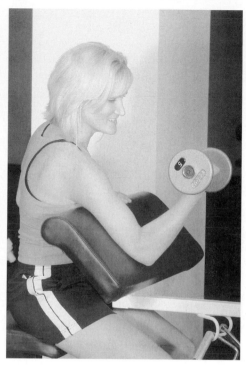

**Figure 7–4** Preacher curls (barbell). Major muscles developed: biceps brachii, brachialis, forearm flexors.

**Figure 7–5** Preacher curls (dumbbells). Major muscles developed: biceps brachii, brachialis, forearm flexors.

♦   THE TECHNIQUE    Stand holding the weight with arms extended, using a pronated grip (palms down, the opposite of preacher curls). Lift the weight by bending your elbows until the bar almost reaches your collarbone; then return to the starting position (Figure 7–6).

## Pole Curls with a Partner (Poleates)

**Poleates** is a resistive exercise routine using a pole, softball bat, or strong broom handle. It is a **functional training** method that builds the target muscle group (i.e., upper arm, forearms, trapezius, etc.) while using the trunk (core) and lower-body muscles as stabilizers.

♦   THE TECHNIQUE    Grasp the pole or bar shoulder-width apart with a supinated grip. Begin with your arms extended and the bar below your waist. Curl the bar to your upper chest while your partner resists the motion (Figure 7–7, p. 101). This exercise produces functional strength for you and your partner because you must stabilize the muscles of your back, abdomen, and legs to complete the movement.

**Figure 7–6** Reverse curl. Major muscles developed: biceps brachii, brachialis, brachioradialis, forearm flexors.

## Curls, Exercise Machines

These machines resemble the preacher-curl exercise with free weights. They are excellent for isolating the biceps muscle.

♦    THE TECHNIQUE    Adjust the seat so that your upper arms are almost parallel to the supporting pad. You should be able to comfortably bend your arms through their full range of motion. Grasp the handles and extend your lower arms (starting position). Flex your arms as much as possible while keeping your elbows on the supporting pad; then return to the starting position.

## Double-Arm Curls, Low Pulley

The same basic technique used with free weights is used for curls on the crossover pulley machine.

♦    THE TECHNIQUE    Adjust the chain of the low pulley station so that the weights you're using go above the weight stack when you stand with the bar at your abdomen. With hands at waist level, grasp the bar with a supinated grip (starting position). Keeping your

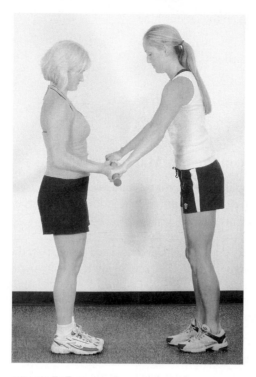

**Figure 7 7** Pole curls with a partner
Major muscles developed: biceps brachii,
brachialis, forearm flexors.

elbows close to your sides, flex your elbows until the weight touches your upper chest; then
return to the starting position.

## Other Exercises for the Front of the Arm

Any exercise that adds stress to the arm muscles as you bend your elbow will work this part
of your body. Exercises that work the biceps, as well as other muscles, include pull-ups,
chin-ups, lat pulls, and rowing exercises. Pulling exercises, such as cleans and, snatches,
also work the biceps. You work the biceps eccentrically (under tension as the muscle lengthens) during upper-body lifts such as the bench, incline, and military presses.

## EXERCISES FOR THE BACK OF THE ARM

The triceps is the major muscle of the back of the arm, and it is trained during all exercises
that involve pressing. Examples of exercises that are particularly good for building the triceps include these:

- Triceps extensions on the lat machine
- French curls
- Bench triceps extensions
- Parallel-bar dips
- Chair dips
- Triceps extensions, exercise machines

## Triceps Extensions on the Lat Machine

The triceps extension on the lat machine is an excellent exercise for isolating the triceps muscles. If you develop elbow pain as a result of doing this exercise, try another of the triceps exercises described previously.

◆   THE TECHNIQUE    Using a narrow, pronated grip, grasp the bar of the lat machine and fully extend your arms with your elbows held closely at your side (Figure 7–8). From this starting position, with elbows locked at your side, allow your hands to be pulled up to your chest; then firmly push the weight back to the starting position. If your elbows move during this exercise, you are cheating.

**Figure 7–8**  Triceps extensions on the lat machine. Major muscles developed: triceps brachii.

## French Curls

This exercise appears to be similar to the behind-the-neck press, which develops the shoulders (see Chapter 6), but it is very effective in isolating the triceps when done properly. The basic difference between the two exercises is that the behind-the-neck press involves movement of both the shoulder and elbow joints, whereas in French curls the shoulders are fixed and the movement occurs in the elbows. Use a spotter for this exercise.

◆    THE TECHNIQUE    Grasp a barbell behind your head, using a pronated grip with your hands approximately 6 to 12 inches apart (Figure 7–9). Keeping your elbows up and stationary, extend your arms until the weight is overhead; then return to the starting position.

## Bench Triceps Extensions

This exercise is similar in many ways to French curls.

| CAUTION | ◆ Be careful not to use too much weight; if you lose control of the bar during the exercise, you could seriously injure yourself. |
|---------|---|

**Figure 7–9** French curls. Major muscles developed: triceps brachii.

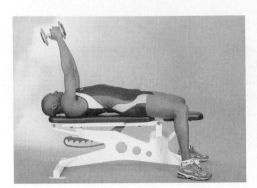 

**Figure 7–10**  Bench triceps extensions. Major muscles developed: triceps brachii.

♦   THE TECHNIQUE   Lie on a bench, grasping a dumbbell with two hands (Figure 7–10). Push the weight above your chest until your arms are extended (starting position). Keeping your elbows fixed, carefully lower the weight until it reaches a point even with the top of your head, and then push the weight back to the starting position. Use a spotter for this exercise.

## Parallel-Bar Dips

This exercise is excellent for helping you improve your bench press as well as for building your triceps. Several equipment manufacturers make parallel-bar-dip machines that actively assist you with the movement.

♦   THE TECHNIQUE   If you are using a machine, adjust the weight according to how much help you need to complete the set. Support yourself between the parallel bars on your fully extended elbows (Figure 7–11). Lower yourself by slowly bending your elbows until your chest is almost even with the bars. Then push up until you reach the starting position. If you aren't using a machine, a good way to improve if you can't do any repetitions initially is to have someone hold your waist and assist you during the motion.

## Chair Dips

This exercise is similar to parallel-bar dips, and you can do it at home using a couple of chairs.

♦   THE TECHNIQUE   Support yourself between two sturdy chairs placed slightly more than shoulder-width apart. Face toward the ceiling with your elbows and legs fully extended. Lower yourself by slowly bending your elbows (Figure 7–12). Then push up until

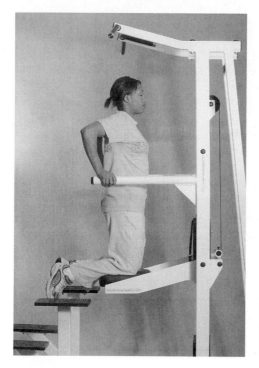

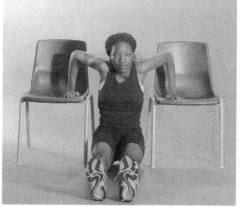

**Figure 7–11** Parallel-bar dips. Major muscles developed: triceps brachii, deltoids.

**Figure 7–12** Chair dips. Major muscles developed: triceps brachii, deltoids.

you reach the starting position. If you are doing this exercise on a bench, keep your back close to the bench during the exercise to avoid putting undue stress on the shoulders.

## Triceps Extensions, Exercise Machines

Triceps machines are excellent for isolating the triceps muscle. The technique may vary slightly on different machines.

♦   THE TECHNIQUE   Adjust the seat so that when you sit down your elbows are slightly lower than your shoulders. Place your elbows on the support cushion and your forearms on bar pads (starting position). Extend your elbows as much as possible; then return to the starting position.

## EXERCISES FOR THE FOREARM

The forearm muscles are essential to any activity requiring a rapid wrist movement (snap), such as in golf, tennis, badminton, and ball throwing. Weakness or overuse of the forearm muscles results in tennis or carpenter's elbow. The forearm muscles are also

**Figure 7–13** Forearm pole twists with a partner. Major muscles developed: forearm flexors and extensors.

largely responsible for grip strength. Exercises that develop the forearm muscles include these:

◆ Pole twists (poleates)
◆ Wrist curls
◆ Wrist rollers

## Pole Twists (Poleates)

This exercise is another example of poleates. It requires a partner and a rubberized pole, a softball bat, or a sturdy broom handle. One partner twists the bar using the forearm muscles while the other partner resists.

◆ THE TECHNIQUE   Grasp the bar in both hands while your partner holds the other end of the bar tightly (Figure 7–13). Twist the bar by turning your wrist—first inward, then outward.

## Wrist Curls

Wrist curls are done using either a supinated or a pronated grip. Supinated wrist curls build the forearm flexors and are important accessory exercises to biceps curls. Pronated or reverse wrist curls build the wrist extensors, the muscles injured in tennis elbow.

◆ THE TECHNIQUE   You can do this exercise with either a barbell or dumbbells. In a seated position, with forearms resting on your thighs and hands extending over your knees, use a supinated grip to hold the weight and lower it as far as possible; then lift your hands upward ("curl" your wrists) by bending at the wrists as much as you can. Repeat this exercise using a pronated grip.

You can do wrist curls on the low pulley of the crossover machine with either the handles or the small bar. A variation of this exercise is the lateral wrist curl. It requires the use of a small bar with the weight affixed at one end. Do the exercise the same way you do wrist curls, except bend your wrist to the side.

## Wrist Rollers

This exercise requires a machine, such as the wrist-roller station on some exercise machines, or a wrist-roller device. The device can be purchased or constructed. To make one, drill a hole through a cylindrical piece of wood and tie a 3-foot piece of rope or small chain to it. Then attach the weight to the other end of the rope.

♦   THE TECHNIQUE   While holding the piece of wood out in front of you with both hands using a pronated grip, lift the weight by winding the rope around the wood.

## Other Exercises for the Forearm and Grip

Grip strength is very important in certain sports—tennis, softball, and rock climbing, for example. People often don't have very good grips because they don't work to develop them. Serious weight-trained athletes have very strong forearms and grips, yet few of them do wrist rollers or wrist curls. Large-muscle weight lifts, such as cleans, snatches, and dead lifts, place considerable stress on the forearms and hands. If you do these kinds of lifts, you will develop a good grip and strong forearms—especially if you do them without using lifting straps.

If you don't want to do these exercises, carry around a small rubber ball and squeeze it every time you think of it. This isometric exercise is very effective for developing grip and forearm strength.

CHAPTER

# 8

# DEVELOPING THE BACK AND NECK

*The quality of people's lives is in direct proportion to their commitment to excellence, regardless of their chosen field of endeavor.*

—VINCE LOMBARDI

MOST PEOPLE HAVE TROUBLE WITH THEIR BACK AND NECK AT SOME POINT DURING THEIR lifetime, yet this part of the body is often neglected by weight trainers.

The spine is composed of a series of bones called *vertebrae,* with the spinal cord running through a channel in these bones. In between the vertebrae lie shock absorbers, the intervertebral disks. The spine has three natural curves, which aid the disks in absorbing shock. Strong muscles are important for maintaining these curves.

Weight trainers must take special care to select exercises that do not damage the intervertebral disks. Nerves that emerge from the spinal cord act as messengers between the tissues and the central nervous system. Pain and muscle spasm result if abnormal pressure is put on these nerves. Strong back and neck muscles help maintain the proper alignment in the vertebrae and prevent pressure on the spinal nerves. See the "Fact or Fiction?" box.

Strong back and neck muscles are critical for movement. Because the neck controls the movement of the head, strong neck muscles are important in any sport. The middle- and upper-back muscles are also vital to almost all movements and provide a balance to the muscles of the front of the body. The lower-back muscles help maintain the body in an upright posture and are important in bending movements. Because the low back is notoriously vulnerable to injury, these muscles must be kept strong and flexible. See the box "Healthy Highlight: Multiple Sets Work Best in Trained Women" on p. 110.

## FACT OR FICTION?

*MYTH: ACTIVITIES SUCH AS YOGA, T'AI CHI, AND PILATES DON'T BUILD MUSCLE STRENGTH.*

These exercises require you to hold certain poses and perform slow, controlled movements, which overloads the muscles. Traditional resistive exercise will strengthen muscles better, but these exercises will build strength to a certain extent.

Most serious weight trainers have good chest and abdominal muscles but fall short in other muscle groups, particularly in the back and neck. The reason is simple—the muscles of the front of the body are the first things they notice when they look at themselves in the mirror. Most weight trainers, particularly beginners and body builders, spend more time working their pecs and abs than any other upper-body muscles.

Overemphasizing chest and arm muscles will give you an unbalanced physique. You should work your back muscles as much as you work the front muscles. Good back development gives your body symmetry and adds stability and balance to your shoulder joints, helping prevent injury and overuse problems.

Many body builders and serious weight trainers lack balanced muscle development because they do only a few exercises and neglect the rest. Despite being much stronger than the average person, they often exhibit muscle imbalances and restricted flexibility during a variety of shoulder and back movements.

## THE BACK MUSCLES

The back is subdivided into the upper, middle, and lower back. To build the back optimally, you should know the major muscles, their actions, and which exercises build those muscles best. The surface muscles of the upper back include the trapezius (traps) and the posterior deltoids. These muscles, which give height and breadth to back development, are discussed later in this chapter. The muscles of the middle back include the latissimus dorsi (lats), rhomboids, and teres major. The lower-back muscles, called collectively the erector spinae, include the longissimus, spinalis, and iliocostalis.

The lats are attached to the upper end of the arm bone (humerus) at one end and fan out down the length of the spine to the pelvis. The latissimus dorsi extends the shoulder, that is, it pulls the arm downward toward the hips. During pull-ups, the lats raise the body toward the arms when the arms are fixed. These muscles also stabilize the trunk during multijoint, large-muscle lifts, such as squats and bench presses.

The rhomboids (major and minor) run from the spine to the scapula (shoulder blade), the large, flat bone that attaches to the humerus. When the rhomboids on both sides work

## HEALTHY HIGHLIGHT

### MULTIPLE SETS WORK BEST IN TRAINED WOMEN

An ongoing controversy in weight training is the ideal number of sets for promoting strength in nonathletes. More than 35 studies have shown that doing 1 set per exercise provides as much benefit as doing 2 or more sets, but other researchers disagree. Dr. Bill Kraemer, in an elegant 6-month study on women, found that they gained strength during the entire study when they did multiple sets per exercise under the supervision of a personal trainer. German researchers, using trained women, found that those who did 1 set per exercise lost strength, while those who did 3 sets gained strength. The take-home message is that weight training works best when you exercise intensely. Most people only go through the motions when they train with weights. Train hard when you work out, and save the socializing for later.

(*Journal of Strength and Conditioning Research* 18: 689–694, 2004)

together, the muscles squeeze the shoulder blades together. The rhomboids draw the scapula toward the spinal column. The teres major muscle connects the scapula to the humerus. This muscle moves the humerus backward, that is, it pulls the arm toward the back. The rhomboids and teres major work together to move the arms backward during movements such as rowing.

The erector spinae muscles support and extend the spine. These muscles attach to the vertebrae, ribs, and pelvis. Well-developed spinal muscles look like two boa constrictors running up your back.

Strive to build all three parts of the back if you want to develop a superior physique and well-balanced muscles. Strong, symmetrical back muscles give balance to the shoulder joint by maintaining uniform tension on the front and back of the shoulder. This in turn promotes joint health and prevents shoulder pain stemming from abnormal stresses on the joint.

## EXERCISES FOR THE LATS (MIDDLE BACK)

Good exercises for the lats include these:

- ◆ Pull-ups
- ◆ Pull-downs on the lat machine (lat pulls)
- ◆ Dumbbell pullovers
- ◆ Barbell pullovers

## Pull-Ups

Use a pull-up bar or an assisted pull-up machine for this exercise. Suspend weights from a weight belt to increase strength more quickly or when you can do more than 10 repetitions.

◆   THE TECHNIQUE   Using a shoulder-width, pronated grip, grasp the bar and hang with your elbows fully extended (Figure 8–1). Pull up your body until your collarbone reaches the bar; return to the starting position and repeat. Use a spotter or an assist machine if you can't do 10 reps.

## Pull-Downs on the Lat Machine (Lat Pulls)

◆   THE TECHNIQUE   Sit on the seat with your knees under the supports. Use a spotter if your lat machine does not have thigh supports. Grasp the bar with a wide grip, with arms and shoulders fully extended (Figure 8–2). Pull the bar steadily to your chest without jerking; then slowly return to the starting position.

**Figure 8–1**  Pull-ups. Major muscles developed: latissimus dorsi, biceps brachii.

**Figure 8–2** Lat pulls. Major muscles developed: latissimus dorsi, biceps brachii.

## Dumbbell Pullovers

♦   THE TECHNIQUE   Use a single dumbbell and lie on your back on a bench (Figure 8–3). Your feet should be flat on the floor, with your hips flexed slightly. Grasp the dumbbell from behind around the nearest set of plates, and position it over your chest (starting position). Flexing your elbows 15 to 30 degrees, lower the dumbbell over and beyond your head until your upper arms are parallel to your head and torso. Return to the starting position and repeat.

## Barbell Pullovers

♦   THE TECHNIQUE   This exercise was described in Chapter 6 (Figure 6–8). It works the pecs and the lats.

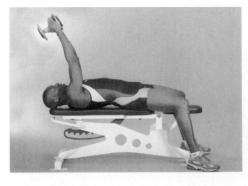
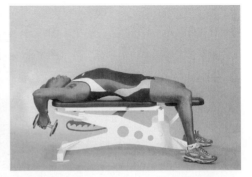

**Figure 8–3** Dumbbell pullovers. Major muscles developed: latissimus dorsi, pectoralis major.

# EXERCISES FOR THE RHOMBOIDS AND TERES MAJOR (MIDDLE BACK)

These exercises isolate and overload the rhomboids and teres major, giving your back a fit, defined appearance:

- One-arm dumbbell rows
- Incline reverse dumbbell rows
- Machine reverse flys
- Machine rows
- Seated cable rows

## One-Arm Dumbbell Rows

◆   THE TECHNIQUE    Place your right knee and right arm on a bench, with your left foot on the floor (Figure 8–4). Your back should be flat. Extend your left arm while holding a dumbbell in your left hand, using a pronated grip. Bring your left arm toward your chest in a rowing motion; return to the starting position and repeat. You can also do this exercise from a standing position with a barbell (bent-over barbell rows). Bending at the waist with your arms extended and spine fixed, pull the barbell toward your chest in a rowing motion; return to the starting position and repeat.

**Figure 8–4**  One-arm dumbbell rows. Major muscles developed: rhomboids, teres major, posterior deltoids, biceps brachii.

## Incline Reverse Dumbbell Rows

♦    THE TECHNIQUE    This exercise was described in Chapter 6 (Figure 6–15).

## Machine Reverse Flys

Some fly machines allow you to exercise the back muscles, as well as the muscles of the chest and shoulders, with an exercise called reverse flys.

♦    THE TECHNIQUE    Put your chest against the pad and extend your arms to the front (Figure 8–5). Pull the bars back, using the muscles of the upper and middle back (posterior deltoids and rhomboids).

## Machine Rows

♦    THE TECHNIQUE    This exercise requires a row or T-bar machine. For the row machine, sit in the chair and grasp the bar in front of you with your arms extended (Figure 8–6). Pull the bar toward you as you pull your shoulder blades together. For the T-bar machine, lie on your front (belly) with your chest firmly on the pad, and grasp the T-bar with your arms fully extended. Pull the T-bar toward your chest; slowly return the bar to the starting position.

## Seated Cable Rows

♦    THE TECHNIQUE    This exercise requires a cable rowing machine. Grasp the handles and place your feet on the rest in front of you. Extend your arms and legs fully; you should feel a stretch in your lats and rhomboids. Without jerking, pull the handles toward your chest, hold the contraction for 1 second, and then return to the starting position. Try to pinch your shoulder blades together during the exercise.

**Figure 8–5** Reverse flys. Major muscles developed: posterior deltoids, rhomboids, teres major, trapezius.

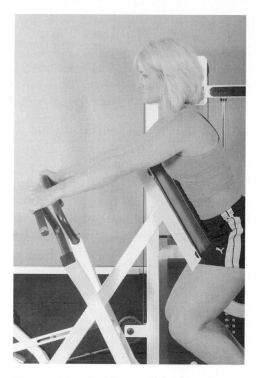

**Figure 8-6** Machine rown. Major muscles developed: posterior deltoids, rhomboids, trapezius, teres major, biceps brachii.

## LOW-BACK PAIN

More than 85 percent of Americans experience back pain at some time in their lives. Low-back pain is estimated to cost as much as $50 billion a year in lost productivity, medical and legal fees, and disability insurance and compensation.

Back pain can result from sudden traumatic injuries, but it is more often the long-term result of weak, inflexible, unfit muscles; poor posture; or improper body mechanics during activities such as lifting and carrying. Any abnormal strain on the back can result in pain. Most cases of low-back pain clear up within a few weeks or months, but some people suffer recurrences or chronic pain.

Back pain can occur at any point along your spine; the lumbar area, because it bears the majority of your weight, is the most common site. Any movement that causes excessive stress on the spinal column can cause injury and pain.

Risk factors associated with low-back pain include age greater than 34 years, degenerative diseases such as arthritis or osteoporosis, family or personal history of back pain or trauma, sedentary lifestyle, low job satisfaction, and low socioeconomic status.

Occupations and activities associated with low-back pain involve physically hard work that requires frequent lifting, twisting, bending, standing up, or straining in forced positions; high concentration demands (such as computer programming); or exposure to vibrations that affect the entire body (such as truck driving).

Underlying causes of back pain include poor muscle endurance and lack of strength in the abdomen, back, hips, and legs; excess body weight; poor posture or body position when standing, sitting, or sleeping; and poor body mechanics when performing actions such as lifting and carrying or sports movements. Abnormal spinal loading from any of these causes can have short-term or long-term direct and indirect effects on the spine. Strained muscles, tendons, or ligaments can cause pain and, over time, can injure the vertebrae (back bones) or the intervertebral disks (back shock absorbers).

## Preventing Low-Back Pain

Incorrect posture when standing, sitting, lying, or lifting is responsible for many back injuries. In general, your posture is good when you think about moving your spine as a unit, with the force directed through its long axis. Follow the same guidelines for posture and movement when you engage in sports or recreational activities. Maintain control over your body movements and warm up thoroughly before you exercise. Take special care when lifting weights as part of a weight-training program.

Regular exercise aimed at increasing muscle endurance and strength in the back and abdomen will prevent back pain, as will physical activity such as walking. Movement helps lubricate your spinal disks and increases muscle fitness in your trunk and legs. The following lifestyle recommendations may also help prevent back pain:

- Lose weight, stop smoking, and reduce emotional stress.
- Avoid sitting, standing, or working in the same position for too long.
- Use a supportive seat and a firm mattress.
- Warm up thoroughly before engaging in vigorous exercise or sports.
- Progress gradually when attempting to improve strength or fitness.

## Managing Acute Back Pain

Sudden back pain usually involves tissue injury. Symptoms may include pain, muscle spasms, stiffness, and inflammation. You may be able to reduce pain and inflammation by applying cold and then heat. Begin with a cold treatment: Apply ice several times a day. Once inflammation and spasms subside, you can apply heat using a heating pad or a warm bath. If the pain is bothersome, an over-the-counter nonsteroidal anti-inflammatory medication such as ibuprofen or naproxen may be helpful; stronger pain medications and muscle relaxants are available by prescription. Bed rest immediately following the onset of back pain may make you feel better, but it should be of very short duration. Limit bed rest to 1 day and begin moderate physical activity as soon as possible. Exercise can increase muscular endurance and flexibility and protect your disks from fluid loss.

Many cases of acute back pain go away by themselves within a few days or weeks, but you should see your physician if acute back pain doesn't resolve within a short time. Other warning signs of a more severe problem that requires a professional evaluation include severe pain, numbness, pain that radiates down one or both legs, problems with bladder or bowel control, fever, and rapid weight loss.

## Managing Chronic Back Pain

Low-back pain is considered chronic if it persists for more than 3 months. Underlying causes of chronic back pain include injuries, infection, muscle or ligament strains, and disk herniations. Because symptoms and causes are so varied, different people benefit from different treatment strategies, and researchers have found that many treatments have only limited benefits. Potential treatments may include over-the-counter or prescription medications; exercise; physical therapy, massage, or chiropractic care; acupuncture; percutaneous electrical nerve stimulation (PENS), in which acupuncture-type needles are used to deliver an electrical current to the muscles and nerves; education and advice about posture, exercise, and body mechanics; and surgery.

The exercises that follow are designed to help you strengthen the major muscle groups that affect the back. If you have back problems, check with your physician before beginning any exercise program. Perform the exercises slowly, and progress very gradually. Stop and consult your physician if any exercise causes back pain. General guidelines for back exercise programs include these:

- Do low-back exercises at least 3 days per week; many experts recommend doing back exercises daily.
- Emphasize muscular endurance rather than strength—endurance may be more protective. Many back injuries are caused by problems with motor control: If you attempt complex trunk movements (such as picking up a book from the floor) when your muscles are tired, you are more likely to strain muscles or put pressure on nerves, thereby causing pain.
- Don't do spine exercises involving a full range of motion early in the morning, because your disks have a high fluid content early in the day and injuries may occur as a result.
- Do regular endurance exercise such as cycling or walking in addition to performing exercises that specifically build muscular endurance and flexibility.
- Be patient and stick with your program. Increased back fitness and pain relief may require as much as 3 months of regular exercise.

## EXERCISES FOR THE LOWER-BACK MUSCLES

Most scientists who study back pain and its causes think people should emphasize muscle endurance and stabilization in the muscles of the back, abdomen, and sides of the abdomen. The three main exercises for developing a stable spine are crunches and side-bridges (described in Chapter 9) and isometric spine extension (the bird-dog exercise, described here). Exercises for the lower back include these:

- Isometric spine extension (bird-dog exercise)
- Back extensions
- Superman on the exercise ball
- Dead lifts
- Back extensions, exercise machines

## Isometric Spine Extension (Bird-Dog Exercise)

The purpose of the isometric extension exercise is to strengthen the lower-back muscles so that they are better able to maintain spinal stabilization and alignment. Most back experts feel that stabilizing the spine and building muscle endurance in the core muscles (abdomen, sides, and back) are the keys to a pain-free back.

◆    THE TECHNIQUE    Balancing on your right hand and left knee, lift your right leg and left arm (Figure 8–7). Extend your right leg to the rear, and reach to the front with your left arm. Hold this position for 10 to 30 seconds. Repeat with the opposite arm and leg.

## Back Extensions

◆    THE TECHNIQUE    Use a flat bench or a back-extension bench. Have a spotter hold your feet, or place your heels under the support (if using an extension bench), and hang over the support at waist level. Place your hands on your chest. Start with the body straight; then bend at the waist, keeping your spine rigid (Figure 8–8). Return to the starting position and hold. Move slowly on this exercise, emphasizing endurance over strength. This exercise is also very good for the hamstring muscles and will help improve whole-body lifts such as dead lifts and squats. Hold a weight plate against your chest to increase resistance.

**Figure 8–7**  Bird-dog exercise. Major muscles developed: erector spinae.

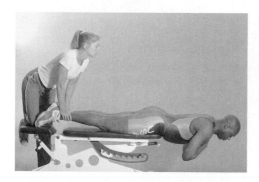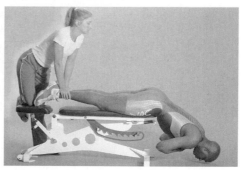

**Figure 8–8** Back extensions. Major muscles developed: erector spinae.

You can also do this exercise on an exercise ball. Lie face down with the ball at stomach level and your legs fully extended behind you, your toes touching the ground, and your hands touching your ears. Lift your head and chest off the ball slowly using your lower-back muscles. Return to the starting position.

## Superman on the Exercise Ball

♦ THE TECHNIQUE  Lie face down with the exercise ball at chest level and with your legs fully extended to the rear and your toes touching the floor (Figure 8–9). Extend your arms and place both hands in front of you as though you were flying like Superman. Hold the position for up to 30 seconds, rest, and repeat.

## Dead Lifts

This is one of the best overall weight-lifting exercises for building the major muscles of the body and developing functional strength (strength that is useful during whole-body

**Figure 8–9** Superman on the exercise ball. Major muscles developed: erector spinae.

movements). It loads the quads, hamstrings, glutes, and spinal muscles, as well as the shoulder and upper-back muscles. There are two dead-lift styles: traditional and sumo. While most power lifters use the sumo style, people interested in overall shaping and conditioning should use the traditional style because it works the quads and glutes better.

♦    THE TECHNIQUE    Stand with feet flat on the floor, shoulder-width apart and toes pointed slightly outward. Squat down and grasp the barbell using either a mixed (right palm facing one way, left palm the other) or pronated (both palms toward the body) grip (Figure 8–10). Keeping your back flat, chest up and out, arms straight, and eyes focused ahead, lift the bar by extending the knees and hips. Keep the weight close to the body as you lift the weight to a standing position. Slowly return to the starting position, taking great care to keep your back straight.

You can also do dead lifts on a Smith machine. Put the weight on the lowest level of the machine, and perform the lift in the manner described above.

## Back Extensions, Exercise Machines

Weak back muscles are easily injured when you do squats and pulling exercises (e.g., cleans and snatches). If your weight-training program includes these exercises, it's a good idea to

**Figure 8–10** Dead lift. Major muscles developed: gluteus maximus, quadriceps, hamstrings, erector spinae.

add low-back exercises. Back extensions help stabilize the spine and prevent fatigue when you stand or exercise in the upright posture.

---

**CAUTION**  ◆  Low-back weight-training exercises may subject the spinal disks to considerable pressure. If you suffer from low-back pain, these exercises may do more harm than good. Straight-leg dead lifts, although popular, are not recommended at all.

---

◆   THE TECHNIQUE    The instructions vary with the machine. For most equipment, sit on the seat, place your upper legs under the large thigh support pads and your back on the back roller pad, and plant your feet firmly on the platform (starting position). Placing your hands on your abdomen, extend backward until your back is straight; then return to the starting position. Try to keep your spine rigid during the exercise.

## BUILDING THE TRAPEZIUS

You've learned the principles of building the lats, rhomboids, and lower-back muscles. Now you'll learn how to build the trapezius (traps)—the major surface muscle of the upper back.

The traps make up much of the muscle mass of the upper body, yet most active people neglect to do exercises to develop them. If you include these exercises as part of your back routine, you will be amazed at how fast you gain strength and power and the positive changes that occur in your body. An added bonus is that you will balance the muscle development in your upper body and help keep your shoulder joints pain free.

The trapezius is one of the largest muscles in the upper body. When well developed, it sticks out prominently on the back of the neck and upper trunk. This large, diamond-shaped muscle attaches at the top of the neck and spreads to the shoulder attachment along the collarbone (clavicle) and down to the middle of the back, tying in the shoulders and lats. Like the lats, the trapezius has an irregular shape. Traps allow you to turn and tilt your head, raise and twist your arms, and shrug or fix your shoulders. The muscle is also important in posture, supporting the upper spine. The traps shrug, squeeze together, and depress the shoulder blades (scapulae).

The trapezius muscle is divided into three regions. The upper part allows you to shrug your shoulders. The middle and lower parts help move your shoulder blades during rowing movements. Building well-developed traps helps balance the muscles in the front of your upper body—the pecs and deltoids. This in turn helps improve posture and reduce the risk of injury by preventing unbalanced stress on the shoulder joint. As discussed earlier, if you work one side of the body, such as the chest and front deltoids, you should do an equal amount of work on the other side of the body—the traps, lats, and posterior deltoids.

You use the trapezius when you lift a weight upward using your shoulders. Any time your arms go below horizontal, you get assistance from your traps. They act as stabilizers during major upper-body lifts, such as the bench press, overhead or military press, and incline press. The traps are also important when you are doing back rows and posterior (backward) lateral raises. Shrugs and their variations are the best exercises for building the traps.

## EXERCISES FOR THE TRAPEZIUS (UPPER BACK)

Good exercises for developing the trapezius include these:

- Barbell shrugs
- Reverse barbell shrugs on the Smith machine
- Cleans, snatches, and high pulls

### Barbell Shrugs

Doing shrugs is the best way to develop the traps. Never roll your shoulders when doing shrugs, because this can cause tendonitis of the rotator-cuff muscles.

◆ THE TECHNIQUE   From a standing position with arms extended, hold a barbell with a pronated grip (Figure 8–11). Shrug your shoulders toward your ears, hold the contraction for 1 second, and then return to the starting position.

**Figure 8–11** Barbell shrugs. Major muscles developed: trapezius.

## Reverse Barbell Shrugs on the Smith Machine

♦   THE TECHNIQUE    Adjust the bar on the Smith machine so that you can grasp it with your arms slightly bent. Load the bar with an appropriate weight. Place the bar behind your back and grasp it at shoulder-width. Unhook the bar from the Smith machine and extend your arms fully. Holding the bar, shrug your shoulders toward your ears; hold the position for 1 to 2 seconds, return to the starting position, and repeat. When you are finished, hook the bar on the machine and walk away.

## Other Exercises That Build the Traps

Large-muscle, whole-body exercises are the best technique for building the trapezius. Exercises such as cleans, snatches, and high pulls involve a dynamic shoulder shrug as part of the lift that overloads the traps. Olympic-type lifts and their modifications should be part of the training program of most power athletes. These exercises are described in Chapter 10.

# EXERCISES FOR THE NECK

Most older weight-training books demonstrated exercises for the neck, while most newer books do not. Good neck strength is important for athletes in sports such as football, wrestling, and boxing. Unfortunately, many people who do neck exercises develop neck pain because they do the exercises incorrectly. As with the lower-back muscles, neck endurance and stabilization are more important than strength for preventing pain and injury. Doing the trapezius exercises described in this chapter will help you stabilize your neck without triggering neck injuries. Also, doing general range-of-motion exercises for the neck will help keep it pain free (Figure 8–12).

Several weight-machine manufacturers, such as Nautilus, make neck machines. Most health clubs and general-use college weight rooms no longer provide them. If you need a strong neck for sports, concentrate on repetitions before building strength. Take great care to do neck exercises slowly and precisely. Do not do exercises such as neck bridges until you have very strong neck muscles. Bridges have the potential for causing serious neck injuries, particularly in young people with weak neck muscles.

Avoid doing neck circles, which can cause excessive strain on the neck and may injure cervical disks. Instead do range-of-motion exercises in single planes: flexion, extension (not hyperextension), and lateral flexion.

## Manual-Resistance Exercises

Manual-resistance neck exercises provide an exercise load in all neck motions. These exercises are an easy, inexpensive way to strengthen neck muscles and can be incorporated almost anywhere in your program. For example, they can be added to your stretching routine prior to running or included as one of your weight-training exercises.

**Figure 8–12**  Neck range-of-motion exercises. Major muscles developed: sternocleidomastoideus, scalene, splenius capitus, splenius cervicus, trapezius.

---

**CAUTION**  ♦  Extreme care is essential: Manual resistance can be very dangerous if you use excessive force. Have your physical therapist, doctor, or coach instruct you in proper technique before attempting these exercises.

---

## Isometric Neck Exercises

You can increase neck strength by using your hand and arm to resist neck movements. Isometric neck exercises can overload neck muscles in flexion (chin toward chest), extension (pulling your head backward), and lateral flexion (bending your head to the right or left side).

♦   THE TECHNIQUE   For neck flexion, place the heel of your palm on your forehead and resist as you attempt to push your chin toward your chest. For neck extension, place the palm of your hand on the back of your head and resist as you attempt to push your head back. For neck lateral flexion, place the palm of your hand on the side of your head and resist as you push your head to the side (do this exercise to the right and left sides).

## Neck-Harness Exercises

Neck-harness exercises involve the same movements as manual-resistance neck exercises, but the resistance is provided by weights suspended from a neck harness. Neck harnesses are relatively inexpensive and can be purchased at almost any sporting goods store.

♦    THE TECHNIQUE    Neck flexion: Wearing the neck harness with weight suspended from the harness chain, lie on your back on a table. Allow your head to slowly roll backward; then pull the weight back up by moving your chin toward your chest. Be sure to hold the sides of the table with your hands so that you don't lose your balance.

♦    THE TECHNIQUE    Neck extension: Wearing the neck harness with weight suspended from the harness chain, stand with your knees bent and your hands on your thighs. Slowly lower the weight with your neck as far as possible; then return to the starting position.

♦    THE TECHNIQUE    Neck lateral flexion: Wearing the neck harness with weight suspended from the harness chain, lie on your side on a table or bench. Allow your head to slowly bend to the lower side; then pull the weight upward by moving your ear toward your higher shoulder. Do this exercise on the right and left sides of your body.

## Neck-Machine Exercises

Several equipment manufacturers make neck exercise machines that provide resistance during neck flexion, extension, and lateral flexion. Nautilus makes a neck-rotation machine, but few facilities have it. Working out on neck machines is probably superior to performing the manual or neck-harness methods, so use the machines if you have access to them.

## Four-Way Neck Machines

Four-way neck machines allow you to do neck flexion, extension, and lateral flexion. Each movement requires you to change your seating position. Do these exercises with your neck muscles, not your trunk.

**CAUTION**    ♦    Progress slowly. Neck muscles are easily strained and take a long time to heal. Do not do these exercises if they cause sharp pains. Do not hyperextend the neck.

C H A P T E R

# 9 DEVELOPING THE ABDOMINAL MUSCLES

Continuous effort—not strength or intelligence—
is the key to unlocking our potential.

—LIANE CARDES

MOST PEOPLE WANT A FLAT STOMACH. WELL, HERE'S SOME BAD NEWS AND SOME GOOD news. No matter how much exercise you do, fat around the middle will remain unless you burn more calories than you take in. There is no such thing as spot reducing—you can't exercise muscles and lose the fat lying over them. Now for the good news. The abdominal muscles (abs) are the major supporting structures of the abdomen. Unlike the legs and arms, which have large bones that provide structure, the abdomen has no bones. Strong muscles add support to the area and act like a biological girdle to "hold you in." If you strengthen the abdominal muscles, the area will look tighter, even though the fat may still be there.

The principal abdominal muscles are the rectus abdominis, which causes the trunk to bend or flex, and the obliques, which assist the rectus and allow you to rotate your trunk and bend to the side.

## ABDOMINAL FAT: THE BAD AND THE UGLY

You already know that a fat abdomen is unattractive, but it's also unhealthy. Everyone wants a firm, cut midsection to improve appearance, but too much abdominal fat can kill you! Although one fat cell looks like another under a microscope, all fat cells are not created equal.

## HEALTHY HIGHLIGHT

### CAN YOU BE FIT AND FAT?

Sixty percent of Americans are overweight, and 25 percent are obese. Many of these people exercise regularly—some vigorously—but are still overweight. Dr. Steven Blair and his colleagues from the Aerobics Center in Dallas showed that carrying a few extra pounds is okay if you are metabolically fit and exercise regularly. Overweight but metabolically fit people often have normal blood pressure, blood sugar, and cholesterol. The Nurse's Health Study from Harvard, which involved more than 115,000 women, showed that regular exercise did not fully erase the consequences of excess weight, however. The healthiest women were thin and active. Both inactivity and obesity independently increased the risk of premature death. Obese inactive women had a death rate 2.4 times higher than that of thin active women, while the rate was 2.0 times higher in obese active women. The statistics were better for women who were overweight but not obese. Overweight inactive women had an increased death risk of 64 percent, while overweight active women had a 28 percent higher risk than thin active women. Thin inactive women had an increased risk of death of 55 percent compared to thin active women. It's best to be lean and active, but you get some health benefit from exercise no matter how much you weigh. It's easier for a fat person to increase physical activity than to lose weight through diet alone.

(*New England Journal of Medicine* 351: 2694–2703, 2004)

See the box "Healthy Highlight: Can You Be Fit and Fat?" Men tend to store fat in their abdomen, giving them an apple shape. Women store it in their legs, hips, and butt, giving them a pear shape. The male "beer belly" is more damaging to health than the female "fat butt" because it is linked to a group of health problems that scientists call the "metabolic syndrome"—high blood pressure, insulin resistance, type 2 diabetes, high cholesterol, and blood-clotting abnormalities. Unfortunately, these days even young women are storing more fat in their abdomens.

Abdominal fat consists of cavity fat (fat surrounding the internal organs) and subcutaneous fat (fat lying just under the skin, the fat that hangs over your belt). Abdominal cavity fat is dangerous because it is easily mobilized and can flood the liver and blood with dangerous fat. Decreasing abdominal fat helps fight the metabolic syndrome; reduces the risk of heart attack, cancer, and stroke, and boosts energy levels and sexual performance.

While men usually have more abdominal fat than women, genetics and age are also important factors. Big abdomens run in families, but you do not have to be a slave to your genes. You can lose abdominal fat if you are willing to change your diet and level of exercise. Both men and women increase abdominal fat as they age. After age 20, fat weight increases by 17 percent per decade, and waist size increases by 2 percent per decade.

Creeping waistlines are not inevitable, however; you can fight them with a lifelong program of exercising, counting calories, and reducing saturated fat and simple sugar intake.

For men, the risk of heart disease and stroke is higher when the waist measures more than 40 inches. The risk increases substantially if the waist measures more than 45 inches. For women, health risks increase when waist circumference exceeds 35 inches. Scientists also use waist-to-hip ratio as an indicator of excessive abdominal fat, but it is a less useful measure than waist circumference. Most people want to have a waist circumference well below the danger point so they will be healthy and look good.

# THE ABDOMINAL MUSCLES

The abdomen, unlike the arms and legs, depends largely on muscles rather than bones for support. Many people store fat around their middles, which makes it difficult to show off well-toned muscles. You will not have that "six-pack" look if your abdominal muscles are covered in fat, no matter how fit and "cut" your abs are. If your muscles are strong and conditioned, you will have a better-looking midsection even if you have some abdominal fat. Your stronger muscles will help hold in your midsection.

Four muscles make up the abs: the rectus abdominis, internal obliques (two muscles, one on each side), external obliques (two muscles), and transversus abdominis (also called transversalis). These muscles allow you to bend forward at the waist, rotate the trunk, and bend to the side. All the abdominal muscles help stabilize the spine and prevent back pain.

## The Rectus Abdominis

This is the muscle everyone sees. It runs down the length of the abdomen, from the lower part of your chest to the top of your pelvis. The rectus flexes the trunk, causing the spine to bend forward. The rectus also tilts the pelvis back and thus is important in maintaining a normal low-back curve and preventing back pain. You use it when you do crunches or pelvic tilts.

The shape of the rectus abdominis is a source of confusion for many people trying to develop it. While the six-pack shape of the muscle suggests a series of muscles that can be developed separately, it is actually one large muscle. Four strips of connective tissue, called tendinous incriptions, divide it. These structures help reinforce the muscle and protect it from rupture during vigorous movements. The linea alba, another connective tissue structure that runs down the center of the muscle, also helps protect the muscle and gives it its six-pack shape. When activated, the entire muscle contracts, so it is extremely difficult to work only its upper or lower part.

## The Internal and External Obliques

You use the obliques to rotate and flex the trunk and bend to the side. These muscles are critical for movements involving weight transfer, such as hitting a baseball or tennis ball; throwing a discus, javelin, or softball; or punching a heavy bag.

The internal and external obliques form the sides of the abdomen and help twist and bend the trunk. They are critical in most sports and help give your body a T shape. Develop the obliques by twisting during crunches and by doing twists and side bends.

The quadratus lumborum is a deep muscle (one muscle on each side) that works with the obliques to help stabilize the spine and bend the trunk to the side. Building this muscle—through exercises such as the side-bridge—is critical to the overall strength of the abdominal (core) muscles.

### The Transversus Abdominis

This underappreciated muscle stabilizes the trunk and compresses your internal organs when you stand, lift, sneeze, cough, or laugh. Anytime you lift a weight or do any whole-body movement, the transversus abdominis helps stabilize your midsection. You develop this muscle when you do large-muscle lifts, such as squats, dead lifts, and bench presses. You can also work this muscle by tensing your abdominal muscles isometrically.

## SIT-UPS FOR SHAPELY ABS?

Sit-ups have been the mainstay of abdominal exercise for more than a hundred years. Anyone who wants great-looking abs does sit-ups—hundreds of them. Is this the best ab exercise? More important, are they safe? (See the "Fact or Fiction?" box.)

The sit-up test is a rite of passage for anyone enrolled in junior and senior high school physical education classes. Also, many people do sit-ups religiously to achieve the Holy Grail of a fit-looking body—firm-looking abs. Conventional wisdom suggests that sit-ups will build firm-looking abdominal muscles and develop core strength for improving performance in everything from waxing the car to hitting a tennis ball.

It's not that simple. Dr. Stuart McGill and colleagues from the University of Waterloo in Canada, in a series of elegant studies on the abdominal muscles and the spine, found that sit-ups put so much stress on the spine that we shouldn't do them at all. Their work also suggests that the sit-up test is dangerous and is not in fact a good measure of fitness.

You can develop shapely abdominal muscles and have a healthy back at the same time. Good abdominal muscle strength contributes to good back health—if you do the exercises correctly. Improperly done exercises can cause back injuries that never heal.

# FACT OR FICTION?

*MYTH: YOU CAN GET TONED, LEAN-LOOKING ABDOMINAL MUSCLES FROM DOING HUNDREDS OF SIT-UPS AND CRUNCHES.*

Abdominal exercises will help strengthen and tone abdominal muscles, but unless you minimize the fat around your middle, you will not have toned abdominal ("six-pack") muscles. Combine exercises from this chapter with a sensible diet, weight training, and aerobic exercise, and you can have better-looking abdominal muscles. It also helps to have good genes.

Chronic back pain is a big price to pay, particularly when you could develop fit-looking abs by doing other exercises. There are also better exercises than sit-ups for generating more powerful movements for sports such as golf, tennis, or volleyball.

The Canadian National Institute of Occupational Safety and Health (NIOSH) sets limits for body stresses in the workplace. Dr. McGill's research shows that repeatedly stressing the back lowers its tolerance to injury. NIOSH set an upper limit of back compression of 3300 Newtons (a Newton, abbreviated N, is a measure of force). One bent-knee sit-up creates 3350 N, while straight leg sit-ups create a whopping 3506 N—much greater than the maximum level set by NIOSH for predicting back injury. Curl-ups, on the other hand, create only 1991 N of spinal compression, and side-bridges (a great exercise for your obliques) create 2585 N.

Part of our preoccupation with sit-ups comes from a misunderstanding of the role of the abdominal muscles in movement. The torso region needs stability to transmit forces between the upper and lower body. The main function of the rectus abdominis—the long, wide muscle on the front of the abdomen—is not to shorten and flex the trunk. Rather, it is an important stabilizer and force transmitter, as suggested by the structure of the muscle. Tendons divide the muscle into four portions, giving the well-developed rectus a six-pack appearance. The muscle is designed to transmit stresses around the spine, which increases the efficiency of the obliques—the muscles on the sides of the abdomen. The rectus abdominis thus is more important as a spinal stabilizer than as a major factor in trunk movement.

## THE CORE AND THE KINETIC CHAIN

Most movements use several joints and many muscles, either as prime movers, assist muscles, stabilizers, or antagonistic muscles. The link that coordinates these joint movements is called the **kinetic chain.**

The key to most linked movements is the core or midsection—the abdominal muscles, deep lateral stabilizing muscles, and spinal extensor muscles. The core is critical to most movements involved in sports because it transmits forces between the lower and upper body. As mentioned above, the rectus abdominis is an important stabilizer and force transmitter.

Build the core muscles by forcing the trunk muscles to stabilize the spine while you are standing, sitting, or lying down. Whole-body exercises—such as curl-ups on the exercise ball, side-bridges, bird-dogs, standing chest presses on a crossover pulley machine, squats, and medicine-ball passes—that stress the upper- and lower-body muscles will also develop the core muscles.

## SAFE, EFFECTIVE EXERCISES FOR THE ABDOMINAL MUSCLES

The goal of your abdominal program is to develop fit, attractive, functional muscles that support the spine and help prevent back pain. It's true that doing sit-ups overloads the abs, but it also causes back injury. If you do enough traditional sit-ups (straight-leg or bent-knee sit-ups), you will probably incur a back injury. The message from scientific studies is clear: *Don't do sit-ups!*

Abdominal-muscle exercise recommendations are based on the results of studies using electromyography, a powerful technique that shows how muscles are activated during exercise. Do abdominal exercises 3 or 4 days per week. Exercises for the abdominal muscles include these:

- Isometric abdominal exercise
- Isometric abdominal stabilizers
- Crunches
- Crunches on the exercise ball
- Side-bridges
- Reverse crunch on a bench
- Bicycle exercise

## Isometric Abdominal Exercise

Perhaps you're not aware that you have your own built-in abdominal exercise machine. You can work on your abdominal muscles anytime, anywhere.

◆  THE TECHNIQUE    Simply tighten your abdominal muscles for 10 to 30 seconds. In other words, hold in your stomach. If you do this periodically during the day, you will notice a difference within a few weeks. Don't hold your breath while holding in your stomach, because this could restrict blood flow to the heart.

## Isometric Abdominal Stabilizers

The abdominal muscles stabilize the body's midsection and help transmit force from the lower to the upper body. As discussed, building endurance in the core muscles (abdomen, sides, and back) will prevent back pain and help you perform better in sports.

◆  THE TECHNIQUE    Do this exercise on a bench with back support (Figure 9–1a) or on the ground (Figure 9–1b). When you first do this exercise, have a spotter hold your feet down and hold your trunk in a 60-degree position relative to horizontal (a flat bench). Hold this position for 10 seconds, rest 30 seconds, and then repeat 3 to 10 times. Gradually build up your endurance until you can hold the position for 30 to 60 seconds. To prevent injury, maintain a straight back during the exercise. You should eventually be able to do this exercise without assistance.

## Crunches

Crunches are a great exercise for isolating the abdominal muscles.

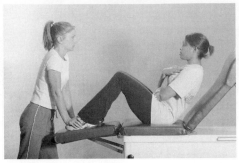

a                                                  b

**Figure 9–1** Isometric abdominal stabilizers. Major muscles developed: rectus abdominis, transversalis, obliques.

◆    THE TECHNIQUE    Lie on the floor on your back, with knees bent and feet flat on the floor (Figure 9–2). Some experts say to bend only one knee and leave the other leg extended. Place your hands across your chest. Contract your front abdominal muscles, drawing your breastbone downward. Try not to lift your shoulders; let your abs do the work.

## Crunches on the Exercise Ball

Electromyography (EMG) shows that this exercise works the abs best on an exercise ball, but it can also be done on the floor. EMG measures muscle activation during exercise.

◆    THE TECHNIQUE    Lie on your back on an exercise ball until your thighs and torso are parallel with the floor (Figure 9–3). Cross your arms over your chest and contract your abdominal muscles, raising your torso to no more than 45 degrees. Increase the stress on your oblique muscles by moving your feet closer together and placing your hands on your ears.

| **CAUTION** | ◆    Don't grasp your hands behind your head when doing crunches or sit-ups, because you might injure your neck. |

## Side-Bridges

Side-bridges are not a well-known exercise. However, EMG studies show that they strengthen the obliques and help stabilize the spine. People who do this exercise regularly will have a lot less back pain.

◆    THE TECHNIQUE    Lying on your side, support your body between your forearm and knees (Figure 9–4). Do this exercise on your left side and right side. As you increase fitness, first move your nonsupport arm across your body as you hold the side-bridge; later support your weight between your forearm and feet. Try to hold your spine straight—don't let it sag during the exercise.

**Figure 9–2** Crunches. Major muscles developed: rectus abdominis, transversalis, obliques.

**Figure 9–3** Crunches on the exercise ball. Major muscles developed: rectus abdominis, transversalis, obliques.

**Figure 9–4** Side-bridges. Major muscles developed: quadratus tumborum, obliques.

### Reverse Crunch on a Bench

♦   THE TECHNIQUE   Lie on a bench and stabilize your body by grabbing the bench above your head (Figure 9–5). Lift your legs so your feet are pointed at the ceiling, and bend your knees slightly. Contract your lower abdominal muscles and lift your tailbone off the bench by pushing your feet slightly toward the ceiling and pushing your lower back into the bench. Return to the starting position.

### Bicycle Exercise

♦   THE TECHNIQUE   Lie flat on the floor on your lower back, with your hands resting beside your head. Bring your knees toward your chest to about a 45-degree angle and make a bicycle-pedaling motion with your legs, touching your left elbow to your right knee and then your right elbow to your left knee.

**Figure 9–5** Reverse crunch on a bench. Major muscles developed: rectus abdominis, transversalis, obliques, erector spinae.

## Abdominal Machines

Abdominal machines from most manufacturers are similar. They provide resistance to trunk flexion at the chest as you bend forward from a seated position.

◆    THE TECHNIQUE    Adjust the seat so that the machine rotates at the level of your navel, the pad rests on your upper chest, and your feet can rest comfortably on the floor (starting position). Move your trunk forward as far as possible and then return to the starting position.

## Hanging Knee Raises (Captain's Chair Exercise)

This exercise is done hanging from a bar, between two bars, or in the captain's chair. It is a good exercise for the abdominal and hip-flexor muscles.

◆    THE TECHNIQUE    While hanging from a bar, bring your knees up toward your chest; then return to the starting position.

◆    THE TECHNIQUE    Captain's chair: Grasp the handles and rest your forearms on the pads (starting position) with your back pressed against the pad. Draw your knees toward your chest; then return to the starting position.

## Twists

Twists are a great way to exercise the obliques. But remember that exercising specific body parts will only help hold in the fat, not get rid of it. It may look better, but it is still there. This exercise may not be good for people who have back pain.

♦ **THE TECHNIQUE**    In either a seated or a standing position, place a pole on your shoulders and rotate as far as possible, first to the left and then to the right. Later, you can use a barbell with weights for added resistance. If you are more interested in definition than in size (as most people are), do many repetitions instead of using a lot of weight. Twisting exercises with medicine balls are also effective.

| **CAUTION** | ♦ Twisting exercises can cause back pain in some people—exercise with caution. |
|---|---|

## Trunk Rotation Machines

The rotary torso machine, made by Nautilus and several other companies, is a high-tech twist machine. There are two sides to it—one for rotating your trunk clockwise, and the other for working your trunk counterclockwise.

♦ **THE TECHNIQUE**    Sit on the seat (adjusted to the right side) and wrap your arms around the handles. Pull with your right arm and twist your trunk toward your left side. After completing your repetitions, adjust the seat to the left, sit on the seat, wrap your arms around the handles, and pull with your left arm, twisting your trunk toward your right side.

# HARNESS YOUR METABOLISM AND FIGHT ABDOMINAL FAT

Positive energy balance—taking in more calories in the diet than you expend through metabolism and exercise—is the major cause of increased fat. Unfortunately, getting rid of fat is more complicated than simply cutting back on calories and exercising. You have trouble losing abdominal fat because your metabolism won't let you.

The body tries to maintain a constant weight (called the weight set-point) by slowing metabolism as you lose weight. Most people who lose weight lose muscle mass as well as fat. Muscle burns a lot of calories—the more muscle you have, the higher your metabolism. As you lose muscle, you burn fewer calories. Also, as you lose weight, the body releases chemicals and sends signals from the nervous system that increase appetite and slow metabolism further.

Late-night television infomercials promise that exercising on ab machines reduces abdominal fat, a method called spot reducing. The classic way to achieve a flat, firm abdomen was to do hundreds of sit-ups. The idea of spot reducing made sense—if you have a fat gut, work the gut muscles to get rid of it. Unfortunately, spot reducing doesn't work. While doing abdominal exercises won't get rid of abdominal fat, burning plenty of calories through exercise will. Several recent studies have shown that people who exercise intensely tend to lose most of the fat from the abdominal cavity as well as the fat covering the abdominal muscles (subcutaneous fat).

You can lose abdominal fat and improve the appearance of your abdominal muscles by developing and toning the abdominal muscles, building muscle mass to increase metabolism, burning plenty of calories through exercise, and speeding up your 24-hour metabolic rate. As discussed earlier, muscle is the most metabolically active tissue in the body. The more muscle you have, the higher your metabolic rate. Also, muscle pushes against the fat near your skin and makes it look smoother. Exercise, particularly intense exercise, burns a lot of calories. If you exercise for 60 to 90 minutes a day, you will lose fat rapidly. Finally, the combination of intense and over-distance exercise will increase the tone of your nervous system so that you burn calories at a faster rate all day and all night. Intense exercise involves multiple, short bouts (10 sec to 2 min) at near maximum intensity, while over-distance training involves prolonged exercise (10 min to 3 hr) at submaximal intensity.

## Weight Training

Weight training is a central part of your abdominal-fat-management program. The workout involves doing 2 or 3 sets of 10 reps of 9 or 10 general weight-training exercises 3 days per week (Table 9–1). Train intensely—use as much weight as possible for each set. You will use less weight for the second set, when you do more repetitions. Weight training will help you burn more calories both during and after exercise.

## Aerobics

Do aerobic exercise for 60 to 90 minutes 3 to 5 times a week. Weight-bearing exercises such as running, power walking, treadmill running, StairMaster, and elliptical training are best for losing fat. Start with 5 to 10 minutes of exercise and build up until you can exercise continuously for 60 to 90 minutes without stopping. Also increase the intensity until you can exercise at 70 percent of maximum effort or harder during your workout. You will burn at least 700 calories during each aerobic workout and will help tip your metabolism toward fat loss.

## Interval Training

**Interval training** consists of intense exercises such as sprinting or cycling interrupted by periods of rest or light exercise. Interval training increases your metabolism so that you continue to burn calories at a higher level 24 to 48 hours after the workout is over. Long-term weight-control studies show that people who train intensely tend to lose more weight than those who exercise slowly. Run, ride a bike, or exercise on a gym aerobics machine (stairclimber, elliptical trainer, ski machine, etc.) for 1 minute at 90 to 100 percent of maximum effort, followed by 2 to 3 minutes of rest. Repeat 10 to 15 times.

## TABLE 9–1
### Example of a Workout to Improve the Appearance of Your Abdomen

There are countless variations on this workout. The program is intense and is designed to produce measurable results within 2 to 3 months. Work hard and stay with the program. You will be pleased with the results. If you haven't been exercising, scale down this program by doing only one set of each exercise and by doing less aerobics and interval training. Work toward completing the entire program.

MONDAY

Weight training (2 or 3 sets of 10 reps for 7–10 exercises):

- Bench press
- Dumbbell rows
- Lat pulls
- Curls
- Triceps extensions on lat machine
- Squats
- Knee flexions (leg curls)

Abdominal exercises:

- Isometric abdominal stabilizers (2 sets of 30 sec each)
- Crunches (2 sets of 10 reps)
- Bicycle maneuver (2 sets of 20 reps)
- Reverse crunches on a bench (2 sets of 10 reps)
- Crunches on the exercise ball (2 sets of 20 reps)
- Side-bridges (hold for 2 sets of 30 sec on each side)

Aerobics (60–90 min):

- Running, cycling, health-club aerobics machines, fast walking

TUESDAY

Interval training: running track 2 miles; sprint straight a ways, walk the turns

Aerobics (60–90 min)

WEDNESDAY (SEE MONDAY)

Weight training

Abdominal exercises

Aerobics (60–90 min)

THURSDAY

Interval training: running track 2 miles; sprint straight a ways, walk the turns

Aerobics (60–90 min)

FRIDAY (SEE MONDAY)

Weight training

Abdominal exercises

Aerobics (60–90 min)

SATURDAY

Aerobics (60–90 min)

Abdominal exercises

SUNDAY

Rest

## Diet

Follow a sensible diet that includes plenty of fruits, vegetables, whole grains, lean meats (beef, chicken, and fish), olive oil, and nuts (see Chapter 12). Minimize high-sugar drinks, simple sugars, salt, desserts, and saturated and trans fats. Try to keep your caloric intake at less than 2000 to 2500 calories per day. Moderation is the key—keep portions small, and avoid junk foods. You must exercise intensely, so avoid low-carbohydrate diets such as the Atkins diet. Your body metabolizes mainly carbohydrates when you exercise more intensely than 65 percent of maximum effort.

## You Can Improve the Appearance of Your Abdomen

In summary, you can improve the appearance of your abdomen by following these steps:

1. Burn plenty of calories during weight training, aerobics, and interval training.
2. Increase muscle mass to speed metabolic rate and smooth the appearance of the abdominal muscles.
3. Increase 24-hour metabolism by boosting muscle temperature during high-intensity exercise.
4. Create a negative caloric balance by consuming less than 1500 to 2500 calories per day (depending on your gender).

This program works. Stick with it, and you will cut down on abdominal fat and get a flatter, firmer midsection.

# 10 DEVELOPING THE LOWER BODY

Run hard, be strong, think big!

NANCY DITTLIT

THE LEG MUSCLES ARE THE LARGEST AND MOST POWERFUL IN THE BODY. POWERFUL movements in most sports are initiated with the leg and hip muscles. For example, golfers, pitchers, shot putters, and tennis players start with movement in their legs and finish the movement with their upper body. Those who fail to use the lower body effectively, relying instead on the weaker and more fragile upper-body muscles, perform inefficiently and are more prone to injury.

Most sports movements begin with the basic athletic position of bent legs and a low center of gravity, with hands to the front (Figure 10–1). This position allows easy movement in any direction and also provides stability. Movement is much easier and more effective if the lower-body muscles are strong and powerful.

This chapter discusses exercise for developing strength, power, and muscle shape in the lower body: multijoint exercises, auxiliary leg-strengthening exercises, and advanced lifts. You will have stronger, more defined legs if you include some of these exercises in your program. See the table "Weight-Training Exercises for Selected Machines and Free Weights" in Appendix 3 for other exercises.

**Figure 10–1**  Basic athletic position.

## MULTIJOINT LOWER-BODY EXERCISES

Multijoint exercises involve movement in two or more joints. Squats and leg presses are multijoint exercises that develop strength in the lower body, which can improve performance in most sports. These exercises also increase strength, to a certain extent, in the back and abdominal muscles. The following exercises are included in this chapter:

- ◆ Squats
- ◆ Power-rack squats
- ◆ Squats, Smith machine
- ◆ Front squats
- ◆ Hack squats
- ◆ Wall squats (phantom chair)
- ◆ Leg presses, exercise machines
- ◆ Lunges
- ◆ Step-ups
- ◆ Isokinetic squat machines

## Squats

Many people avoid squats because of reports that deep knee bends overstretch the knee ligaments. In fact, you can squat very low before the knee ligaments are stretched significantly. Good form is essential in this lift. Try to squat down "between your legs"—squat with your weight on your heels, and let your buttocks drop between your thighs. Beginners often use too much weight; consequently, they bend their backs excessively during the lift and sometimes injure themselves. See the box "Healthy Highlight: NSCA Supports Squats."

♦ THE TECHNIQUE    Many experts recommend using a weight-lifting belt when doing squats with maximum weights. No belt is needed when warming up or doing lighter sets. Too many people rely on a belt to protect the back rather than concentrating on using good technique. You will not develop your back and trunk muscles if you always use a belt. Begin the exercise standing with your feet shoulder-width apart and toes pointed slightly outward. Rest the bar on the back of your shoulders and hold it in that position with your hands (Figure 10–2). Keep your head up and your lower back straight. Squat down (under control) until your thighs are approximately parallel with the floor and your gluteals are about 1 inch lower than the knee. Drive upward toward the starting position, keeping your back in a fixed position throughout the exercise. A general strategy for this lift is to go down slowly and up quickly.

**CAUTION**    ♦    Never "bounce" at the bottom of the squat—bouncing could injure the ligaments of your knee.

# HEALTHY HIGHLIGHT

### NSCA SUPPORTS SQUATS

Most people don't like to do squats because they've been told the exercise causes knee injuries. To avoid injuries, many people do partial squats, going down just a few inches. The National Strength and Conditioning Association (NSCA) issued a position statement that supports squats as an important exercise. Squats are safe and effective and prevent injuries—if they're performed correctly. The squat doesn't hurt knee stability. In fact, it strengthens the muscles, bones, ligaments, and tendons in the lower body and trunk. Make sure your muscles are fit and conditioned before using heavy weights, and don't bounce in the bottom position. Do the lift with your legs and avoid excessive movement with the trunk. The squat is a favorite of many body builders because it builds the muscles in the quads, hamstrings, calves, and trunk.

(NSCA Position Statement, 2002)

**Figure 10–2**  Squats. Major muscles developed: quadriceps, gluteus maximus, hamstrings, erector spinae.

Safety should be of primary concern. A good squat rack is an important prerequisite. The rack should be sturdy and adjustable for people of different heights. Some racks have a safety bar at the bottom that can be used if the lift cannot be completed. Two spotters are also required—one standing on each side of the lifter, prepared to assist in case the person fails to complete the lift. Use a third spotter behind the lifter when squatting with a heavy weight. Some people wrap their knees and use weight-lifting boots to provide additional support.

You can do many variations of this exercise to increase your squatting power, such as power-rack squats and bench squats. Because of the high risk of injury, I do not recommend bench squats.

---

| CAUTION | ◆ Bench squats can be dangerous. You may unintentionally slam down on the bench during the exercise and injure your spine. |

---

## Power-Rack Squats

Power-rack squats allow you to use the power rack to overcome sticking points in the range of motion of the squat exercise. As with the power-rack bench press described in Chapter 6, you select three positions along the range of motion and work out at each one.

♦  THE TECHNIQUE   Place the bar on the first pair of pegs that allows it to rest on your shoulders with your thighs nearly parallel to the ground. Push the weight upward until you are standing upright. After your workout at the first position, move the pegs so that the bar lies in the middle of the range of motion. Repeat the exercise sequence. Finally, move the pegs so that the bar travels only a few inches during the exercise. At this peg stop, you will be capable of handling much more weight than you can from the parallel squat position.

## Squats, Smith Machine

The Smith machine, described in Chapter 6, is excellent for doing squats because it helps keep your back in a good position during the exercise. Perform squats on the Smith machine in the same way as with free weights. If you are experiencing back pain, step forward slightly when doing the exercise so that you are leaning slightly into the bar. This will take pressure off your lower back.

## Front Squats

The front squat is a variation of the squat used mainly in the training programs of Olympic-style weight lifters. This lift is better for isolating the leg muscles than the regular squat, because you cannot use your back as much to assist in the movement; consequently, you cannot lift as much weight in this exercise.

♦   THE TECHNIQUE   Standing with your feet shoulder-width apart and toes pointed slightly outward, hold the bar on your chest and squat down until your gluteals are 1 inch lower than the knee (Figure 10–3). Keep your elbows high and rest the weight above your collarbone. Do this exercise with good control, because you can easily lose your balance. You can improve stability by using weight-lifting shoes.

## Hack Squats

Hack squats isolate the thigh muscles more than regular squats do because they force you to keep your back straighter—even more so than during front squats. This exercise is generally used as an auxiliary to regular squats rather than as the primary leg exercise.

♦   THE TECHNIQUE   In a standing position, hold a barbell behind you with your arms fully extended down so that the weight rests on the back of your thighs (Figure 10–4). Slowly squat until the weight nearly reaches the ground; then push up to the starting position.

## Wall Squats (Phantom Chair)

The wall squat is an excellent exercise for your thigh muscles that requires no equipment. It is a particularly good exercise for ski conditioning.

♦   THE TECHNIQUE   Lean against a wall and bend your knees as though you were sitting in a chair. Support your weight with your legs. Begin by holding that position for 5 to 10 seconds. Build up to 1 minute or more.

**Figure 10–3**  Front squats. Major muscles developed: quadriceps, gluteus maximus, hamstrings, erector spinae.

<table>
<tr><td>CAUTION</td><td>♦ Wall squats may cause pain under or around the kneecap in some people. If you experience kneecap pain, particularly the day after doing the exercise, don't do this exercise—or decrease the time you stay in the squat position.</td></tr>
</table>

## Leg Presses, Exercise Machines

Leg presses are done on leg-press exercise machines and can be substituted for squats. They are safer and more convenient than squats because they don't involve handling weight, place less stress on the back, and don't require a spotter. However, leg presses are less effective than squats for developing strength in the quadriceps, gluteals, and hamstrings. Most manufacturers of weight-training equipment make leg-press machines.

♦   THE TECHNIQUE   Platform leg-press machine: Adjust the seat so that your knees are bent approximately 90 degrees when beginning the exercise (starting position). Push out forcefully until your knees are fully extended; then return to the starting position (Figure 10–5).

**Figure 10–4** Hack squats. Major muscles developed: quadriceps, gluteus maximus, hamstrings, erector spinae.

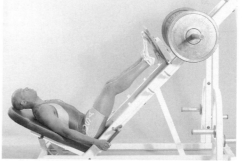

**Figure 10–5** Leg press. Major muscles developed: quadriceps, gluteus maximus, hamstrings.

| CAUTION | ♦ When doing leg presses, extend the knees fully but do not lock them because you could damage the menisci (shock-absorber pads in the knee joint). |

## Lunges

Lunges are a great exercise for the quadriceps (front of thigh), hamstrings, gluteus maximus (buttocks), and, to a lesser extent, calf and lower-back muscles.

♦   THE TECHNIQUE    Stand with one foot in front of the other, holding a dumbbell in each hand (Figure 10–6). Lunge forward with one leg, bending it until the thigh is parallel to the floor. The heel of the lead leg should stay on the ground. Do not shift your weight so far forward that the knee moves out past the toes. Repeat the exercise using the other leg. Keep your back and head as straight as possible and maintain control while performing the exercise.

## Step-Ups

Step-ups are a great way to build strength in your legs and help you make the transition to more difficult exercises, such as front and back squats.

♦   THE TECHNIQUE    Use an aerobics step, bleacher step, or gym bench. Hold a dumbbell in each hand or put a barbell on your back. Step up on the bench with your right foot, return to the starting position, and then step up on the bench with your left foot. Return to the starting position slowly, maintaining control.

**Figure 10–6** Lunges. Major muscles developed: quadriceps, gluteus maximus, hamstrings.

## Isokinetic Squat Machines

The isokinetic, or high-speed, squat machine is a relatively new product. These machines add resistance to the movement when you are going relatively fast. They present a tremendous risk of injury and have no place in the weight room. Squat machines that load the spine more slowly—such as those made by Hammer, Bowflex, and Soloflex—are safe and effective. See the "Fact or Fiction?" box.

| CAUTION | ♦ Sudden loading of the spine at high speed may cause severe damage to the intervertebral disks. High-speed squat machines are not recommended. |

# AUXILIARY EXERCISES FOR THE LOWER BODY

Several accessory exercises for the lower body isolate distinct muscle groups, such as the quadriceps, hamstrings (back of thigh), and calf. Auxiliary exercises include these:

- ♦ Knee extensions (leg extensions)
- ♦ Knee flexions (leg curls)
- ♦ Heel raises
- ♦ Heel raises, leg-press machines

## Knee Extensions (Leg Extensions)

Knee extensions are done on a knee-extension machine. Most equipment manufacturers have these machines. Knee extensions are excellent for building the quadriceps muscle group and are good supplements to squats or leg presses in the general program. Doing knee extensions with weighted boots is not recommended because it may strain the ligaments of the knee.

| CAUTION | ♦ Knee extensions may cause kneecap pain in some people. (See "Kneecap Pain" in Chapter 2.) These exercises, particularly if done through a full range of motion, increase pressure on the kneecap and cause pain. If you have pain in your kneecaps, check with an orthopedic specialist before doing this exercise. |

Doing knee extensions during the last 20 degrees of the range of motion (just before the knee is fully extended) builds up the muscle that tends to draw the kneecap toward the center of the joint. This exercise is often prescribed for people who have kneecap pain. Several companies make knee-extension machines that allow you to restrict the motion done during the exercise.

♦   THE TECHNIQUE   Sit on the knee-extension bench and place your shins on the knee-extension pads (Figure 10–7). Extend your knees until they are straight; then return to the starting position.

## Knee Flexions (Leg Curls)

Knee flexions, more commonly known as leg curls, require the use of a leg-curl machine. This exercise is done in either a prone or a standing position, depending on the machine. Upright leg-curl machines put the leg in a more functional position than do prone leg-curl machines. Instructions for this exercise are similar to those for most leg-curl machines. The exercise develops the hamstrings, the muscles on the back of the thighs. Most sports build the quadriceps muscles, but few work on the hamstrings. Because injuries can be caused by an imbalance between muscles, it is important to work on your hamstrings in addition to your quadriceps.

♦   THE TECHNIQUE   Lie on your stomach or stand, resting the pads of the machine just below your calf muscles (Figure 10–8). Flex your knees (either one at a time or together, depending on the machine) until they approach your buttocks; then return to the starting position. Because the hamstrings are weaker than the quadriceps, you will be unable to handle as much weight during this exercise as on the knee-extension machine.

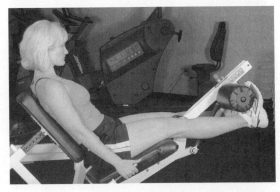

**Figure 10–7** Knee extensions. Major muscles developed: quadriceps.

**Figure 10–8** Knee flexions. Major muscles developed: hamstrings.

## Heel Raises

Heel raises strengthen the calf muscles—the soleus, gastrocnemius, and plantaris—and the Achilles tendon, which connects the calf muscles to the heel. While you can do them on a calf exercise machine, these exercises can be done anywhere using a step or a block of wood. They do not necessarily require weights.

♦    THE TECHNIQUE    Place the pads of the calf exercise machine on your shoulders and stand on your toes, with your heels hanging over the back of the base (Figure 10–9). Rise up on your toes as high as possible, hold the contraction for 1 second, and then return to the starting position. Other calf exercise machines may work the calf muscles from a seated position.

If you don't have access to a calf exercise machine, stand on the edge of a step or a block of wood with a barbell resting on your shoulders and slowly lower your heels as far as possible; then raise them until you are up on your toes. The calf muscles are very strong, and increasing their size and strength requires a lot of resistance. You can add calf exercises at the end of your squat or leg-press routine by doing some heel raises after your last repetition.

## Heel Raises, Leg-Press Machines

Heel raises can be done conveniently on a leg-press machine immediately after doing leg presses.

**Figure 10–9** Heel raises. Major muscles developed: soleus, gastrocnemius (calf muscles), plantaris.

◆　THE TECHNIQUE　Sit in the leg-press machine and fully extend your legs (starting position). Press down with your toes and lift your heels; then return to the starting position. You can work different portions of the calf muscles by pointing your feet straight ahead, inward, and outward.

## ADVANCED LIFTS

Popular with serious weight trainers, advanced lifts are complex exercises that take a considerable amount of time to learn. They are very valuable because they develop strength from the basic athletic position (see Figure 10–1) and help improve strength and power for many sports. Advanced lifts include the following:

- ◆ The clean
- ◆ The high pull
- ◆ The snatch
- ◆ The dead lift

## The Clean

The clean is a lift used to get the weight to the starting position for the overhead press (see "Overhead Press" in Chapter 6) or the jerk (part of the clean and jerk). It is an important exercise in the program of power athletes such as throwers, football players, multievent athletes (e.g., decathletes and heptathletes), and volleyball and basketball players—or anyone wanting to improve whole-body power.

♦   THE TECHNIQUE   The clean consists of a first pull, second pull, catch, and recovery. Each movement is continuous with the next.

First pull: Place the bar on the floor in front of your shins. With your feet approximately 2 feet apart, grasp the bar with palms facing you (supinated grip), and your hands at shoulder-width. Squat, keeping your arms and back straight and your head up (Figure 10–10a). Extend your legs and raise your head, shoulders, and hips as a unit (Figure 10–10b). Make sure that the pull is controlled and the arms remain extended.

Second pull: Pull the weight up past your knees to your chest while driving your hips and shoulders upward. After pulling the weight as high as you can, squat down suddenly.

Catch: Catch the bar on your chest at a level just above your collarbone (Figure 10–10c). Keep your elbows as high as possible, and hold the bar on the end of your fingers. The depth of the squat depends on both your experience and your goals. Catching the bar in a full squat is better for building whole-body power but takes more practice than catching it in only a partial squat.

Recovery: Stand up straight with the bar at chest level, with your feet shoulder-width apart and your elbows up.

The main power for this exercise should come from your hips and legs. Think of the middle phase of the lift as a vertical jump—this will make you drive up the weight with your legs rather than with your arms. Keep your arms straight for as long as possible, and hold the bar as close to the body as possible.

## The High Pull

The high pull (Figure 10–11) is a variation of the clean used to improve pulling power. It is identical to the power clean except that you don't turn the bar over at the top of the lift and catch it at your chest. This variation allows you to handle more weight and places less stress on your wrists and forearms, particularly if you use straps.

## The Snatch

The snatch (an Olympic lift) is another pulling exercise that is fun and fairly easy for the novice to master. Learn the technique using a broom handle or a wooden dowel, and progress to an Olympic weight-lifting bar before adding weight plates. This exercise develops whole-body power that eventually will make you stronger and faster on the playing field.

The object of the lift is to pull the bar over your head in one continuous motion and catch it overhead from a squat with your arms straight. As with the clean and jerk, good coaching is essential to mastering this lift.

a

b

c

**Figure 10–10** The clean. Major muscles developed: gluteus maximus, quadriceps, hamstrings, erector spinae, biceps brachius, trapezius, deltoids.

**Figure 10–11** The high pull. Major muscles developed: gluteus maximus, quadriceps, hamstrings, erector spinae, biceps brachius, trapezius, deltoids.

◆ THE TECHNIQUE    Place the bar on the floor in front of your shins, with your feet approximately shoulder-width apart (Figure 10–12a). Grasp the bar with palms facing you (supinated grip) and your hands placed as wide apart as possible. Squat, keeping your arms and back straight and your head up. Pull the weight up past your knees to your chest while throwing your hips upward and shrugging your shoulders (Figure 10–12b). After pulling the weight as high as you can, go into a squat and catch the weight overhead with your arms straight (Figure 10–12c). In competition, the lifter must stand and control the weight until the referee signals a completed lift. Stand up straight with the bar overhead. Return the bar to the starting position. The lift is divided into a first pull, second pull, catch, and recovery (or second movement).

First pull: The lifter extends the legs and raises the head, shoulders, and hips as a unit. The pull is controlled, and the arms remain extended.

Second pull: The second pull begins as the bar passes the knees; the lifter extends the hips, plantar-flexes the ankle (i.e., pushes on the toes while lifting the heels), and elevates the shoulders to propel the bar upward. During the second pull, the lifter exerts the maximum force over the greatest distance possible before dropping under the bar.

Catch: The squat and catch occur after the completion of the second pull. The lifter jumps and lands with feet parallel and toes pointing out and squats under the bar. The hips

a

b

c

**Figure 10–12**  The snatch. Major muscles developed: gluteus maximus, quadriceps, hamstrings, erector spinae, biceps brachius, trapezius, deltoids.

are brought forward close to the heels. The catch occurs with the lifter in the low squat position; the bar is secured overhead with elbows locked.

Recovery: The recovery, or second movement, occurs when the lifter drives upward out of the squat to a standing position. The lifter then lowers the weight to the floor under control.

## The Dead Lift

The dead lift is one of the three events in **power lifting** (a weight-lifting competition); the other two are the bench press and the squat. It is an excellent exercise for the legs, buttocks, and back. Because it is possible to handle a great deal of weight in this exercise, proper form is critical in order to avoid back injury.

♦   THE TECHNIQUE    Place the bar on the floor in front of your shins (Figure 10–13). Keep your feet approximately shoulder-width apart. Using a mixed grip (see "Grips" in Chapter 5), grasp the bar at shoulder-width and squat, keeping your arms and back straight and your head up. Pull the weight past your knees until you are in a fully erect position. Return the weight to the floor under control, being careful to bend only your knees and to maintain a straight back. Sumo is another style of dead lift, done with a narrow grip and feet spread wide apart.

**Figure 10–13** The dead lift. Major muscles developed: glutius maximus, quadriceps, hamstrings, erector spinae.

## FUNCTIONAL TRAINING MACHINES AND EQUIPMENT

Most modern weight machines isolate specific muscle groups, such as those of the chest, shoulder, upper back, or legs. While these machines are good for building muscle groups one at a time, they do little to build strength in several muscle groups at once—the way the muscles are used in everyday movements and sports skills. Functional training machines, made by companies such as Life Fitness, Nautilus, and Cybex, require that you do traditional exercises (such as chest presses and cable rowing) in a standing position and can simulate sports movements such as the golf swing. You must stabilize your legs, abdomen, and back to complete the lifts (see Figure 10–14).

**Figure 10–14**  Chest presses on a functional training machine.

C H A P T E R

# 11 EXERCISES TO DEVELOP SPEED AND POWER

The more I train, the more I realize I have more speed in me.

—LEROY BURRELL

JUMPING, PLYOMETRIC, AND SPEED EXERCISES ARE EXCELLENT FOR BUILDING BASIC muscle strength, power, and speed. New research shows that they help build bone mass in girls and young women that will protect them against fractures as they age. These fun, challenging exercises are excellent additions to most fitness programs.

Jumping, plyometric, and speed exercises enhance performance in sports because they increase leg power and train the nervous system to activate large-muscle groups quickly during movement. The exercises in this chapter enhance the capacity for single "explosive" movements such as jumping, throwing a baseball or softball, and hitting a golf ball or tennis ball.

## PLYOMETRIC AND SPEED EXERCISES

Plyometric exercises involve rapid stretching and then shortening of a muscle group during highly dynamic movements. The stretching causes a stretch reflex and an elastic recoil in your muscles. Combined with a vigorous muscle contraction, this creates a force that overloads the muscles and increases strength and power.

Plyometrics range in difficulty from calf jumps off the ground to multiple one-leg jumps to and from boxes. Calf jumps, a simple plyometric exercise involving jumping in

157

place repeatedly, use mainly your calf muscles. As you land on the ground after the first jump, your calf muscles stretch to help control your landing. The recoil from this stretch adds to the force of the muscle contraction used for the next jump.

The basic principle in all jumping and plyometric exercises is to absorb the shock with your arms or legs, then immediately contract your muscles. For example, if you are doing a series of squat jumps, jump again as quickly as possible as soon as you land after one jump. The more quickly you jump, the more you overload your muscles. These exercises train your nervous system to react rapidly.

In untrained people, the nervous system reacts slowly in activating the muscles during repeated muscle contractions, such as those that occur during calf jumping. This protective reflex is designed to protect the legs against injury. With conditioning, you can train the nervous system to react more quickly and to activate leg muscles rapidly. Stronger muscles and joints no longer need the protection of the reflex.

As discussed in Chapter 2, groups of muscles and nerves form motor units. Your body uses small, slow motor units to lift light objects and perform ordinary movements, such as standing and sitting. You use larger and faster motor units for rapid, powerful movements, such as sprinting or jumping. Because most sports require maximum effort at least part of the time, developing fitness in the large motor units is very important.

A basic principle of sports physiology is that *a motor unit is trained in proportion to its recruitment.* This means you can improve your capacity for powerful movements only if you train the motor units used during the activity. If you want to improve power for sports, overload your muscles at high speeds.

Sports movements use many muscles and joints at the same time. For example, jumping requires a coordinated action of muscles that move the ankle, knee, and hip joints as well as many other joints in the upper body and spine. Most weight-training exercises overload muscles that move only one or two joints. Although weight-training exercises build muscle, they don't train the muscles to work in coordinated muscle movements. Plyometric and speed exercises overload muscles in a way similar to the way muscles work during sports movements.

## INJURY RISK OF POWER EXERCISES

Any high-intensity sport or exercise increases the risk of injury because you push your tissues closer to their breaking point. When doing plyometric and speed exercises, start gradually and progress slowly. If any pain persists after doing the exercise, modify the program by doing fewer sets and repetitions of the exercise, fewer exercises, or avoiding the advanced, high-impact exercises. See the "Fact or Fiction?" box.

The intensity of plyometric and speed exercises ranges from simple bounces (jumping rapidly in place) to box jumping (jumping up and down from a box or bench). Start with the basic exercises and progress slowly to the more advanced movements. Don't advance until you can do the exercises without post-exercise pain. If you progress slowly, you won't get hurt, and you will become faster and more powerful in sports activities.

Jumping and plyometric exercises can cause stress to your muscles, bones, and joints, and all the exercises in this chapter are considered moderate to high impact. Don't do these exercises more than 2 or 3 days per week. If you feel pain in your muscles and joints for

## FACT OR FICTION?

*MYTH: YOUNG WOMEN SHOULD AVOID HIGH-IMPACT EXERCISES.*

Women develop peak bone mass during their teens and early 20s. After age 30, most women lose bone continuously as they age. Developing as much bone as possible during growth years and early adulthood will keep bones strong and viable longer. Studies show that loading bone develops bone during growth and maintains it during adulthood. The rate at which bone is loaded is as important as the absolute load. Plyometric exercises—such as jumping in place, box jumping, and rope jumping—load bone quickly and help build or maintain bone mass. You can reduce the risk of injury from plyometrics by ensuring that your major muscle groups are well trained through weight training and endurance exercises.

hours or days after a workout, modify your program or stop doing the exercises that give you trouble.

## BASIC SPEED AND POWER EXERCISES: LOWER BODY

Hundreds of speed and power exercises exist. This chapter introduces some basic exercises that will help you improve speed and power. For a more comprehensive discussion of this training technique, read specific books on plyometrics, such as *Jumping into Plyometrics* by Donald Chu.

An important principle of these exercises is that when you complete 1 repetition, you must begin the next rep *immediately.* This overloads your muscles and trains your nervous system. The list of exercises begins with simple, relatively low-impact movements (see the box "Healthy Highlight: Stretching before Exercise Decreases Strength and Performance"). More difficult exercises are presented later in the chapter. Don't attempt advanced exercises until you're in good condition and can do the exercises without pain. Start off by doing 1 or 2 sets of about 3 or 4 exercises. As you become better conditioned, build up to 3 sets of 6 to 10 exercises. Do these exercises correctly and intensely—it is better to do only 1 set correctly than to do many sets incorrectly or at half-speed.

**CAUTION** ♦ Always maintain control of your spine when doing plyometric and speed exercises. Try to direct forces through the length of the spine rather than across it. This will help you avoid back injuries.

Although the exercises described here develop power mainly in the lower body, they also develop coordination between upper- and lower-body muscles for whole-body power movements.

# HEALTHY HIGHLIGHT

### STRETCHING BEFORE EXERCISE DECREASES STRENGTH AND PERFORMANCE

Stretching before exercise is a time-honored ritual practiced by athletes in most sports. Surprisingly, stretching offers little or no benefit. Several recent studies have shown that pre-exercise stretching decreases muscle strength and performance in explosive muscle activities, such as jumping, for 15 to 30 minutes after doing the stretches. The best warm-up involves large-muscle range-of-motion exercises similar to those used in the sport or exercise program. For example, body builders should lift light weights when doing large-muscle lifts such as the bench press and squats before they lift heavy weights. Tennis players should hit forehands, backhands, serves, and volleys at relatively low intensities before playing a match. Runners, swimmers, cyclists, and skiers should do those activities at lower intensities before doing them intensely. Stretching is important for building strength and range of motion and for improving athletic performance. Stretch after exercise, when the muscles are warm. Many fitness experts claim that stretching is important for preventing injury and speeding recovery from muscle strains. However, in a review of literature, researchers from the Centers for Disease Control and Prevention concluded that there is insufficient evidence to either endorse or recommend against routine stretching before or after exercise to prevent injury among competitive or recreational athletes.

*(Medicine and Science in Sports and Exercise* 36: 371–378, 2004)

## Calf Jumps

The calf jump is a simple plyometric exercise that develops power mainly in the calf muscles.

◆　THE TECHNIQUE　　From a standing position, with hands on hips and knees slightly flexed, jump off the ground using mainly the muscles of your calves and feet (Figure 11–1). Try to "bounce" as quickly as possible when performing the exercise.

*Variations:* Advanced variations of this exercise include calf jump spins and one-leg calf jumps. With calf jump spins, attempt to spin as you jump, eventually turning 360 degrees between jumps. Do one-leg calf jumps the same way you do two-leg jumps, but lift one leg off the ground when doing the exercise.

## Rope Skipping

Rope skipping is essentially the same as calf jumping, except that it is more vigorous. It is an excellent exercise for conditioning the nonoxidative energy system and developing jumping

**Figure 11–1** Calf jumps.

power, particularly in the calf muscles. Do this exercise using either "boxer" or playground style. In boxer style, you use a short rope and jump by yourself. In playground style, two people swing the rope while a third person jumps. For most people, boxer style is more practical.

Good jump ropes can be purchased at almost any sporting goods store. The best ones are made of leather and have wooden handles and ball-bearing swivels. Ropes with these features turn easily in the hand without tangling. Buy one that fits you—it shouldn't be so short that you can't turn the rope without hunching over during the exercise or so long that turning it is difficult.

♦   THE TECHNIQUE    Hold one handle in each hand with the rope behind you. Swing the rope over your head and jump over it when it reaches your feet. Continue swinging the rope and jumping over it. Speed up the tempo as your skill improves. Start off with 5 to 10 segments of 15 seconds each and progress to 5 to 20 segments of 1 to 3 minutes.

As your skill improves, try some of the many rope-skipping variations. These include crossing your hands in front of you as you jump over the rope and swinging the rope to the side for two revolutions between jumps. You can also vary your foot movements so that they mimic running or dancing. Using a heavy rope or wearing a weighted vest increases the conditioning effect of rope skipping.

## Squat Jumps

The squat jump is a basic exercise that should be a cornerstone of any program designed to develop jumping and lower-body power. This type of leg power is important in all power sports.

♦ THE TECHNIQUE    Standing with your weight on the balls of your feet, squat until your thighs are 3 to 4 inches above **parallel** (Figure 11–2). Jump up vigorously, fully extending your ankle, knee, and hip joints. As in all plyometric exercises, when you land, *immediately* repeat the exercise. During the exercise, rotate your arms forward in an arc.

   *Variation:* Single-leg squat jumps. Same as above, except use one leg at a time (see "One-Leg Squat Jumps"). This is an advanced exercise and should be attempted only after you have adapted to the basic exercises.

## Mule-Kick Squat Jumps

This exercise is another variation of the squat jump.

**Figure 11–2** Squat jumps.

♦    THE TECHNIQUE    Stand with your feet shoulder-width apart and knees slightly bent (Figure 11–3). Jump up, driving your arms upward. As you reach the highest point of the jump, kick your heels backward and touch the back of your thighs. As you land, extend your legs, retract your arms, and prepare to jump again. Do 5 to 10 repetitions, taking as little time as possible between jumps.

## Double-Leg Tuck Jumps

The double-leg tuck jump is a more difficult variation of the squat jump.

♦    THE TECHNIQUE    Standing with your weight on the balls of your feet, squat until your thighs are 3 to 4 inches above parallel. Jump up vigorously, fully extending your ankle, knee, and hip joints. As you complete the jump but are still in the air, draw (tuck) your knees in vigorously toward your chest (Figure 11–4). *Move your knees to your chest, not your chest toward your knees.* Your arms use a "delayed rotation" movement to help you gain full lower-body extension. During the jump phase, your arms rotate upward to help you gain momentum. Delay the downward rotation of your arms as you tuck your knees to your chest. As you release your knees and descend to the ground, move your arms downward in preparation for the next jump.

**Figure 11–3** Mule-kick squat jumps.    **Figure 11–4** Double-leg tuck jumps.

## 360-Degree Squat Jumps

This exercise, another variation of the squat jump, is similar to the 360-degree calf jump described earlier. It requires more fitness than most squat jumps. Start with 45- to 90-degree turns and progress to 360-degree turns.

♦    THE TECHNIQUE    Stand with your feet shoulder-width apart and your knees slightly bent (Figure 11–5). Jump up and drive your arms upward, spinning in the air as much as possible. As you land, retract your arms and prepare to jump again. Start off by rotating in only one direction. As you become more advanced, rotate to the left on one repetition and to the right on the next. Do 5 to 10 repetitions, taking as little time as possible between jumps. Advanced variations of this exercise include tuck and mule-kick 360s.

## One-Leg Squat Jumps

Don't do these jumps until you have conditioned your legs with two-leg squat jumps. Progress slowly; if you feel ankle, knee, or hip pain after doing this exercise, cut down on the number of repetitions or eliminate the exercise from your program.

♦    THE TECHNIQUE    Stand on one leg and bend your knee slightly (Figure 11–6). Jump up and drive your arms upward. As you land, retract your arms and immediately jump again. Do 5 to 10 repetitions, taking as little time as possible between jumps.
    *Variations (all advanced exercises):* One-leg tuck squat jumps; one-leg mule-kick squat jumps; one-leg 360-degree squat jumps.

## Ice-Skater Exercise

The ice-skater exercise develops lateral leg power and helps stabilize the back against lateral (shear) forces.

**Figure 11–5**  360-degree squat jumps.

**Figure 11–6** One-leg squat jumps.

♦   THE TECHNIQUE   From a standing position, with your weight placed on the inside of the feet, extend with your legs and arms and jump to the right, using a speed-skating motion (Figure 11–7). Do the movement with your lower body; do not allow your trunk to sway in the direction of the skate. One jump to the left and one to the right make up one repetition of this exercise.

*Variations:*

♦   Sand ice skaters. Same as above, except do the exercise in the sand (i.e., long-jump pit).

♦   Slide-board ice skaters. Same as above, except do the exercise on a slide board. Slide boards are available commercially, or you can make one by building a wooden frame around a Formica board sprayed with silicone.

## Lunge Jumps

The lunge or split jump builds your thigh, gluteal, and back muscles. It is an excellent exercise for developing striding power for sprinting and lower-body flexibility.

**Figure 11–7** Ice-skater exercise.

♦ THE TECHNIQUE   From a standing position, jump up, and then land in a split position with your right leg bent and your left leg extended in back of you (Figure 11–8). After you land, immediately jump up, and again land in a split position, with your legs reversed. One repetition occurs when each leg has been in the forward position. During this exercise, try to keep your body straight and jump up as high as possible.

**Figure 11–8** Lunge jumps.

# HORIZONTAL JUMPS AND HOPS

These more advanced exercises involve jumping and hopping horizontally. They are excellent for developing basic leg power for jumping and running.

## Standing Long Jump

In addition to being excellent for increasing basic leg power, this exercise is a good gauge of your progress. Measure your standing long jump every few weeks. If you do speed and plyometric exercises regularly, you will be amazed at how rapidly you improve.

◆   THE TECHNIQUE   Stand with your feet shoulder-width apart and your toes just behind the starting (scratch) line (Figure 11–9). Bend your knees, bringing your hands below your waist, and then jump as far as you can. Try to extend your ankles, knees, hips, and arms fully to jump as far as possible.

**Figure 11–9**  Standing long jump.

## Multiple Standing Long Jump

This exercise is similar to the standing long jump, except that you take three jumps in succession.

♦ THE TECHNIQUE  Stand with your feet shoulder-width apart and your toes just behind the starting (scratch) line. Bend your knees, bringing your hands below your waist, and then jump as far as you can, extending your ankles, knees, hips, and arms fully. As soon as you land, try to jump again, and repeat until you have jumped three times.

## Standing Triple Jump

The triple jump is contested in track and field competitions. It used to be called the "hop, step, and jump," a name that describes its basic movements.

♦ THE TECHNIQUE  Stand with your feet shoulder-width apart and your toes just behind the starting (scratch) line. Bend your knees and bring your hands below your waist; then hop as far as you can on one leg, extending your ankles, knees, hips, and arms fully. Land on the same leg from which you took off, and then step vigorously with the other leg. As you land, immediately jump with that leg to complete the exercise. A sequence might be to hop with the right leg, extend and land on the left leg (step), and then complete the jump with the left leg.

## Skiers

Skiers are good for alpine and cross-country skiers, skaters, and athletes who must change direction rapidly when running.

♦ THE TECHNIQUE  Stand with your feet together (Figure 11–10). Keeping both feet together, jump forward and to the left, land, and then jump forward and to the right. Jump as quickly as possible for 5 to 10 repetitions. You have done one repetition when you've jumped to both the left and right sides.

## Four Squares (Dot Drills)

This exercise also helps build leg power for lateral, forward, and backward movements. Some gyms have rubber mats with dot patterns to facilitate the exercise.

♦ THE TECHNIQUE  Keeping your feet together, jump in various patterns to the front, back, and sides (Figure 11–11). For example, jump front, back, left, and right and repeat. Many combinations are possible.

## Cone Hops

This exercise is similar to the multiple standing long jump, except that you jump for height over the cones as well as distance.

**Figure 11–10**  Skiers.

♦   THE TECHNIQUE   Space three to five 2-foot cones (or similar objects) approximately 3 feet apart (Figure 11–12). Stand in front of the first cone with your feet shoulder-width apart and then jump over the cones as quickly as possible.

## Hurdle Hops

This exercise is an advanced form of cone hops using hurdles. Don't attempt it unless you are well conditioned and have good jumping ability and technique. If the hurdles have adjustable stabilization weights, make sure they are set so that the hurdle falls down easily when hit. Mini-hurdles constructed from PVC pipe are safer for the beginner.

♦   THE TECHNIQUE   Place three to five hurdles approximately 3 feet apart (Figure 11–13). Start with the hurdles at their lowest height. Keeping your feet shoulder-width apart, hop over the hurdles as quickly as possible, using both legs.

**Figure 11–11**  Four squares (dot drills).

# BOUNCE PUSH-UPS

You can do bounce push-ups against a wall or steeplechase hurdle or on the floor. They are excellent for developing upper-body pushing power.

## Wall Bounce Push-Ups

Wall bounce push-ups are the simplest, least stressful push-ups. Start with them, and stay with them until your muscles and joints become accustomed to the stress of upper-body plyometric exercise.

◆    THE TECHNIQUE    Lean against a wall or steeplechase hurdle at a 45- to 60-degree angle. Push up forcefully; then allow yourself to fall back against the wall, absorbing your fall with your arms. Immediately push off again.

## Floor Bounce Push-Ups

These push-ups are much more stressful and difficult than wall bounce push-ups. Don't attempt them until you can do at least 10 to 15 push-ups. They can be done from a standard

**Figure 11–12**  Cone hops.          **Figure 11–13**  Hurdle hops.

or modified push-up position. In the modified push-up position, you rest your weight on your knees instead of your toes.

♦   THE TECHNIQUE    From a standard or modified push-up position, push up force-fully, extending your elbows fully until your hands leave the ground (Figure 11–14). Bounce back to your hands; then repeat the exercise.

   *Variation: "Clap" bounce push-ups (Marine push-ups):* Do this exercise as described above, but clap your hands after they leave the ground (Figure 11–15). In this sequence, you push up and leave the ground, clap your hands, bounce back to the push-up position, and repeat.

   *Variation: "Rocky Balboa" one-arm push-ups:* This difficult exercise was popular-ized by the movie *Rocky.* Do it the same way as floor bounce push-ups, but use only one arm. Start off using the modified push-up position and graduate to the standard push-up po-sition when you gain the necessary strength and power to do the exercise.

## Box Jumping

Box jumping involves jumping to and from boxes, benches, or steps. Landing from a height creates greater stress on the muscles and joints, so these exercises should be attempted only after you do exercises in which you jump to and from the ground. Box height varies between

**Figure 11–14** Floor bounce push-ups.

**Figure 11–15** Clap bounce push-ups.

approximately 6 inches and 5 feet. Start off with smaller boxes and progress slowly to higher ones. As in other plyometric exercises, the object is to attempt to jump again as soon as possible after you land.

## Step-Downs

Step-downs are the simplest, least stressful box jump. Begin with a low box (approximately 1 to 2 feet high). This exercise progresses from simply stepping down from the box and absorbing the shock with the legs to jumping down, landing, and then vigorously jumping into the air and finally to jumping between a series of boxes.

◆   THE TECHNIQUE    Phase 1, step down: Stand on a box or bench with your feet at shoulder-width, knees bent, and spine erect. Step off the bench and land with bent knees (Figure 11–16a,b).

Phase 2, step down and jump up: Stand on a box or bench with your feet at shoulder-width, knees bent, and spine erect. Step off the bench and land with bent knees, then immediately jump up, extending both legs and arms (Figure 11–16c).

Phase 3, step down, jump up, and repeat: Place three to six boxes or benches approximately 3 feet apart. Jump from the first box to the ground, then up to the next box, then back to the ground, and so on (Figure 11–16d). Jump as quickly as possible between benches.

## Standing Long Jumps from a Box

This exercise is similar to the standing long jumps described above, except that it stresses your legs much more when you land. It is sometimes called "depth jumping."

◆   THE TECHNIQUE    Stand on a box or bench with your feet shoulder-width apart (Figure 11–17). Jump as far as possible, fully extending your ankles, knees, hips, and arms. Land with bent knees. As your fitness improves, increase the height of the box. A variation of this exercise is to land on the ground and then jump again immediately (standing long jump).

a   b   c

d

**Figure 11–16** Step-downs.

**Figure 11–17** Standing long jumps from a box.

**Figure 11–18**  Ski box jumps.

## Ski Box Jumps

This exercise is similar to the skiers exercise described earlier, except that you jump to and from a box as you jump side-to-side.

♦   THE TECHNIQUE    Stand with your side to a box or bench. With your feet together, jump up vigorously onto the bench, then immediately jump to the ground on the other side, then jump back to the bench, then jump back to the starting position, and so on (Figure 11–18).

## Single-Leg Jump-Ups

Single-leg jump-ups are excellent for isolating powerful thigh muscles and are good for developing jumping power in activities involving a single-leg take-off (e.g., lay-ups in basketball, jumping for a ball when running, and so on).

♦   THE TECHNIQUE    Stand to the side of a bench or box and place your foot on top of it. Drive hard with your leg and jump into the air, fully extending your ankle, knee, and hip. Land on the bench and return to the starting position, and then repeat immediately.

## MEDICINE-BALL EXERCISES

A medicine ball resembles a basketball in size but is heavier and softer. It usually is made of leather, but newer medicine balls sometimes are made of rubber, and some have handles. Medicine balls weigh between 2 and 20 pounds. Because of their weight, medicine balls are excellent for plyometrics. When you catch them, your muscles stretch and contract eccentrically as you attempt to slow down and control the ball. You can do medicine-ball exercises by yourself or with a partner. These exercises are excellent for developing power in the upper and lower body. Variations are limited only by your imagination.

# Catch with Yourself

Do this exercise with the ball starting at your chest, behind your neck, or at your waist. This is a good whole-body exercise because you must use your legs, arms, and trunk to perform it properly.

♦   THE TECHNIQUE   Chest-high catch: Stand with your feet shoulder-width apart and hold the ball with both hands at chest level. Vigorously press the ball overhead with both hands until it flies into the air straight above you, using your legs to help push the ball (Figure 11–19). Catch the ball with both hands and then immediately throw the ball into the air again. Repeat.

♦   THE TECHNIQUE   Behind-the-neck catch: Stand with your feet shoulder-width apart and hold the ball behind your head with both hands. Vigorously press the ball overhead with both hands until it flies into the air straight above you, using your legs to help push the ball. Catch the ball behind your head with both hands and then immediately throw the ball into the air again. Repeat. Start with a light medicine ball (2 to 5 pounds) before progressing to a heavier one. Don't do this exercise if you have shoulder problems.

**Figure 11–19** Catch with yourself.

♦    THE TECHNIQUE    Waist-high catch: Stand with your feet shoulder-width apart and place your hands under the ball at waist level. Vigorously push the ball overhead with both hands until it flies into the air straight above you, using your legs to help push the ball. Catch the ball with both hands and then immediately throw the ball into the air again. Repeat. As you become accustomed to this exercise, jump into the air as you throw the ball, land to catch the ball, and repeat.

## Medicine-Ball or Shot-Put Throws

You can develop power by throwing a medicine ball or a shot in various ways. Exercises include overhead, underhand, and side-rotation throws.

♦    THE TECHNIQUE    Overhead throw: The motion for this exercise is similar to that for the underhand waist-high catch described above, except that you throw a medicine ball or shot over your head and behind you (Figure 11–20). Try to throw the object as far overhead as possible, fully extending your ankles, knees, hips, and arms and jumping above the ground as you throw.

♦    THE TECHNIQUE    Front waist throw: This exercise is also an underhand throw initiated at the waist, except that you throw the ball or shot in front of you.

**Figure 11–20** Overhead throw.

♦    THE TECHNIQUE    Waist throw to the side: Hold the ball or shot in both hands. Rotating to the right and then to the left, throw the object as far as possible. Try to transfer your weight from your rear foot to your front foot during the throw. Repeat the exercise, releasing the ball to the other side.

## Chest Passes with a Partner

This exercise is excellent for developing the pushing muscles in the upper body. It also strengthens the muscles of the trunk and lower body.

♦    THE TECHNIQUE    Stand with one foot in front of the other and with knees bent slightly, about 6 to 10 feet from a partner (Figure 11–21). Hold the ball in both hands at chest level and throw it to your partner using a motion similar to a basketball chest pass. Your partner should catch the ball and immediately throw it back to you. The catching motion should blend continuously with the throwing motion in a semicircular pattern. You can also do this exercise from a kneeling position if you want to isolate the upper-body muscles.

## Overhead Passes with a Partner

This exercise is excellent for developing power in your triceps and shoulder muscles. Don't do this exercise if you have shoulder problems.

♦    THE TECHNIQUE    Kneel facing your partner, about 6 to 10 feet apart. Hold the ball in both hands behind your head. Throw the ball forward over your head so that your partner catches it with arms extended overhead. Your partner then retracts the ball overhead and throws it back to you.

## Medicine-Ball Sit-Ups

You can do this exercise with a partner or by yourself with a spotter. Don't attempt to do this exercise until you have conditioned your abdominal and back muscles through standard exercises (e.g., crunches, back extensions, and so on). This exercise is not appropriate for people who suffer from back pain.

**Figure 11–21**  Chest pass with a partner.

**Figure 11–22** Medicine-ball sit-ups.

♦ THE TECHNIQUE    Two-person sit-ups: Sit facing each other with knees bent, feet flat on the floor, and one person holding the medicine ball. Each person should lean back, with hands overhead, until their back reaches the ground. Then both sit up at the same time. On reaching the top of the sit-up, the person with the ball tosses the ball to the other person, who then catches it. Repeat. The sequence for each person is do sit-up with ball and throw ball to partner, do sit-up without ball and catch ball from partner, repeat.

♦ THE TECHNIQUE    One person with spotter: This exercise is similar to two-person sit-ups except that a spotter or coach stands 3 to 5 feet from the person doing the sit-ups (Figure 11–22). At the top of the sit-up, the person tosses the ball to the spotter, then completes a sit-up without the medicine ball. As the person returns to the top of the sit-up, he or she catches the ball thrown by the spotter. The sequence is do sit-up with ball and throw ball to spotter, do sit-up without ball and catch ball from spotter, repeat.

## OTHER EXERCISES TO DEVELOP SPEED AND POWER

Variations of plyometric exercises are limited only by your imagination. Obviously, you can't include in your exercise program all the exercises presented in this chapter. Choose those whose movements most closely resemble your favorite sports. In general, choose about 6 to 12 speed–power exercises and integrate them into a program that includes cardiovascular, strength, and flexibility exercises. Sample exercise routines and exercise programming are discussed later in the chapter.

Remember, the gains you make from doing these exercises will not transfer automatically to increased power in sports. You need to practice the sports skill and gradually integrate your increased power into your movements. If you work consistently on sports skills and exercise to increase strength and power, you eventually will become more powerful in your sport.

## Sprint Starts, Running

These exercises are excellent for developing power and acceleration capacity in the legs. The photo sequence (Figure 11–23) shows proper sprint-starting technique. The athlete in this sequence is a world-class sprinter. Notice the incredible extension he gets as he bursts from the blocks. Training to develop this kind of "explosive" strength can carry over to other sports requiring power and speed.

When you work on sprint starts, it's best to use starting blocks, but they are not absolutely necessary. If you are a football player, do sprint starts from the football stance. If you are a tennis player, soccer player, or baseball player, do some of your starts from the ready position for your sport. The ready position is your waiting position before you initiate a movement.

♦    THE TECHNIQUE    "On your marks" position: Stagger your feet 10 to 14 inches apart, with your front foot placed about 20 inches from the starting line (see Figure 11–23a). Try to relax in this position.

"Set" position: Raise your back and hips, with your front leg bent about 90 degrees and your rear leg about 120 degrees (see Figure 11–23b). Right-handed people generally start with their left foot forward. With your back flat and your hips slightly higher than your

a                                        b                                        c

**Figure 11–23** Sprint starts.

shoulders, contact the ground with your fingertips, raising your shoulders as high as possible. Don't put too much weight on your fingertips.

"Go": Raise your shoulder so that you can direct force through the length of your body with your front, driving leg. Drive the front leg fully so that your body forms a straight line from your hip to your heel (see Figure 11–23c). Push your rear foot hard against the block or ground as you drive your knee forward. As you drive forward, the arm on the side of the front foot drives straight forward, while the arm on the side of the rear foot drives straight backward. Both arms should be bent approximately 90 to 110 degrees. Try to fully extend your hips and knees and use your arms dynamically during the driving phases of the movement. After the start, run as fast as possible for three to five strides.

Start off with three sprint starts, and progress to 10 to 20 starts as fitness increases. After a few weeks, have someone time your starts so that you can gauge your progress. Also videotape your starts to ensure that you are extending fully at the hips and knees.

## Harness Sprinting

Harness sprinting builds leg and core strength (Figure 11–24). It involves wearing a harness around your waist and pulling a weight sled, a truck tire, or another person who's providing resistance. Vary the speed and resistance—the higher the resistance, the slower the speed, and vice versa.

## Stadium Stairs

Running stairs, a tried-and-true technique for developing leg power, overloads your body during the sprinting motion. The local football stadium is a great place to do this exercise.

♦   THE TECHNIQUE   Find some unobstructed stairs that will support your weight. Beware of old wooden football-stadium seats that could collapse when you run on them. The number of repetitions will vary with the size of the stadium (Figure 11–25). Running up the stairs at a major university's football stadium will be much more difficult than doing it at the local high school. As with other sprint exercises, start conservatively and build up the intensity and duration as your fitness improves.

Variations of stadium-stair running include running two steps at a time, hopping up the stairs on one or both legs, and hopping up the stairs using a side-to-side motion. The last is a good exercise for Alpine skiers. Advanced trainers can increase the resistance by doing stadium-stair exercises while wearing a weighted vest, available at sporting goods stores and through track-and-field supply catalogues.

Be especially careful when running or hopping up or down stadium stairs. You can easily lose your balance and suffer serious injury. Stop if you find yourself losing your balance or equilibrium. This exercise may not be a good idea if you have kneecap pain. Stair climbing, particularly going down stairs, puts a lot of pressure on your kneecaps. If you experience kneecap pain the next day or several hours after running stadium stairs, cut down on your training volume or eliminate the exercise from your program.

Stair-climbing machines, while excellent for developing cardiovascular endurance, are less effective than stadium stairs for developing lower-body power. While doing stadium

**Figure 11–24**  Harness sprinting.

**Figure 11–25**  Stadium stairs.

stairs, you force your legs to extend vigorously during the push-off phase of the running stride and absorb the shock as you land. The resulting development of dynamic strength in your legs is not possible to achieve with stair-climbing machines, which require minimal stride length and involve little or no impact.

## High Knees, Fast Arms

This exercise is excellent for developing sprint power. It helps increase stride frequency, one of the two factors that determine sprint speed (the other is stride length). Do this exercise on a grass field or a wooden gym floor to minimize impact. This is a maximum-intensity exercise. It is better to do 1 set of 10 seconds at maximum effort than 10 sets of 20 seconds at 50 percent effort. This exercise only works if you exercise at maximum intensity—don't just go through the motions.

◆    THE TECHNIQUE    Simulating a sprint motion in a nearly stationary position, pump your arms and lift your knees as quickly as possible (Figure 11–26). Try to complete 20 strides in only 10 yards. Begin with 3 reps (3 sets of 10 yards). Progress to 10 to 20 reps.

**Figure 11–26**  High knees, fast arms.

## Bounding Strides

This exercise helps build stride length for sprinting. Rather than take many strides over a short distance (as in the high-knees, fast-arms exercise), you attempt to take as few strides as possible over a longer distance.

◆   THE TECHNIQUE   Do this exercise on a grass field or a running track over a distance of 50 to 100 yards. Take the longest strides possible, moving your arms vigorously in synchrony with your legs (Figure 11–27). Your strides should resemble bounding jumps. Begin with 2 or 3 reps and progress to 10 reps.

| CAUTION | ◆ Proceed conservatively with high-impact plyometric exercises. Do not progress to more advanced exercises until you have gained the necessary fitness and skill. |
|---|---|

## Additional Lower-Body Speed–Power Exercises

This chapter has discussed elementary and some advanced speed–power exercises. Many other exercises will help you increase power for high-power sports. These exercises include the following:

◆ *Downhill sprinting:* Sprinting down a slight incline (e.g., 3 degrees) to overload the large motor units used during sprinting.

**Figure 11–27**  Bounding strides.

- *Skipping:* This is the same movement you did as a child, except attempt to extend your ankles, knees, and hips fully during the push-off phase of the movement.

- *Water sprinting:* Sprinting in waist-deep or deeper water, wearing a life jacket.

- *Sand sprinting:* Sprinting in loose or hard sand.

- *Uphill sprinting:* Sprinting 50 to 100 yards to the top of a moderately steep hill. This is a great exercise for increasing leg power and preventing hamstring injuries.

- *Weight lifting (Olympic):* Exercises such as the power clean (see Chapter 10), snatch, hang clean or snatch, box clean or snatch, and jerks off the rack are excellent for developing power in most of the major muscle groups. Consult a competent weight-lifting coach for instruction in these lifts.

## INTEGRATING POWER TRAINING INTO WORKOUTS

Power training requires the athlete to exercise at maximum intensity. It is the only way to overload the large, fast motor units. Power training is very effective and will improve your power in sports provided you also practice the sports skill. This extremely high intensity training carries a high risk of injury. It is also easy to overtrain by failing to balance training and recovery. Athletes overtrain when they don't get enough rest between workouts or when the workouts are too hard.

Start off gradually and progress slowly. Choose one or two power exercises, and add more as you get in better shape. Gauge the appropriateness of your workouts by how you feel the next day. If you are extremely sore for 1 or 2 days after a power workout, you have done too much. In other words, listen to your body.

## PEAK-POWER WEIGHT TRAINING

You can also use the peak-power training technique with weight training. The principle is the same as for the stationary bicycle. Calculate your **peak power** (maximum combination of weight and speed) for 5 repetitions of an exercise. In general, use a weight that is 50 to 60 percent of the maximum weight you can lift for 1 repetition. Time how long it takes you to do 5 reps. Do the lift as rapidly as possible. It's essential to practice good lifting technique when using the peak-power method.

- THE TECHNIQUE    Calculate the peak-power workout weight for your lift. Following is an example for the bench press. In this example, the lifter can bench-press 300 pounds for 1 repetition. Begin with a weight that is 40 to 45 percent of your best 1-rep lift. It's a good idea to use a rubber bounce pad on the bar to protect against injury. Time how long it takes you to bench-press 5 reps, lifting the weight as rapidly as possible. Don't cheat on the lift—go all the way down and all the way up. Repeat this procedure for weights that are 50, 60, and 70 percent of your maximum bench press for 1 rep. Your workout weight will be the one that results in the highest number of pounds per second.

In this example, peak-power output is at 50 percent of maximum. The workout weight should be between 150 and 170 pounds. Do 3 to 5 sets of 5 reps at that weight, lifting the weight as quickly as possible. Increase the weight when you can do your sets in less than 5 or 6 seconds. This highly effective training technique produces rapid gains in strength and power.

## COMBINING WEIGHT-TRAINING AND POWER EXERCISES

A new technique for developing muscle power combines weight-training exercises, such as squats and bench presses, with power exercises, such as squat jumps, bounce push-ups, and sprint starts. For example, do 1 set of 5 repetitions of the squat and follow this immediately with 5 squat jumps. Alternatively, do a set of squats and then do a 30-meter sprint. For the upper body, do a set of bench presses followed immediately by a set of bounce push-ups or medicine-ball tosses with a partner.

Strength–power combination exercises can be specific to your sport. Volleyball players could do a set of squats followed by 5 spiking drills. Shot-putters could do some squats and then put the shot several times. The rationale behind this technique is to maximize the load on the muscles and nervous system. Although the technique has not been validated scientifically, it has become very popular with coaches in many sports.

## SPEED–POWER TRAINING PROGRAM

Because speed–power training is intense and presents a high risk of injury, it must be done gradually and conservatively. People respond differently to the stress of the program; some people can train almost every day without feeling overly tired or getting injured. Others find the workouts extremely stressful. Take it slowly and you probably won't have any problems. Table 11–1 offers an example of a beginning speed–power workout.

---

### TABLE 11–1
### Beginning Speed–Power Exercise Program

Begin with 1 set of each exercise and progress slowly until you can complete the entire program. Practice this program 2 or 3 days per week. This program is most effective for developing power for sports if it is combined with a weight-training program and skill practice.

| EXERCISE | SETS | VOLUME (REPETITIONS OR OTHER) |
|---|---|---|
| Calf jumps | 1–3 sets | 10 reps |
| Squat jumps | 1–3 sets | 10 reps |
| Ice skaters | 1–3 sets | 10 reps |
| Rope skipping | 1–3 sets | 1 minute |
| Bounce push-ups | 1–3 sets | 10 reps |
| Medicine-ball chest passes | 1–3 sets | 10 reps |

The ideal speed–power training program includes weight training, speed–power training, and sports practice. Don't overtrain. An example of a balanced program is to train with weights 3 days a week, practice speed–power exercises 2 days a week, and practice your sport 4 or 5 times a week. During the off-season (when you are not actively playing the sport), emphasize weight training and speed–power training. The off-season is an excellent time to develop "base" strength. As the active season begins, cut back on your weight training and emphasize **skill** development and speed–power training.

## YOU CAN DEVELOP MORE SPEED AND POWER!

Until recently, many athletes and coaches thought you had to be born with speed and power. These qualities seemed almost impossible to gain through training alone. However, although genetics are very important, you *can* learn to sprint faster and jump higher. Start with these beginning exercises, and you will be amazed at how much you can improve in 2 to 3 months of training.

CHAPTER

# 12 NUTRITION FOR WEIGHT TRAINING

Obstacles are those frightening things that become visible
when we take our eyes off our goals.

—HENRY FORD

NUTRITION PLAYS AN IMPORTANT ROLE IN DETERMINING THE EFFECTIVENESS OF A FITNESS and weight-control program. Keeping off excess body fat through exercise alone is difficult. Weight training helps build muscle but is not a good way to burn off many calories. Unless you combine it with good nutrition and endurance exercise, you probably are doomed to failure in fighting the "battle of the bulge."

We are bombarded with nutritional information—some of it helpful but too much of it junk. Beware of nutritional advice that seems too good to be true. No nutritional supplement or drug can turn a weak, flabby individual into a strong, healthy person. Major changes call for hard work and dedication. Instant "cures," such as megavitamin therapy or "fat-burning" pills, don't work and are either dangerous or expensive. You are better off staying with the proven principles of nutrition and participating in a steady, progressive fitness program.

Nutrition is also important for exercise performance. Scientists are beginning to appreciate the role of diet and nutritional manipulation in athletic success. Although the **balanced diet** is still the cornerstone of the well-rounded fitness program, various dietary techniques also have been effective in improving performance.

# PLANNING A HEALTHY DIET

Several government agencies and professional groups provide guidelines for proper nutrition. You can use these guidelines to choose a dietary pattern that will help you obtain the energy and nutrients you need today and avoid diet-related chronic diseases in the future.

## USDA and DHHS Dietary Guidelines for Americans

In 2005 the U.S. Department of Agriculture and the Department of Health and Human Services issued the Dietary Guidelines for Americans (Table 12–1). The guidelines, which were developed by panels composed of leading researchers in nutrition, biochemistry, medicine, and exercise physiology, recommend substantial changes in the American diet. People should eat 100 percent more fruits, 50 percent more vegetables (particularly dark green and orange), 75 percent more low- or nonfat dairy foods, 25 percent less meat, 10 percent fewer enriched-grain products but more whole-grain foods, 10 percent fewer oils, 60 percent fewer high-sugar foods, and 50 percent fewer solid fats. The USDA and DHHS have devised a series of food pyramids based on age, gender, and physical activity (see www.mypyramid.gov for more information).

For the first time, the guidelines include specific exercise recommendations. A description of these diet and exercise guidelines follows.

### Exercise

- Exercise regularly and reduce the time you spend on sedentary activities. Physical activity promotes health, psychological well-being, and a healthy body weight.
- Older adults should exercise regularly to slow down age-related decline in body function.
- To reduce the risk of chronic diseases such as heart disease, stroke, and diabetes, do at least 30 minutes of moderate-intensity physical activity on most days of the week.
- Exercise intensely or for a longer duration to achieve greater benefits than the basic exercise recommendations offer.
- To help manage body weight and prevent weight gain, do at least 60 minutes of moderate- to vigorous-intensity activity on most days of the week and avoid eating too much.
- To sustain weight loss, do 60 to 90 minutes of moderate-intensity physical activity daily and avoid exceeding caloric intake requirements.
- The exercise program should include aerobics, resistance training, and flexibility exercises.

### Nutrients and calories:

- Approximate daily caloric intake should be 1600 to 2000 calories for inactive women, 2200 to 2400 calories for active women, 2000 to 2400 calories for inactive men, and 2400 to 3000 calories for active men. Caloric requirements vary with age, weight, muscle mass, and level of physical activity.
- Eat a variety of healthy foods and limit the intake of saturated and trans fats, cholesterol, added sugars, salt, and alcohol.

**TABLE 12–1**

**Sample USDA and DHHS Dietary Guidelines Eating Plan
at the 2000-Calorie Level**

Amounts of various food groups that are recommended each day or each week in the Dietary Guidelines for Americans 2005 (amounts are daily unless otherwise specified) at the 2000-calorie level. Also identified are equivalent amounts to illustrate serving size.

| FOOD GROUPS AND SUBGROUPS | DIETARY GUIDELINES AMOUNT[a] | EQUIVALENT AMOUNTS |
|---|---|---|
| Fruit group | 2 cups (4 half-cup servings) | ½ cup equivalent is:<br>• ½ cup fresh, frozen, or canned fruit<br>• 1 med fruit<br>• ¼ cup dried fruit<br>• USDA and DHHS: ½ cup fruit juice |
| Vegetable group | 2.5 cups (5 half-cup servings) | ½ cup equivalent is: |
| • Dark green vegetables | 3 cups/week | • ½ cup of cut-up raw or cooked vegetable |
| • Orange vegetables | 2 cups/week | |
| • Legumes (dry beans) | 3 cups/week | • 1 cup raw leafy vegetable |
| • Starchy vegetables | 3 cups/week | • USDA and DHHS: ½ cup vegetable juice |
| • Other vegetables | 6.5 cups/week | |
| Grain group | 6 ounce-equivalents | 1 ounce-equivalent is: |
| • Whole grains | 3 ounce-equivalents | • 1 slice bread |
| • Other grains | 3 ounce-equivalents | • 1 cup dry cereal<br>• ½ cup cooked rice, pasta, cereal |
| Meat and beans group | 5.5 ounce-equivalents | 1 ounce-equivalent is:<br>• 1 ounce of cooked lean meats, poultry, fish<br>• 1 egg<br>• USDA and DHHS: ¼ cup cooked dry beans or tofu, 1 tbsp peanut butter, ½ oz nuts or seeds |
| Milk group | 3 cups | 1 cup equivalent is:<br>• 1 cup low-fat/fat-free milk, yogurt<br>• 1½ oz of low-fat or fat-free natural cheese<br>• 2 oz of low-fat or fat-free processed cheese |

**TABLE 12–1 (continued)**
**Sample USDA and DHHS Dietary Guidelines Eating Plan**
**at the 2000-Calorie Level**

| | | |
|---|---|---|
| Oils | 24 grams (6 tsp) | 1 tsp equivalent is:<br>• 1 tbsp low-fat mayo<br>• 2 tbsp light salad dressing<br>• 1 tsp vegetable oil |
| Discretionary calorie allowance<br>• Example of distribution:<br>  Solid fat[b]<br>  Added sugars | 267 calories<br><br>18 grams<br>8 teaspoons | 1 tbsp added sugar<br>equivalent is:<br>• ½ oz jelly beans<br>• 8 oz lemonade |

[a] Appropriate for many sedentary males 51 to 70 years of age, sedentary females 19 to 30 years of age, and some other gender/age groups who are more physically active.

[b] The oils listed in this table are not considered to be part of discretionary calories because they are a major source of vitamin E and polyunsaturated fatty acids, including the essential fatty acids, in the food pattern. In contrast, solid fats (i.e., saturated and trans fats) are listed separately as a source of discretionary calories.

*Source:* U.S. Department of Agriculture and Department of Health and Human Services, Dietary Guidelines for Americans 2005.

*Food groups:*

◆ Eat plenty of fruits (1 to ½ cups per day, depending on energy needs) and vegetables (1 to 4 cups per day, depending on energy needs).

◆ Choose a variety of fruits and vegetables each day. Eat selections from all five vegetable subgroups (dark green vegetables, orange vegetables, legumes, starchy vegetables, and other vegetables) several times a week.

◆ Depending on energy needs, consume 3 to 10 servings of grains per day, half of them whole-grain.

◆ Depending on energy needs, consume 2 to 3 cups per day of fat-free or low-fat milk or equivalent dairy foods.

*Fluids*

◆ Quenching thirst, drinking fluids with meals, and taking in water in the foods you eat are usually enough to maintain hydration. Healthy people who have access to fluids and who are not exposed to heat stress consume adequate water to meet their needs.

◆ Drink extra water if you exercise vigorously or are exposed to heat.

*Fats*

♦ Restrict saturated fats to less than 10 percent of caloric intake, restrict cholesterol intake to less than 300 milligrams per day, and keep consumption of trans fatty acids as low as possible.

♦ Fat should make up 20 to 35 percent of daily calories. Most fats should be from foods containing polyunsaturated and monounsaturated fatty acids, such as fish, nuts, and vegetable oils.

♦ Buy lean, low-fat, or fat-free food products.

*Carbohydrates*

♦ Eat plenty of fiber-rich fruits, vegetables, and whole grains often.

♦ Limit intake of foods containing added sugars or caloric sweeteners, particularly soft drinks.

*Sodium and potassium:*

♦ Consume less than 2,300 milligrams of sodium (approximately 1 tsp of salt) per day. Beware of food products containing significant amounts of added salt. People with high blood pressure or a susceptibility to the condition should consume less than 1500 milligrams of sodium per day.

♦ Eat potassium-rich foods, such as fruits and vegetables.

*Alcoholic beverages*

♦ Drink alcoholic beverages sensibly and in moderation—up to one drink per day for women and up to two drinks per day for men. Don't drive or operate machinery after consuming alcohol.

♦ People with addiction problems, women of childbearing age who may become pregnant, pregnant and lactating women, children and adolescents, and people taking medications that can interact with alcohol should not drink alcohol.

*Weight control*

♦ Maintain a healthy body weight by balancing calories consumed from foods and beverages with calories expended through metabolism and exercise.

♦ Prevent gradual weight gain by cutting down on calorie-dense foods and high-sugar beverages and increasing exercise.

*Food safety*  Improper food handling can cause disease.

♦ Clean your hands and food-contact surfaces after handling meat and poultry. Rinse fruits and vegetables before serving them.

♦ Separate raw, cooked, and ready-to-eat foods while shopping, preparing, or storing foods. Refrigerate perishable food promptly.

♦ To kill germs, cook foods to a safe temperature.

♦ Don't eat raw eggs, raw or undercooked meat and poultry, unpasteurized juices and dairy products, or raw sprouts.

## Fluids

Fluids are a particularly important part of an active person's diet because they directly affect exercise capacity. Body water is an important component in most of the body's biochemical reactions and helps maintain blood volume and control body temperature. Many people avoid drinking water or other fluids because they are afraid of gaining "water weight." However, fluids are critical for health and performance. Worry about body fat rather than body weight.

A variety of effective fluid replacements have been developed for active people. These not only satisfy the body's fluid requirements but also provide energy during exercise and hasten recovery after a vigorous workout. (These products are discussed later in this chapter.)

## Vitamins

Incredible amounts of money are spent on **vitamins** and minerals every year, by both athletes and nonathletes. In the United States, however, the only common documented deficiencies are iron and calcium. Therefore, with a couple of possible exceptions, anything more than a balanced diet and maybe a "one-a-day" vitamin/mineral supplement is useless and a waste of money.

Vitamins act as coenzymes (i.e., they work with enzymes to drive the body's metabolism) and aid in the production and protection of red blood cells. While vitamins are not produced in the body and must be consumed in the diet, they are needed only in extremely small amounts. Exercise may increase requirements for vitamin C, thiamine, pyridoxine, and riboflavin. Only vitamins C and E, pantothenic acid, and thiamine have been shown to have any effect on exercise performance. Many positive studies of these vitamins have used animal subjects or vitamin-deficient human subjects.

Vitamin C supplementation has been a fertile area of debate ever since Linus Pauling suggested that megadoses of the vitamin can cure and prevent the common cold. His contention has been extremely controversial, and only a few medical studies have supported his claims. It is certain that debate on this issue will continue for many years.

It appears that vitamin supplements improve performance only if there is a nutritional deficiency. To be on the safe side, you might consider taking a basic vitamin supplement. There apparently is no justification for the megadoses of vitamins taken by many athletes, though. Moreover, high doses of vitamins have been shown to have toxic side effects in some people. The best advice is to eat a balanced diet from the six basic food groups.

## Iron

Iron intake in active women is often inadequate. As many as 25 to 80 percent of women endurance athletes could be iron-deficient. A great deal of iron is lost through feces, urine, sweat, and menstrual blood.

Menstruating women need about 18 milligrams of iron a day but typically take in only 12 milligrams per day. This can lead to a drop in iron stores in the bone marrow and, eventually, to iron-deficiency anemia (low blood count). Bone marrow is found inside many bones and is the site for red blood cell production. Iron deficiency, even without anemia, leads to impaired performance and fatigue.

Iron from meat, fish, and chicken is absorbed by the body much more easily than iron from other foods. It is recommended, therefore, that active women eat meat, fish, or chicken or take an iron supplement every day. Some people, however, cannot tolerate iron supplements. Check with your doctor for advice about your iron needs. A simple test that measures blood ferritin can tell your doctor if you are iron-deficient.

To sum up, iron supplements are beneficial if you are iron-deficient. Iron has a marked effect on the body's endurance capacity and ability to transport oxygen.

## Calcium

Osteoporosis, or weakening of the bones, is a common problem in postmenopausal women and in some men over 50 years of age. Three factors that affect bone weakening in women are estrogen (a female hormone), calcium in the diet, and exercise. Until recently, this condition was of little interest to younger women. However, it has been found that active women who have irregular menstrual cycles sometimes have decreased bone density. (In general, the bones of active women are denser than those of inactive women.)

Decreased bone density in active young women is thought to be due to low levels of estrogen. Heavy exercise training can depress estrogen production. Calcium in the diet may also be an important factor. Women with normal estrogen levels should take in at least 1200 milligrams of dietary calcium per day. Those with low estrogen levels do not absorb calcium as well, so they need at least 1500 milligrams per day. Dairy products—such as milk, yogurt, cottage cheese, ice cream, and hard cheese—are excellent sources of calcium. Another good source is soft-boned fish, such as salmon, trout, or sardines.

Take a calcium supplement if you can't get enough in your diet. The best calcium supplements are calcium carbonate and calcium citrate, because they are more readily absorbed than calcium phosphate. Beware of calcium supplements containing bonemeal and dolomite—they often contain high levels of lead, mercury, and arsenic.

## Energy Requirements of Active People

Most body functions, including muscle contractions that allow people to lift weights and do other physical tasks, are made possible by the energy supplied by foods. Carbohydrates, fats, and protein are the three basic food components. All three are essential for supplying the body's energy needs.

Active people must take in enough calories to satisfy the energy requirements of physical activity and provide the nutrients necessary for good health. Again, this can be accomplished by consuming a well-balanced diet containing enough calories to satisfy the body's needs but not so many that you become overweight. (See the box "Healthy Highlight: Weight Training Burns an Extra 325 Calories per Day.")

## DEVELOPING AN ATTRACTIVE BODY: THE ROLE OF EXERCISE AND NUTRITION

The main reason for the tremendous popularity of weight training is that it improves physical appearance. People who train with weights often look more athletic, tighter, and more

## HEALTHY HIGHLIGHT

### WEIGHT TRAINING BURNS AN EXTRA 325 CALORIES PER DAY

A pound of fat contains 3500 calories. It takes 10 days to lose a pound of fat if you burn 350 calories in a workout and don't increase your food intake. University of Colorado at Denver scientists, led by Edward Melannson, found that women who weight-trained burned an extra 325 calories per day compared to women not exercising, equivalent to the number of calories expended by running for 20 to 30 minutes. This is yet another study that shows the importance of weight training for fat loss. Weight training increases calorie use both during and after exercise. It also increases muscle mass, which further boosts metabolic rate. Don't worry about gaining excessive bulk from weight training. Muscle is denser than fat, which means that it takes up less space per pound. Your waist, hips, and arms will get smaller as you gain muscle and lose fat.

*(Journal of Strength and Conditioning Research* 19: 61–66, 2005)

muscular than other people. Paradoxically, some people use weight training to help them gain weight whereas others use it to lose weight. Is this possible? Yes, if you understand the principle of energy balance as it applies to body composition.

## Weight Training, Energy Balance, and Body Composition

All the energy absorbed by the body in the form of food must be accounted for—as energy used for body functions, energy stored as fat, or energy wasted, in the form of heat. There is no other place for food energy to go. If less energy is taken in than is needed, fat is lost.

Intense weight training speeds calorie use during and after exercise. Lifting weights increases muscle mass, one of the most metabolically active tissues in the body. People who go on low-calorie diets to lose weight usually lose a lot of muscle mass. Consequently, their metabolic rate decreases and lost fat is regained easily. Weight training spares muscle mass and helps maintain metabolic rate so that weight-loss programs are more successful.

Contrary to popular belief, spot reducing is not possible—you cannot reduce fat in a particular area through exercise. Studies have shown that spot reducing doesn't happen from exercise. However, weight training can have an enormous effect on physical appearance, even if body fat is unaltered.

Strengthening a body part, such as the abdominal muscles, increases muscle tone and "tightens up" the area. Strong abdominal muscles are less likely to sag, so that area of the body looks more attractive. Excess fat stays—but it looks better. Weight training can play a role in helping people gain or lose weight, or simply look more attractive, if it is practiced as part of a comprehensive diet and exercise program.

## Losing Weight

Weight loss is a national obsession. Many people train with weights or do other exercises so that they can control their weight. Ultimately, the body's energy balance determines whether body fat increases, decreases, or stays the same. Fat increases when more energy is consumed than is expended. Although exercise is an important part of a weight-control program, caloric restriction is essential if the program is to be successful.

The goal of a weight-control program should be to lose body fat and maintain the loss. Quick-loss programs often lead to loss of muscle tissue and body water. They do nothing to instill healthy long-term dietary habits that will maintain the new weight. The following principles for losing body fat will increase the chances of success for a weight-control program:

- Stress fat loss. Rapid weight loss from fad diets is often caused by the loss of muscle mass and body water. Fat loss, not weight loss, should be the goal.
- Restrict the weight you lose. Lose no more than $1\frac{1}{2}$ or 2 pounds per week. More rapid weight loss results in loss of muscle tissue and body water.
- Lose fat by eating less and exercising more.
- Exercise, particularly endurance exercise, is critically important for a successful weight-loss program. The best exercises for losing weight include running, walking, and cycling. Weight training helps burn calories and maintain muscle mass during weight loss.
- Monitor your body composition. Make sure that most of the weight loss is from a reduction in body fat instead of a reduction in fat-free weight.
- Avoid taking weight-loss supplements and drugs—particularly without the advice of a physician. While these drugs are sometimes effective, most people regain their lost weight when they stop taking them. The leading weight-loss supplements and drugs include orlistat, sibutramine, and a combination of ephedrine and caffeine. Each has unpleasant or potentially dangerous side effects.

## Gaining Weight

Many people are naturally underweight and seek to gain weight. There are two basic ways to increase body weight: increasing muscle and increasing fat. Lean people can often increase body fat with little or no adverse effect on appearance or health; nevertheless, they should strive to gain "quality weight." This can be done only through a vigorous weight-training program that stresses the large-muscle groups in the legs, hips, shoulders, arms, and chest.

Muscle weight takes many years to gain but is surely preferable to the fat that is quickly added with expensive high-calorie weight-gain supplements or unhealthy high-fat diets. Following are basic guidelines for gaining weight:

- Stress quality over quantity (increase muscle rather than fat). Carrying extra fat does little to improve your physical performance or appearance.

# FACT OR FICTION?

*MYTH: ACTIVE PEOPLE NEED MORE PROTEIN THAN SEDENTARY PEOPLE DO.*

Scientists have argued this point for more than 100 years. Current evidence suggests that extremely active people need a little more protein than the average person does. The daily protein requirement for a healthy adult is 0.8 gram per kilogram of body weight. Some experts think that the protein requirement for athletes who weight-train or do intense training is about 1.5 grams per kilogram of body weight, but other experts disagree. New research shows that eating high-protein meals—such as high-protein energy bars—before or after training increases the rate of muscle hypertrophy. When it comes to protein intake, timing is more important than quantity.

---

◆ Use weight training to increase the size of major muscle groups. Emphasize exercises that work large-muscle groups: mainly presses (e.g., bench press, seated press) and high-resistance leg excrcises (e.g., squats, leg presses). For lifts, use heavy resistance and many reps (e.g., 5 sets of 5 repetitions).

◆ Concentrate on long-term gains. Do not expect to increase fat-free weight by more than 4 to 6 pounds per year.

◆ Don't use drugs to gain weight. Avoid anabolic steroids and growth hormone. Anabolic steroids increase the risk of coronary artery and liver disease and have many serious side effects. Growth hormone can cause permanent disfigurement and permanently impair insulin metabolism. The benefits are not worth the risks.

◆ Eat a well-balanced diet containing slightly more calories than normal. If you are training vigorously, your protein requirement may increase slightly to 1 to 1.5 grams per kilogram of body weight. Eating 10 to 20 grams of protein (a small meal or protein bar) before or immediately after weight training may speed muscle growth. See the "Fact or Fiction?" box.

◆ Monitor your body composition. Keep track of your progress by measuring your fat-free weight and body fat. The underwater weighing and DEXA techniques are the most accurate. These tests are done in many college and university physical education departments and sports-medicine centers. The skinfold and electrical impedance techniques of body-composition measurement are also widely available. Ask your instructor for further information.

◆ Consult a physician if you do not progress. There are a variety of explanations for being chronically underweight, including family history, maturational level, smoking, and metabolic status.

Weight control is important for health, appearance, and athletic performance. However, excessive preoccupation with weight control and food can lead to eating disorders.

# EATING DISORDERS

Being thin and young is presented by the media as ideal for women. This representation has resulted in an epidemic of eating disorders in industrialized countries. Over 90 percent of all people with anorexia nervosa and bulimia are women.

Men are not immune from such compulsive behavior, but they display it differently. Men who exercise to excess, even when severely injured, are called obligatory runners or body builders. These men run more than 50 miles a week or lift weights to excess. When they can't exercise, they become extremely depressed. The common denominator in these conditions in men and women is not known.

## Anorexia Nervosa and Anorexia Athletica

These two eating disorders are closely related. **Anorexia nervosa** is an obsessive preoccupation with food and fear of weight. The person uses extreme diets and becomes focused on becoming thin at the expense of other goals. **Anorexia athletica** is a variation of anorexia nervosa in which, besides severe dieting, the person overdoes exercise.

Typically, the person with anorexia is a young woman of high school or college age. She is seen by parents and friends as extremely conscientious, with an overly organized life. She usually has low self-esteem and an extreme wish to please others. She may have a slight weight problem. However, these are only generalizations. Sometimes, anorexia may develop because of depression, illness, or peer pressure.

Women often report experiencing a type of "high" when they first follow their punishing diet routine. Researchers have speculated that this may be a result of the increased attention they get from losing weight. It has also been suggested that the "high" comes from the body's release of chemicals, known as endorphins, to combat the intense feelings of hunger accompanying the diet. Endorphins produce an effect similar to that of opium and are one of the body's ways of dealing with pain.

As the condition develops, the person follows a stricter diet and does more exercise. Physical signs common to individuals with anorexia include extreme weight loss, dry skin, hair loss, brittle fingernails, cold hands and feet, low blood pressure and heart rate, swelling around the ankles and hands, and weakening of the bones. Anorexia nervosa is characterized by the following:

- *Extreme weight loss.* A woman with anorexia typically loses at least 25 percent of her original weight. With the weight loss, she often experiences insomnia (inability to sleep) and a decreased ability to tolerate cold. She may wear many layers of clothes to keep herself warm and hide her extreme weight loss.

- *Unrealistic body image.* She sees herself as overweight, even when others describe her as painfully thin. This self-image becomes more distorted as she loses weight.

- *Extreme diets.* She restricts food intake for extended periods, even when extremely hungry. She usually will try to eliminate carbohydrates from the diet and often becomes a vegetarian.

- *Obsession with food.* She will often daydream about food, able to think of nothing else. She may prepare elaborate meals for others as part of her obsession with food. She also has a great fear of losing control and gaining back all the weight she has lost. She lives by the notion that she can't lose enough weight and still has a long way to go.

- *Drug use.* She may abuse drugs, particularly stimulants such as amphetamines, which depress appetite. She may use emetics to help her vomit, diuretics to lose water weight, and laxatives to clear out the digestive tract. (The excessive use of laxatives leads to constipation in people with anorexia.)

- *Amenorrhea.* It is likely she will stop menstruating. This happens early in the condition, even before much weight is lost.

- *Excessive exercise.* She uses exercise as a way of losing more weight. She often runs herself to exhaustion and extreme weakness.

- *Depression.* The woman with anorexia probably feels extremely depressed. She has very low self-esteem, decreased sex drive, feelings of hopelessness, and, sometimes, suicidal thoughts.

## Bulimia

A person with **bulimia** will go on an eating binge and consume thousands of calories. Usually, but not always, the person induces vomiting after the binge. People with bulimia are often, but not necessarily, also anorexic. After the eating binge, the person typically is very depressed and ashamed and usually resolves to go on a stricter diet. This leads to a vicious cycle of binge eating and dieting.

People with long-standing bulimia usually are dehydrated and have decayed teeth, enlarged salivary glands, abnormally low levels of potassium and chloride in the blood, and abnormal heart rhythms and brain waves.

## Treating Eating Disorders

Because eating disorders are so common, you should be aware of their warning signs and risk factors. The physical signs—excessive weight loss, low blood pressure, obsessive behavior, dry skin, cold hands and feet—have been discussed. Young women who are slightly overweight and have low self-esteem are at greatest risk. The best thing you can do is to recognize the problem early. Treatments are not very effective for people who have suffered from these eating disorders for a long time.

Treatment should fit the severity of the problem. You could have one or two physical symptoms typical of anorexia without actually having the condition. Perhaps you just need to learn good eating habits. You should get a checkup, too. If there is any possibility that you or one of your friends has an eating disorder, seek psychological counseling and medical help right away.

Medical treatment includes hospitalization to stabilize serious cases, medications to treat depression, and behavior modification to change eating habits. Anorexia and bulimia can cause serious health problems and even death. They should not be taken lightly.

Certain social and psychological factors increase the risk of developing these disorders:

◆ The belief that the only way to be beautiful and happy is to be thin

◆ Family history of eating disorders

◆ Lack of emotional support from one's family

◆ Overemphasis on achievement

◆ Rigid, overprotective parents

If you have any risk factors or overt symptoms of an eating disorder, seek help from your physician or counselor before you have a serious problem on your hands. You don't have to commit to long-term treatment. A meeting may help you understand whether you have an eating disorder or are just undergoing the normal, temporary setbacks of life.

## DIET AND PERFORMANCE

**Carbohydrates** are the essential fuel for muscular work (Figure 12–1). They are stored in your muscles and liver as **glycogen.** Although fats and proteins are used for energy during exercise, carbohydrates' contribution to supplying energy increases with the intensity of physical activity. When your body or individual muscles are depleted of glycogen, fatigue and sluggishness set in, limiting performance.

The amount of glycogen present in the liver and muscles when exercise begins will affect endurance, the capacity for intense exercise, and even mental outlook. If your muscles feel tired, you are unlikely to have an effective workout or a successful competition. Glycogen depletion causes fatigue, and if normal glycogen levels are not restored, performance levels will be impaired. The goal of an optimal athletic nutrition program is to prevent glycogen depletion during exercise and replenish glycogen stores in the muscles and

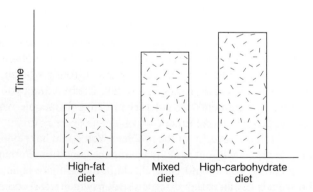

**Figure 12–1** Effect of diet on performance.

**TABLE 12–2**
**Example of a Diet High in Energy and Carbohydrates**

| BREAKFAST | Fruit |
|---|---|
| 1 cup fruit juice (orange, grapefruit, guava) | Spinach salad |
| | Nonfat milk |
| Pancakes (2 or 3) with syrup | |
| 2 eggs (cholesterol-free egg substitutes) | DINNER |
| Turkey sausage | Pasta with meat sauce (spaghetti, lasagna, etc.) |
| Nonfat milk or hot chocolate | Vegetables (broccoli, spinach, or carrots) |
| LUNCH | Green salad |
| Tuna salad sandwich (made with low-fat mayonnaise) | Fruit |
| | Nonfat milk |

the liver immediately after exercise. This can be accomplished by eating a high-energy, high-carbohydrate diet during periods of intense training or competition and consuming carbohydrate beverages during and after training.

## The High-Carbohydrate Diet

A high-carbohydrate diet is critical for athletes involved in heavy training. It contains the six basic food groups but stresses food from the carbohydrate groups, such as cereals, fruits, and grains.

Many studies have shown that this diet enables active people to exercise longer and more intensely and to recover faster than those on mixed or high-fat diets. Table 12–2 gives an example of a high-energy, high-carbohydrate diet that is suitable for any active person involved in intense training. This diet includes fresh vegetables for vitamins and minerals and meats and meat substitutes for protein, and it avoids refined-sugar products, such as cakes, pies, and candy. Alcoholic beverages should also be avoided or minimized.

Most people do not train hard enough to benefit fully from a high-carbohydrate diet, but active people should take great care in designing their diets. It is important to consume enough calories and protein to optimize muscle growth. Too much carbohydrate in the diet, particulary high-sugar soft drinks, will lead to fat gain. There is no one perfect diet. Experiment with a variety of foods to find a diet that's agreeable and palatable.

## Carbohydrate Drinks during Exercise

Consuming carbohydrate drinks during exercise improves performance. These drinks enhance glycogen stores in the liver, maintain blood-sugar levels during exercise, and decrease the rate of glycogen breakdown in muscles—all of which improve exercise performance.

Just as important, the use of carbohydrate drinks immediately after exercise results in a rapid resynthesis of glycogen. Researchers have found that the 2-hour period immediately after exercise is the best time for restoring glycogen in the muscles and liver. If you consume carbohydrate drinks during this time, you can increase glycogen levels by 20 percent. If you also take in protein with the carbohydrate drink, you can accelerate the rate of protein synthesis—and muscle growth—after exercise.

Specially formulated athletic fluid-replacement drinks containing carbohydrates are excellent for maintaining blood sugar and replacing lost glycogen. Drinking a carbohydrate beverage during and immediately after exercise allows you to come back sooner after a hard workout and possibly avoid the feeling of fatigue that accompanies low glycogen levels.

## Avoidance of High-Fat Diets

In years past, a breakfast of bacon, eggs, and toast smothered in butter was almost a tradition in the United States. Today many people avoid such meals because of their high fat and cholesterol content. Studies show that diets high in fat and cholesterol increase the risk of coronary artery disease (hardening of the arteries) and some types of cancer.

Both the American Heart Association and the American Cancer Society recommend diets low in fat and cholesterol. So the recommended high-carbohydrate diet not only will improve your physical performance but may improve your health as well. Figure 12–2 summarizes how to read a food label to help you choose healthy foods.

## Protein Requirements for Weight Trainers

Protein supplements have been popular among weight trainers for many years. However, most people who train with weights don't need any more protein than the average person does. The daily requirement for protein in healthy adults is about 0.8 to 1.0 gram of protein per kilogram of body weight. However, several recent studies suggest that athletes involved in extremely intense programs may have a higher protein requirement than average.

Protein requirements are determined by a complicated and difficult procedure called "nitrogen balance." Proteins are composed of different combinations of **amino acids.** Amino acids contain nitrogen, and the nitrogen must be eliminated before amino acids can be used as fuel. Nitrogen is an important marker of protein metabolism because its elimination from the body is directly proportional to the breakdown of amino acids.

Protein breakdown in the body can be estimated by measuring nitrogen loss in waste products such as urine, feces, and sweat and in nail clippings, hair, and so on. Protein intake can be estimated by measuring the quantity of nitrogen ingested in the diet. If the body is using more protein for fuel than is being taken in (a net loss of nitrogen), the person is said to be in "negative nitrogen balance." If the person is incorporating more protein into body tissues than is being expended as fuel (a net gain in nitrogen), then the person is said to be in "positive nitrogen balance."

The goal for people involved in a weight-training program is to achieve a positive nitrogen balance (or at least to prevent a negative nitrogen balance). A positive nitrogen

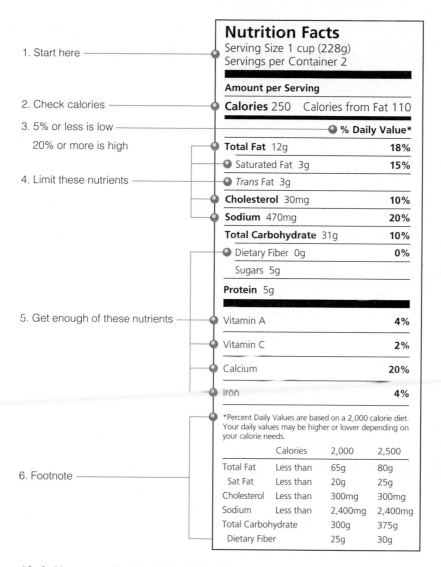

1. Start here

2. Check calories

3. 5% or less is low
   20% or more is high

4. Limit these nutrients

5. Get enough of these nutrients

6. Footnote

**Nutrition Facts**
Serving Size 1 cup (228g)
Servings per Container 2

**Amount per Serving**

**Calories** 250    Calories from Fat 110

**% Daily Value***

| | |
|---|---|
| **Total Fat** 12g | **18%** |
| Saturated Fat 3g | **15%** |
| *Trans* Fat 3g | |
| **Cholesterol** 30mg | **10%** |
| **Sodium** 470mg | **20%** |
| **Total Carbohydrate** 31g | **10%** |
| Dietary Fiber 0g | **0%** |
| Sugars 5g | |
| **Protein** 5g | |

| | |
|---|---|
| Vitamin A | **4%** |
| Vitamin C | **2%** |
| Calcium | **20%** |
| Iron | **4%** |

*Percent Daily Values are based on a 2,000 calorie diet.
Your daily values may be higher or lower depending on
your calorie needs.

| | Calories | 2,000 | 2,500 |
|---|---|---|---|
| Total Fat | Less than | 65g | 80g |
| Sat Fat | Less than | 20g | 25g |
| Cholesterol | Less than | 300mg | 300mg |
| Sodium | Less than | 2,400mg | 2,400mg |
| Total Carbohydrate | | 300g | 375g |
| Dietary Fiber | | 25g | 30g |

**Figure 12–2** How to read a food label. The information in the main or top section (see 1–5 on the sample nutrition label) can vary with each food product; it contains product-specific information (serving size, calories, and nutrient information). The bottom part (see 6 on the sample label) contains a footnote with Daily Values (DVs) for 2000- and 2500-calorie diets. This footnote provides recommended dietary information for important nutrients, including fats, sodium, and fiber. The footnote is found only on larger packages and does not change from product to product.

*Source:* U.S. Food and Drug Administration, Center for Food Safety and Applied Nutrition, November 2004.

balance means that the body is adding protein and suggests that muscles are getting bigger and stronger. Factors important in muscle growth include muscle tension from weight training, presence of anabolic hormones such as testosterone, adequate protein and calories in the diet, and sufficient rest between workouts.

Nitrogen-balance studies usually show that most active people do not need more protein in their diets. The average requirement of 0.8 to 1.0 gram of protein per kilogram of body weight is easily satisfied by the average American diet. Extra protein probably is necessary only for elite or experienced weight-trained athletes involved in very intense training. However, the need for added protein in active people is vigorously debated by scientists. As discussed, ingesting a protein supplement before or after weight training accelerates muscle hypertrophy, but, for people training at less intense levels, protein supplements are unnecessary.

## Proteins as an Energy Source

Most energy used during exercise comes from carbohydrates and fats. However, proteins are used for energy, and they help maintain blood sugar through a process called "gluconeogenesis" (the formation of new blood sugar in the liver). Maintenance of blood sugar during exercise is critical for sustaining exercise intensity. Low blood sugar causes fatigue, sluggishness, and disorientation.

Because of its effects on blood sugar and metabolic regulation, the pregame or pre-exercise meal should contain some protein. For many years, physicians treating people with diabetes mellitus, a disease related to faulty blood-sugar regulation, have recommended a diet with a significant protein component because the amino acids are very effective in ensuring long-lasting release of sugar into the blood. In essence, the amino acids act like tiny blood-glucose-releasing capsules that prevent hunger and mainain energy levels.

## Amino Acid and Polypeptide Supplements

Amino acid and polypeptide supplements have been hailed as "natural" anabolic steroids that accelerate muscle development, decrease body fat, and stimulate the release of growth hormone. Amino acids are the basic building blocks of proteins, and polypeptides are combinations of two or more amino acids linked together. Proponents point to the more rapid absorption of amino acid and polypeptide supplements as proof of their superiority over normal dietary sources of protein.

Presently, there is little scientific proof to support amino acid or polypeptide supplementation for most active people—except when the supplements are consumed immediately before or after exercise. The protein requirement of most people who train with weights is no higher than that for sedentary individuals, so the rate of amino acid absorption from the gastrointestinal tract is not important. For recreational weight trainers, these supplements are a waste of money.

Some indirect proof exists, however, that amino acid or polypeptide supplements may be beneficial for elite weight-trained athletes. Muscle hypertrophy (enlargement) depends on the concentration of amino acids in the muscle—the more amino acids available, the faster the rate of muscle hypertrophy. Several studies have shown that elite weight-trained athletes often do not consume enough protein. Also, when very large amounts of protein were consumed, muscle hypertrophy was accelerated. This issue is controversial among exercise physiology researchers.

These supplements do involve risks. Consuming an unbalanced amino acid formula, one high in some amino acids and deficient in others, may cause negative nitrogen balance. Also, substituting amino acid or polypeptide supplements for protein-rich foods may cause deficiencies in important nutrients such as iron and the B vitamins. Clearly, amino acid supplementation is of little use to the average recreational weight trainer. Unless you are an elite athlete, stick to the well-balanced diet.

CHAPTER

# 13 ERGOGENIC AIDS: DRUGS AND SUPPLEMENTS

The most important thing about motivation is goal setting.
You should always have a goal.

—FRANCIE LARRIEU SMITH

SUBSTANCES TAKEN TO ENHANCE PERFORMANCE ARE CALLED **ERGOGENIC AIDS.** MANY
active people consume a wide variety of drugs and nutritional supplements in their quest
for improved performance and the "perfect body." They take these substances for several
reasons:

1. To enhance muscle hypertrophy (increase in size)
2. To speed recovery and prevent the effects of overtraining
3. To increase training intensity and aggressiveness
4. To control fat, body water, and appetite

Table 13–1 describes the principal performance aids used by weight trainers.
    Many of these drugs and supplements are banned for use in amateur and professional
sports, and some are illegal. Also, little is known about the effectiveness and long-term
health consequences of these substances. You should be aware of the latest information
about drugs and supplements and be careful about what you put into your body.

# TABLE 13–1
## Performance Aids Used by Some Weight Trainers

| SUBSTANCE | SUPPOSED EFFECTS | ACTUAL EFFECTS | SELECTED POTENTIAL SIDE EFFECTS |
|---|---|---|---|
| Adrenal androgens: DHEA, androstenedione (andro) | Increased testosterone, muscle mass, and strength; decreased body fat. | Increased testosterone, strength, and fat-free mass and decreased fat in older subjects (no effects in younger people). | Gonadal suppression, prostate hypertrophy, breast development in males; masculinization in women and children. Long-term effects unknown. Andro is a controlled substance.[a] |
| Amino acids | Increased muscle mass. | No effects if dietary protein intake is adequate. | Minimal side effects; unbalanced amino acid intake can cause problems with protein metabolism. |
| Anabolic steroids | Increased muscle mass, strength, power, aggressiveness, and endurance. | Increased strength, power, fat-free mass, and aggressiveness; no effects on endurance. | Minor to severe: gonadal suppression, liver disease, acne, breast development in males; masculinization in women and children; coronary artery disease, cancer. Steroids are controlled substances.[a] |
| Chromium picolinate | Increased muscle mass; decreased body fat. | No effects on fat-free mass or on body fat. | Moderate doses (50–200 µg) appear safe; higher doses may cause DNA damage and other serious effects. Long-term effects unknown. |
| Creatine monohydrate | Increased muscle creatine phosphate, muscle mass, and capacity for high-intensity exercise. | Increased muscle mass and performance in some types of high-intensity exercise. | Minimal side effects; some anecdotal reports of muscle cramping and exacerbation of existing kidney problems. |

*(continued)*

**TABLE 13–1 (continued)**

| SUBSTANCE | SUPPOSED EFFECTS | ACTUAL EFFECTS | SELECTED POTENTIAL SIDE EFFECTS |
|---|---|---|---|
| Ephedra (usually sold combined with caffeine or another stimulant) | Decreased body fat; increased training intensity due to stimulant effect. | Decreased appetite, particularly when taken with caffeine; some evidence for increased training intensity. | Abnormal heart rhythms, nervousness, headache, and gastrointestinal distress. Ephedra and ephedrine are controlled substances.[a] |
| Ginseng | Decreased effects of physical and emotional stress; increased oxygen consumption. | No effect on performance. | No serious side effects; high doses can cause high blood pressure, nervousness, and insomnia. |
| Growth hormone | Increased muscle mass, strength, and power; decreased body fat. | Increased muscle mass and strength. | Diabetes, acromegaly (disease characterized by increased growth of bones in hands and face), enlarged heart and other organs. An extremely expensive controlled substance.[a] |
| HMB (hydroxy-beta-methylbutyrate) | Increased strength and muscle mass; decreased body fat. | Some studies show increased fat-free mass and decreased fat; more research needed. | No reported side effects. Long-term effects unknown. |
| "Metabolic-optimizing" meals for athletes | Increased muscle mass, energy supply; decreased body fat. | No proven effects beyond those of balanced meals. | No reported side effects; extremely expensive. |
| Protein | Increased muscle mass. | No effects if dietary protein intake is adequate. | Can be dangerous for people with liver or kidney disease. |

[a] Possession of a controlled substance is illegal without a prescription, and physicians are not allowed to prescribe controlled substances for the improvement of athletic performance. In addition, the use of anabolic steroids, growth hormone, or any of several other controlled substances listed in this table is banned for athletic competition.

*Source:* Brooks, G. A., et al. 2005. *Exercise Physiology: Human Bioenergetics and Its Applications.* 4th ed. New York: McGraw-Hill.

# ANABOLIC–ANDROGENIC STEROIDS

People take **anabolic steroids** to gain weight, muscle size, strength, power, speed, endurance, and aggressiveness. These drugs are widely used both by serious athletes and by active people trying to improve their appearance and performance.

In the United States, the Anabolic Steroid Control Act of 1990 classified anabolic steroids as a Schedule III substance. The law gave the Drug Enforcement Administration (DEA) power to restrict the importation, exportation, distribution, and dispensing of anabolic steroids. These restrictions have led to a thriving "black market" for illegal anabolic steroids in the United States.

Anabolic steroids increase protein synthesis, which enhances lean body mass. The binding of anabolic steroids with receptor molecules in the cells stimulates the cells to make proteins. Anabolic steroids also help users recover more quickly after exercise by interfering with the activity of hormones that break down tissue. They may also increase aggressiveness, which allows people to train harder. Steroids work better at higher dosages (more than 400 mg of testosterone a week), but side effects increase with higher dosages. See the Fact or Fiction? box.

 FACT OR FICTION?

*MYTH: LOW DOSES OF STEROIDS GIVE BENEFITS WITH DECREASED RISK OF SIDE EFFECTS*

Anabolic steroids increase strength, muscle mass, and power. However, as with any drug, the side effects of steroids increase with dosage. High doses of anabolic steroids (equivalent to more than 600 mg of testosterone per week) increase red blood cells (hematocrit) to dangerous levels, may promote coronary artery disease, accelerate the development of atherosclerosis (arterial disease) and existing cancer cells, promote mental illness in some people, and suppress testicular function. Steroid users often take low doses of the hormone in order to get some benefits while minimizing the risk of side effects, not realizing that testosterone supplements shut down normal production of the hormone. People who take moderate doses (200 mg of testosterone per week), for example, substitute expensive injected testosterone for testosterone the body makes for free. Higher doses of the hormone are necessary to get greater gains than those expected from naturally circulating testosterone. Dosage presents a serious problem for anabolic steroid users. Low to moderate doses shut down natural production of testosterone so that the steroids provide no additional benefit beyond that of the hormones the body makes naturally, while high doses have greater effects on performance and muscle mass but increase the risk of side effects.

## How Steroids Work in the Body

◆ *Increase in the size and perhaps the number of muscle cells:* Steroids make muscles larger, but they also have several effects that radically affect muscles' strength, power, speed, and endurance. Steroids may increase the number of muscle fibers, a process called hyperplasia. Muscle biopsies of trained steroid-using weight lifters showed that they had larger and more numerous muscle fibers than control subjects. Steroids may turn on cell structures called satellite cells, which may make new muscle cells. Most top muscle physiologists doubt that hyperplasia is important in making muscles bigger.

◆ *Increased speed of calcium release:* Power athletes—ranging from baseball players to Olympic lifters—have long appreciated the effects of steroids on quickness and power. Calcium triggers muscle contraction, and steroids increase the speed of calcium release and make the muscle cells more sensitive to calcium. The muscles then contract faster and more powerfully.

◆ *Increased androgen receptor activity:* Steroids work by binding to **testosterone receptors** in the tissues. In the past, scientists claimed that taking high doses of steroids was ineffective because there were not enough testosterone receptors to accommodate the high levels of the hormone. However, the activity of the receptor increases in the face of high blood levels of testosterone. Also, intense weight training increases both the number and the activity of receptors. Heavy training and high doses of testosterone combine to promote muscle growth.

◆ *Anticatabolic effects:* Muscle growth occurs when protein synthesis in the muscle exceeds protein breakdown. If you can slow protein breakdown after a workout, you can make gains by having only a small amount of net protein synthesis. Animal studies show that steroids can cross-bind with corticosteroid binding sites, catabolic hormones that cause protein breakdown. High doses of steroids may promote cross-binding, but not all studies show that steroids have such **anticatabolic** effects.

◆ *Release of growth hormone and muscle growth factor:* Steroids trigger the release of growth hormone (GH) from the brain and muscle growth factor (IGF-1) from the liver. They do this only when the weekly dosage of anabolic steroids equals 400 milligrams per week. IGF-1 and GH are highly anabolic. Athletes have not seen significant gains from taking GH by itself. More impressive gains occur when the drugs are combined with anabolic steroids.

◆ *Psychological effects:* Steroids increase euphoria, energy, and sexual arousal. High blood testosterone increases androgen receptors in the brain—just as it does in muscle. Steroids increase important brain chemicals such as serotonin, GABA (gamma-aminobutyric acid), and acetylcholine, which could stimulate the mental drive to train harder.

## Health Risks of Anabolic Steroids

Side effects of steroids include liver toxicity and tumors (from oral steroids), decreased high-density lipoproteins (good cholesterol), cardiac arrhythmia (abnormal heart rhythm), reduced sperm count, lowered testosterone production, high blood pressure, increased risk of AIDS (due to shared needles), depressed immune function, glucose intolerance, psychological disturbances, masculinization in women and children, premature closure of the bone growth centers, and increased risk of cancer (Table 13–2). Steroids can also make adolescent acne much worse in both young men and women. Severe side effects of anabolic steroid use have been reported among athletes, including myocardial infarction (heart attack), ventricular tachycardia (accelerated heart rate), liver cancer, and severe psychiatric disturbances. Recent studies have shown that "roid rage" is largely a myth, but the drugs do have severe psychiatric effects in about 10 percent of users. Athletes may be particularly prone to side effects because they often take high dosages of the drugs for prolonged periods of time.

Because people must take high doses of steroids to achieve significant results, the stage is set for heart enlargement and eventual heart failure, prostate enlargement, and cancer. Also, high doses of steroids increase levels of IGF-1—a potent growth stimulator of muscle and cancer cells. While it is true that steroid users from the 1970s and 1980s have not been dying in large numbers from cancer and heart disease, they didn't take as many steroids as some modern athletes do.

# GROWTH HORMONE

Growth hormone (GH) is popular with athletes, who use it to increase muscle mass and strength. Reports in the news media suggest that, like anabolic steroids, its use has filtered down to nonathletes interested in improving their appearance and speeding weight loss. The development of recombinant human growth hormone and the easy availability of imported growth hormone through the Internet have led to the hormone's increased popularity.

GH speeds the rate at which proteins enter muscle cells, which increases the cells' growth rate. It also stimulates another growth-promoting hormone, insulin-like growth

| TABLE 13–2 | |
|---|---|
| **Reported Side Effects of Anabolic Steroids** | |
| Abnormal bleeding and blood clotting | Gastrointestinal distress |
| Acne | Impaired immune function |
| Breast enlargement in males | Increased aggressiveness |
| Coronary artery disease | Liver cancer |
| Decreased male-hormone levels | Liver toxicity |
| Depressed sperm production | Masculinization in women and children |
| Dizziness | Prostate cancer |
| Elevated blood pressure | Stunted growth in children |
| Elevated blood sugar | Tissue swelling |

factor. Because GH mobilizes fats from the fat cells, it is also used to help control body composition.

Human growth hormone has no apparent beneficial effects on muscle size or performance. Animal studies have found that the administration of GH stimulates muscle growth. Observations among athletes suggest that GH is highly anabolic in intensely training elite body builders, but the side effects can be severe. Prolonged administration of growth hormone may result in low blood sugar, elevated insulin levels, heart enlargement, and elevated blood fats. Long-term use could also lead to acromegaly (characterized by enlarged bones in the head, face, and hands), cardiomyopathy, peripheral nerve damage, osteoporosis (weakening of the bones), arthritis, heart disease, insulin resistance, and carpal tunnel syndrome. These side effects occur at high doses.

Some athletes also take drugs that increase the secretion of natural growth hormone. These drugs include propranolol, vasopressin, clonidine, and levodopa. There is no evidence that using these drugs enhances muscle hypertrophy.

# Insulin-Like Growth Factor (IGF-1)

Recombinant **insulin-like growth factor (IGF-1),** also called somatomedin C, has recently become a popular drug among athletes. Production of IGF-1 is stimulated by growth hormone. It is released mainly by the liver but may also be secreted by the testes, fat cells, bone, and heart. IGF-1 is an extremely anabolic (muscle-building) hormone. The side effects are thought to be similar to those of growth hormone. The long-term effects are unknown.

# Dehydroepiandrosterone (DHEA) and Androstenedione (Andro)

**Dehydroepiandrosterone (DHEA)** and **androstenedione (andro)** are relatively weak androgen hormones produced mainly in the adrenal glands. They are broken down to testosterone, which explains their popularity with athletes. DHEA is widely available in health-food stores and supermarkets, but because the Food and Drug Administration no longer recognizes andro or related compounds as food supplements they are available only by prescription.

Athletes take these hormones to stimulate muscle hypertrophy and to lose weight. Administration of DHEA or andro in middle-age and older adults improved "energy levels" and increased muscle mass, mental acuity, and immune function. These hormones may boost performance by increasing blood testosterone levels.

High doses of DHEA (1600 mg/d) in young men led to a reduction in HDL cholesterol (good cholesterol). In elderly subjects, DHEA reduced LDL (bad cholesterol) and had no effect on HDL. Doses of 150 to 300 milligrams per day have a marked effect on testosterone levels that could lead to masculinization in women and interfere with hormone controls in both sexes.

Androstenedione administration could have side effects similar to those of DHEA. These "pro-hormones" have the same side effects in young people as testosterone—stunted growth, skin problems, interference with normal sex hormones, and psychological disorders. Women should avoid them because they can interfere with the menstrual cycle and potentially cause reproductive and bone problems.

## INSULIN

Some active people take insulin injections to promote muscle hypertrophy. Insulin promotes carbohydrate and fat storage and speeds protein synthesis. It helps build muscle by enhancing amino acid transport into cells, increasing the rate of incorporation of amino acids into protein, and suppressing protein breakdown. The effects of insulin supplements on muscle size and strength are unknown. The most serious side effect of exogenous insulin administration (insulin injection) in exercising body builders is insulin shock, a condition marked by dangerously low blood-sugar levels.

## CLENUBUTEROL

Athletes take **clenubuterol** (an anti-asthma drug) to prevent muscle atrophy, increase lean body mass, and decrease body fat. Beneficial effects have been shown in animals, but few studies have been done on humans. Side effects include insomnia, abnormal heart rhythm, anxiety, depressed appetite, and nausea. More serious side effects include enlarged heart, heart failure, and heart attack. This drug is easy to get, but its side effects can be serious.

## MYOSTATIN BLOCKERS

While IGF-1 stimulates muscle growth, myostatin prevents it. French researchers studied the balance between these two chemicals in chickens bred to have large breasts (pectoralis major muscles). After birth, the chickens showed an increase in IGF-1 and a decrease in myostatin, coinciding with a rapid increase in muscle. Scientists have been working on drugs that will promote protein synthesis in muscle by increasing IGF-1 and decreasing myostatin in hopes of increasing meat yields from cows, pigs, chickens, and sheep. The drugs are of obvious interest to body builders and power athletes, but their side effects are unpredictable.

## OTHER SUBSTANCES TAKEN TO ENHANCE PERFORMANCE

Other substances sometimes used as ergogenic aids include human chorionic gonadotropin (HCG), periactin, conjugated linoleic acid (CLA), vanadyl sulfate, dibencozide, and organ extracts. These agents are not very popular, and their effectiveness is questionable.

# SUPPLEMENTS TAKEN TO SPEED RECOVERY

Other supplements are taken primarily to replenish depleted body fuels (e.g., creatine phosphate: creatine supplementation; muscle and liver glycogen: glucose and lactate polymers) and to serve as sources of postexercise protein synthesis (e.g., amino acids).

## Creatine Monohydrate

**Creatine monohydrate (creatine),** one of the most popular and widely used supplements among athletes and serious weight trainers, is used to build strength and muscle mass, enhance recovery, and improve exercise capacity.

Creatine supplementation increases the creatine phosphate content of the muscle by about 20 percent. Creatine phosphate is an important high-energy chemical used to maintain the level of ATP, which supplies the energy for most physiological functions in the body. Creatine supplementation has been shown to improve performance in short-term, high-intensity, repetitive exercise, which might make it a valuable supplement for active people. It may improve performance by augmenting the availability of creatine phosphate and possibly regulating the rate of sugar breakdown in muscle. It may increase muscle-building capacity during resistive exercise by allowing more intense training.

Creatine has been anecdotally linked to diarrhea, dehydration, muscle cramping, and muscle strains. In more than thirty studies—some conducted for as long as 3 years—creatine use showed no side effects. The often-cited links between creatine, dehydration, and cramps have repeatedly been refuted by scientific studies. College football players who took creatine monohydrate supplements (5 to 20 g/d for up to 5 years) showed no evidence of kidney or liver damage based on the results of standard blood tests.

## Hydroxy-beta-methylbutyrate (HMB)

**Hydroxy-beta-methylbutyrate (HMB)** is a breakdown product of the amino acid lysine. Combining all the studies on HMB indicates that the supplement has been shown to increase net lean mass by 0.28 percent per week and strength by 1.40 percent per week. Other studies have shown that taking HMB together with creatine monohydrate causes greater improvements in muscle mass and strength than does taking either supplement alone. The few studies on the side effects of HMB suggest that it is safe.

# SUPPLEMENTS TAKEN TO INCREASE AGGRESSIVENESS AND TRAINING INTENSITY

Serious exercisers often spend several hours per day training for their favorite activities, and monotony and fatigue sometimes make it difficult to show significant improvement. Many athletes use stimulants, such as amphetamines and caffeine, to help them train harder and combat fatigue.

## Amphetamines

Some athletes and other active people take amphetamines to prevent fatigue and to increase confidence and training intensity. Examples of amphetamines include benzedrine, dexedrine, dexamyl, and methedrine. These drugs act by stimulating the nervous system. Side effects include increased blood pressure, heart rate, arousal, wakefulness, and confidence and the feeling of an enhanced decision-making capability.

Amphetamines mask fatigue and increase static strength but do not improve cardiovascular capacity or muscle endurance. They appear to aid power-oriented movement skills in activities that employ constant motor patterns, such as shot putting and hammer throwing, and theoretically could provide some benefit to body builders and weight lifters by allowing them to train harder.

Amphetamines can have severe neural and psychological effects, including aggressiveness, paranoia, hallucinations, compulsive behavior, restlessness, and irritability. They can cause arrhythmia, hypertension, and angina (heart-related chest pain). Amphetamines are highly addictive and dangerous drugs.

## Caffeine

Caffeine—found in coffee, cola, tea, and chocolate—is a stimulant favored by active people. It stimulates the central nervous system by effecting the release of adrenaline (epinephrine). In athletics, caffeine is used as a stimulant and as a fatty-acid mobilizer. While some evidence indicates that caffeine may improve endurance, the drug does not appear to enhance short-term maximal exercise capacity.

The diuretic and cardiac stimulatory properties of caffeine can combine to increase the risk of arrhythmias such as ventricular ectopic beats and paroxysmal atrial tachycardia. Caffeine also can cause insomnia and is addictive. Caffeine was removed from the Olympic doping control list in early 2004.

## Other Agents

Other agents used by some active people to enhance training intensity include cocaine, ephedrine, modafinil (Provigil), GHB (gamma-hydroxybutyric acid; see the box "Healthy Highlight: GHB Is Bad News"), and ginseng. Cocaine use is not thought to be widespread among athletes, but some athletes reportedly use it to increase training intensity.

Ephedra, a weak stimulant, previously was widely used by athletes during workouts, but it was banned by the FDA in April 2004. Despite a slight stimulating effect on blood pressure and on exercise and recovery heart rates, ephedra has no effect on physical work capacity. Ephedra supplements have become controversial and have been associated with the deaths of several professional athletes.

Modafinil (Provigil), a medication used to treat narcolepsy (excessive daytime sleepiness), acts as a minor stimulant and may improve concentration and endurance capacity. It was recently added to the Olympic banned-drug list. Ginseng is also very popular with athletes, but little evidence supports its use as an ergogenic aid.

# HEALTHY HIGHLIGHT

## GHB IS BAD NEWS

For many years, gamma-hydroxybutyric acid (GHB) was popular with body builders and weight trainers. It was legal and readily available on the Internet. However, the drug became associated with date rape and also was linked to many deaths among people who combined it with alcohol. GHB and similar drugs were subsequently banned and made schedule I drugs. GHB is one of the most addictive street drugs—even more addictive than heroin. One study found that only 1 in 25 patients addicted to GHB was able to successfully get off the drug. People withdrawing from GHB suffer from delirium, psychosis, loss of normal movement capacity, and resistance to drug therapy. Just a small amount of the drug (1 tsp) causes intoxication, and only a little more (2 tsp) can cause respiratory failure and death. The drug is not detected on standard hospital emergency-room screening tests. The FDA has warned consumers about the dangers of GHB and its chemical cousin GBL. These drugs are extremely addictive, suppress the central nervous system, and trigger seizures, vomiting, and coma. Stay away from this drug—it's bad news!

(*Forensic Science International* 148: 139–142, 2005)

# SUPPLEMENTS TAKEN TO AID WEIGHT CONTROL

Substances used in weight control include drugs that suppress appetite, thermogenic drugs, drugs that affect the gastrointestinal tract, and diuretics to control weight and increase muscle definition. Athletes such as gymnasts, dancers, figure skaters, and weight-class athletes use a variety of techniques to decrease the amount of body fat, either immediately before a contest or chronically due to the requirements of their sport.

Appetite-suppressing drugs work by acting on catecholamine neurotransmitters or serotonin neurotransmitters or by blocking opioid receptors. **Thermogenic** drugs affect metabolic rate. Gastrointestinal drugs are used to affect nutrient absorption. Other agents include human chorionic gonadotropin, growth hormone, glucagon, progesterone, and biguanides. The effectiveness and desirability of these agents are questionable.

Appetite suppressants include amphetamine, ephedrine, sibutramine, diethylpropion, fenfluramine, and phenylpropanolamine. While these drugs depress appetite and lead to weight loss, some have serious side effects. Amphetamine, for example, is highly addictive and can cause cardiac arrhythmia and impair temperature regulation.

Thermogenic drugs include thyroid hormone, ephedrine, and dinitrophenol. Thyroid hormones, in common use in the 1970s, reduce lean body mass and increase the incidence of cardiac arrhythmia. Ephedrine and β-agonists have been suggested as useful agents, but more research is necessary to establish their effectiveness. Uncoupling agents, such as dinitrophenol, are toxic at effective dosages and are associated with neuropathy (nerve damage) and cataracts (eye damage).

Drugs affecting the gastrointestinal tract include Orlistat, dietary fiber, and sucrose polyester. Orlistat, one of two weight-loss prescription drugs approved in the United States, partially blocks fat absorption. While effective, it has side effects—such as abdominal cramping and oily stools—that are unacceptable to many people. Dietary fiber causes gastrointestinal distention and may restrict energy intake. Limited clinical trials suggest that including fiber supplements may aid weight loss. Sucrose polyester (Olestra) is a new diet ingredient that holds some promise. This substance cannot be digested and can be substituted for fats in the diet. The few studies on Olestra have shown conflicting results.

The combination of ephedrine and caffeine is an effective weight-loss agent, comparable to either Orlistat or sibutramine. However, these supplements are controversial and may have severe side effects. The FDA is attempting to ban over-the-counter sales of ephedra.

Before a contest, body builders attempt to accentuate their muscle definition through use of diuretics, potassium supplements, and low-calorie diets. Some body builders also take potassium supplements to promote fluid retention in their muscle cells, leading to increased muscle size. Athletes and people trying to lose weight sometimes combine these practices with very-low-calorie diets and dehydration in their quest for leanness.

There is no evidence that these unhealthy practices improve performance in body building. Serious complications have developed from them, including rhabdomyolysis (suggested by elevated serum creatine kinase and phosphorus), hypotension, (abnormally low blood pressure) marked hemoconcentration, hyperkalemia (high levels of potassium, due to the use of potassium-sparing diuretics and potassium supplements), cardiac arrhythmia, and heart failure.

# SUPPLEMENTS AND YOUR EXERCISE PROGRAM

To sum up, active people and athletes often take a wide variety of drugs and nutritional supplements in their quest for improved performance and the "perfect body." They take these substances to enhance muscle mass; speed recovery and prevent the effects of overtraining; increase training intensity and aggressiveness; and control fat, body water, and appetite. Many of these agents have serious side effects. It's always best to seek the advice of a health professional before using any supplements or drugs as part of your exercise program.

APPENDIX 1

# Muscular System

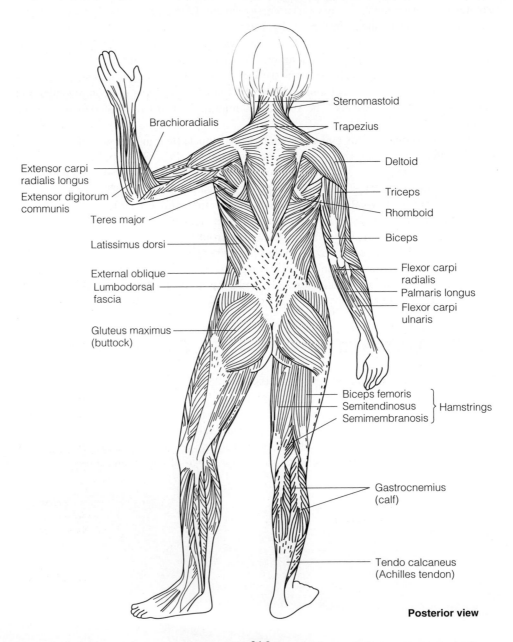

Brachioradialis

Extensor carpi
radialis longus

Extensor digitorum
communis

Teres major

Latissimus dorsi

External oblique

Lumbodorsal
fascia

Gluteus maximus
(buttock)

Sternomastoid

Trapezius

Deltoid

Triceps

Rhomboid

Biceps

Flexor carpi
radialis

Palmaris longus

Flexor carpi
ulnaris

Biceps femoris
Semitendinosus    } Hamstrings
Semimembranosis

Gastrocnemius
(calf)

Tendo calcaneus
(Achilles tendon)

**Posterior view**

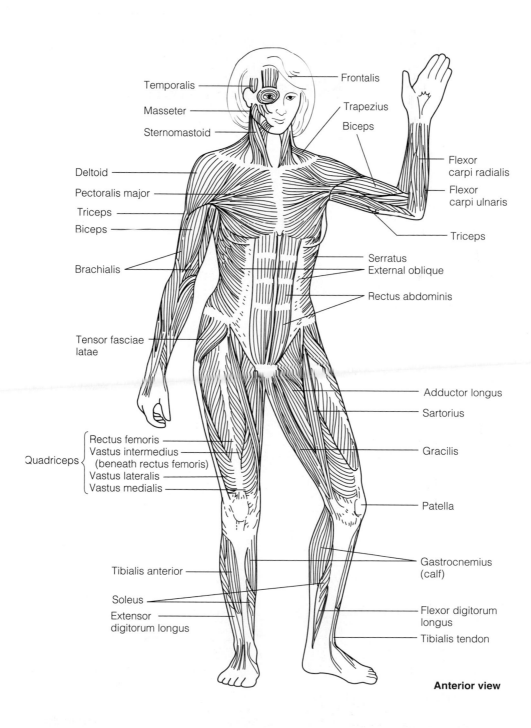

Temporalis

Masseter

Sternomastoid

Frontalis

Trapezius

Biceps

Deltoid

Pectoralis major

Triceps

Biceps

Brachialis

Flexor
carpi radialis

Flexor
carpi ulnaris

Triceps

Serratus
External oblique

Rectus abdominis

Tensor fasciae
latae

Adductor longus

Sartorius

Gracilis

Quadriceps
{
Rectus femoris
Vastus intermedius
(beneath rectus femoris)
Vastus lateralis
Vastus medialis
}

Patella

Tibialis anterior

Soleus

Extensor
digitorum longus

Gastrocnemius
(calf)

Flexor digitorum
longus

Tibialis tendon

**Anterior view**

A P P E N D I X  2

# Skeletal System

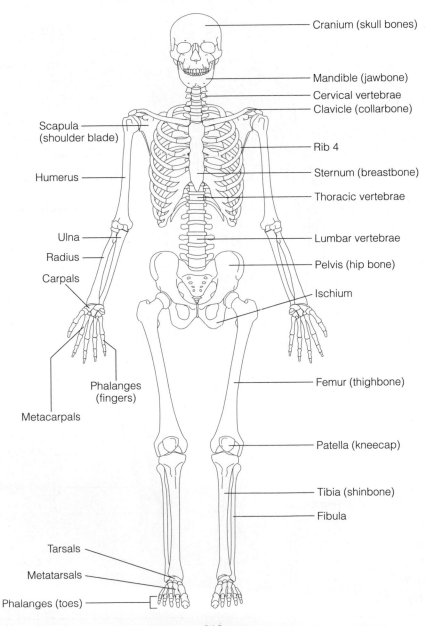

Cranium (skull bones)

Mandible (jawbone)

Cervical vertebrae

Clavicle (collarbone)

Scapula
(shoulder blade)

Rib 4

Humerus

Sternum (breastbone)

Thoracic vertebrae

Ulna

Lumbar vertebrae

Radius

Pelvis (hip bone)

Carpals

Ischium

Phalanges
(fingers)

Metacarpals

Femur (thighbone)

Patella (kneecap)

Tibia (shinbone)

Fibula

Tarsals

Metatarsals

Phalanges (toes)

# Machine and Free-Weight Exercises for Sports and Activities

## WEIGHT TRAINING FOR SPORTS AND ACTIVITIES

Emphasize these body parts when training for the following sports and activities. Although it is important to condition all major muscle groups, specific activities require extra conditioning in specific muscles.

| Activity or Sport | Neck | Shoulders | Chest | Arms | Forearms | Upper Back | Lower Back | Abdominals | Thighs | Hamstrings | Calves |
|---|---|---|---|---|---|---|---|---|---|---|---|
| Badminton | | ✓ | ✓ | ✓ | ✓ | ✓ | | | ✓ | ✓ | ✓ |
| Basketball | | ✓ | ✓ | ✓ | | ✓ | ✓ | ✓ | ✓ | ✓ | ✓ |
| Billiards | | ✓ | | ✓ | ✓ | ✓ | ✓ | | | | |
| Canoeing | | ✓ | ✓ | ✓ | ✓ | ✓ | ✓ | ✓ | | | |
| Cycling | | ✓ | | ✓ | ✓ | ✓ | ✓ | ✓ | ✓ | ✓ | ✓ |
| Dancing | | | | | | | ✓ | ✓ | ✓ | ✓ | ✓ |
| Field hockey | | ✓ | ✓ | ✓ | ✓ | ✓ | ✓ | ✓ | ✓ | ✓ | ✓ |
| Fishing | | | | ✓ | ✓ | | | | ✓ | ✓ | ✓ |
| Football | ✓ | ✓ | ✓ | ✓ | ✓ | ✓ | ✓ | ✓ | ✓ | ✓ | ✓ |
| Golf | | ✓ | | ✓ | ✓ | ✓ | ✓ | ✓ | ✓ | ✓ | ✓ |
| Gymnastics | | ✓ | ✓ | ✓ | ✓ | ✓ | ✓ | ✓ | ✓ | ✓ | ✓ |
| Jogging | | ✓ | | ✓ | | ✓ | ✓ | ✓ | ✓ | ✓ | ✓ |
| Scuba diving | | | | ✓ | | ✓ | ✓ | ✓ | ✓ | ✓ | |
| Skiing, snow | | ✓ | | ✓ | | ✓ | ✓ | ✓ | ✓ | ✓ | ✓ |
| Skiing, water | ✓ | ✓ | | ✓ | ✓ | ✓ | ✓ | ✓ | ✓ | ✓ | ✓ |
| Squash | | ✓ | ✓ | ✓ | ✓ | ✓ | ✓ | ✓ | ✓ | ✓ | ✓ |
| Swimming | | ✓ | ✓ | ✓ | ✓ | ✓ | ✓ | ✓ | ✓ | ✓ | |
| Table tennis | | ✓ | | ✓ | ✓ | ✓ | | | ✓ | ✓ | ✓ |
| Tennis | | ✓ | ✓ | ✓ | ✓ | ✓ | ✓ | ✓ | ✓ | ✓ | ✓ |
| Volleyball | | ✓ | ✓ | ✓ | ✓ | ✓ | ✓ | ✓ | ✓ | ✓ | ✓ |
| Wrestling | ✓ | ✓ | ✓ | ✓ | ✓ | ✓ | ✓ | ✓ | ✓ | ✓ | ✓ |

# WEIGHT-TRAINING EXERCISES FOR SELECTED MACHINES AND FREE WEIGHTS

| Company | Legs | Arms | Shoulders and Chest | Torso |
|---|---|---|---|---|
| **Atlantis** | Butt machine<br>Donkey calf<br>Leg abduction<br>Leg adduction<br>Leg curl<br>Leg extension<br>Leg press<br>Total hip | Arm curl<br>Preacher curl<br>Triceps extension<br>Triceps pushdown | Chest press<br>Deltoid raise<br>Incline press<br>Pec dec<br>Rear deltoid<br>Rotator cuff<br>Shoulder press | Crossover<br>Lat pull-down<br>Low-back extension<br>Pullover<br>Row |
| **Body Master** | Abductor<br>Adductor<br>Glute trainer<br>Leg curl<br>Leg extension<br>Seated leg curl<br>Standing calf<br>Standing leg curl<br>Super leg curl<br>Super leg extension<br>Super leg press | Arm curl<br>Overhead triceps<br>  extension<br>Triceps press | Chest press incline<br>Chest press vertical<br>Lateral raise<br>Seated pec dec vertical<br>Shoulder press | Abdominal<br>Abdominal crunch<br>Lat pull-down<br>Low-back extension<br>Low row<br>Rowing |
| **Cybex** | Hip abduction<br>Hip adduction<br>Leg extension<br>Leg press<br>Prone leg curl<br>Rotary calf<br>Seated leg curl | Arm curl<br>Triceps extension | Chest press<br>Incline press<br>Overhead press | Ab crunch<br>Pull-down<br>Torso rotation |
| **Flex Fitness** | Leg curl<br>Leg extension<br>Seated leg press | Biceps machine<br>Overhead triceps | 30-degree pec<br>  contractor<br>Deltoid raise<br>Pectoral fly<br>Shoulder press<br>Vertical press | Abdominal machine<br>Lat flexor<br>Low-back machine<br>Uni-lateral lat<br>Vertical row |
| **Hammer** | Abductor<br>Adductor<br>Calf<br>H squat<br>Iso lateral leg press<br>Iso leg curl<br>Iso leg extension<br>Leg curl<br>Leg extension<br>Leg press<br>Seated calf raise<br>Seated leg curl | Behind-neck press<br>Bench press<br>Flat back chest<br>Front military press<br>Incline press<br>Iso behind-neck press<br>Iso incline press<br>Iso wide chest<br>Seated bicep<br>Seated triceps | Bench press<br>Flat back chest<br>Iso wide chest<br>Lateral raise<br>Rear deltoid<br>Rotator cuff<br>Seated dip | Behind-neck<br>  pull-down<br>Bilateral row<br>Dead lift<br>Front pull-down<br>High row<br>Iso pullover<br>Low row<br>Pullover<br>Row<br>Shrug |

| Company | Legs | Arms | Shoulders and Chest | Torso |
|---|---|---|---|---|
| **Hoist** | Inner and outer thigh<br>Leg curl<br>Leg extension/lying<br>Leg press/calf raise<br>Multihip | Standing biceps/triceps | Chest press/mid row<br>Chin-dip assist<br>Lateral raise<br>Lat pull-down/high row<br>Pec fly/rear deltoid | Ab crunch<br>Chin-dip assist<br>Low back<br>Mid row<br>Rotary torso |
| **Icarian** | Leg curl<br>Leg extension<br>Leg press | Camber curl<br>Triceps pushdown | Incline pec dec<br>Shoulder press<br>Vertical chest press | Ab crunch<br>Low-back extension<br>Seated row |
| **Life Machines** | Calf raise<br>Leg abduction<br>Leg adduction<br>Leg curl<br>Leg extension<br>Leg press<br>Seated leg curl | Biceps curl<br>Triceps extension | Chest press<br>Incline press<br>Lateral raise<br>Pec fly<br>Seated raise<br>Shoulder press | Ab crunch<br>Lat pull-down<br>Low-back extension<br>Seated row<br>Shoulder pullover |
| **Magnum** | Glute/ham<br>Leg abduction<br>Leg adduction<br>Leg curl<br>Leg extension<br>Leg press<br>Multihip<br>Seated calf | Arm curl<br>Biangular arm curl<br>Triceps extension<br>Triceps pushdown | Bench press<br>Bilateral chest<br>Lateral raise<br>Pec rear deltoid<br>Shoulder press<br>Vertical bench press | Biangular lat row<br>Cable crossover<br>Lat pull-down<br>Rogers row<br>Rotary back<br>Upper back |
| **McdX** | Hip abduction<br>Hip adduction<br>Leg extension<br>Leg flexion<br>Leg press<br>Prone leg curl<br>Seated leg curl | Arm curl<br>Triceps | Chest press<br>Overhead press<br>Seated dip | Pullover<br>Torso arm<br>Torso flexion |
| **Muscle Dynamics** | Calf seated<br>Calf/squat<br>Donkey calf<br>Inner thigh<br>Leg curl<br>Leg extension<br>Leg press<br>Outer thigh | Arm curl<br>Triceps press | Bench press horizontal<br>Bench press vertical<br>Incline press<br>Pec deck<br>Shoulder press<br>Side lateral raise<br>Triceps dip | Abdominal<br>Back<br>Lat pull-down<br>Long pull<br>Low row<br>Pullover<br>Rogers row<br>Rotary torso |
| **Nautilus** | Calf raise<br>Leg curl<br>Leg extension<br>Leg press | Biceps curl<br>Preacher curl<br>Triceps extension | 10-degree chest<br>50-degree chest<br>Bench press<br>Incline press<br>Lateral raise<br>Military press<br>Seated dip | Abdominal<br>Compound row<br>Hip and back<br>Hip flexion<br>Lat pull-down<br>Pullover<br>Rotary torso |

*(continued)*

| Company | Legs | Arms | Shoulders and Chest | Torso |
|---|---|---|---|---|
| **Parabody** | Abduction | Biceps curl | Dumbbell shoulder press | Abdominal crunch |
| | Adduction | Dumbbell curl | Front raises | Back butterfly |
| | Back kicks | Incline dumbbell curl | Military press | Bench press |
| | Leg extension | Reverse biceps curl | Side raises | Bent-over row |
| | Leg press | Triceps extension | | Decline press |
| | Prone leg curl | Triceps kick back | | Dumbbell fly |
| | Standing calf raise | Triceps pushdown | | Incline press |
| | Standing leg curl | | | Lat pull-down |
| | | | | Pec dec butterfly |
| | | | | Upright row |
| | | | | Vertical butterfly |
| **Paramount** | Glute | Arm curl | Chin/dip | Abdominal |
| | Leg curl | Biceps curl | Seated chest | |
| | Leg extension | Triceps extension | Shoulder press | |
| | Leg press | Triceps pushdown | | |
| **Trotter** | Hip abduction | Arm curl | Chest press | Abdominal |
| | Hip adduction | Triceps press-down | Fly | Back extension |
| | Leg curl | | Incline press | Lat pull-down |
| | Leg extension | | Shoulder press | Upright row |
| | Leg press | | | |
| **Tuff Stuff** | Abductor | French curl | Deltoid raise | Abdominal crunch |
| | Adductor | Seated arm curl | Seated chest press | Back extension |
| | Angled donkey calf | | Seated vertical fly | High lat pull-down |
| | Horizontal leg press | | Shoulder press | Low lat pull-down |
| | Multihip | | | Seated long pull |
| | Seated leg curl | | | Seated row |
| | Seated leg extension | | | |
| **Universal Gym** | Abductor kick | Biceps curl | Bench press | Bent-over row |
| | Adductor kick | Dips | Front raise | Crunch |
| | Calf raises (leg press) | Lat pull | Incline press | Lat pull |
| | Knee extension | | Rip-up | Pullover |
| | Knee flexion | | Shoulder press | Pull-up |
| | Leg press | | Upright row | Side bend |
| **Free weights** | Back squat | Barbell curl | Bench press | Abdominal crunch |
| | Front squat | Dumbbell curl | Decline press | Abdominal sit-ups |
| | Hack squat | French curl | Dumbbell back raise | Bent-over row |
| | Leg curl | Preacher curl | Dumbbell flys | Dead lift |
| | Leg extension | | Dumbbell front raise | Incline lever row |
| | Leg press | | Dumbbell lateral raise | Lat pull-down |
| | Lunges | | Incline press | Pullover |
| | Seated calf | | Overhead press | Seated row |
| | Smith machine | | | Shrug |
| | Step-ups | | | Upright row |

# A P P E N D I X   4

# Norms and Test Procedures for Measuring Strength

## NORMS FOR BODY COMPOSITION, PERCENT FAT

Percent fat can be calculated by many methods, including underwater weighing, Bod Pod, skinfold, bioelectrical impedance, and ultrasound. *Source:* The Cooper Institute for Aerobics Research, Dallas, TX, 1995.

| MEN | AGE (YEARS) | | | | |
|---|---|---|---|---|---|
| *Rating* | *20–29* | *30–39* | *40–49* | *50–59* | *60+* |
| Very lean | 5.2 | 9.1 | 11.4 | 12.9 | 13.1 |
| Excellent | 9.4 | 13.9 | 16.3 | 17.9 | 18.4 |
| Good | 14.1 | 17.5 | 19.6 | 21.3 | 22.0 |
| Fair | 17.4 | 20.5 | 22.5 | 24.1 | 25.0 |
| Poor | 22.4 | 24.2 | 26.1 | 27.5 | 28.5 |
| Very poor | 29.1 | 29.9 | 31.5 | 32.4 | 33.4 |

| WOMEN | AGE (YEARS) | | | | |
|---|---|---|---|---|---|
| *Rating* | *20–29* | *30–39* | *40–49* | *50–59* | *60+* |
| Very lean | 10.8 | 13.4 | 16.1 | 18.8 | 16.8 |
| Excellent | 17.1 | 18.0 | 21.3 | 25.0 | 25.1 |
| Good | 20.6 | 21.6 | 24.9 | 28.5 | 29.3 |
| Fair | 23.7 | 24.9 | 28.1 | 31.6 | 32.5 |
| Poor | 27.7 | 29.3 | 32.1 | 35.6 | 36.6 |
| Very poor | 35.4 | 35.7 | 37.8 | 39.6 | 40.5 |

# NORMS FOR 1-MINUTE SIT-UPS

*Instructions:* Determine the number of bent-knee sit-ups you can do in 1 minute, with feet held by a spotter and hands folded across the chest. Some experts think this test puts excessive stress on the spinal discs. *Source:* The Cooper Institute for Aerobics Research, Dallas, TX, 1995.

| MEN | | | AGE (YEARS) | | | |
|---|---|---|---|---|---|---|
| *Rating* | *< 20* | *20–29* | *30–39* | *40–49* | *50–59* | *60+* |
| Superior | 62 | 55 | 51 | 47 | 43 | 39 |
| Excellent | 51 | 47 | 43 | 39 | 35 | 30 |
| Good | 47 | 42 | 39 | 34 | 28 | 22 |
| Fair | 41 | 38 | 35 | 29 | 24 | 19 |
| Poor | 36 | 33 | 30 | 24 | 19 | 15 |
| Very poor | 27 | 27 | 23 | 17 | 12 | 7 |

| WOMEN | | | AGE (YEARS) | | | |
|---|---|---|---|---|---|---|
| *Rating* | *< 20* | *20–29* | *30–39* | *40–49* | *50–59* | *60+* |
| Superior | 55 | 51 | 42 | 38 | 30 | 28 |
| Excellent | 46 | 44 | 35 | 29 | 24 | 17 |
| Good | 36 | 38 | 29 | 24 | 20 | 11 |
| Fair | 32 | 32 | 25 | 20 | 14 | 6 |
| Poor | 28 | 27 | 20 | 14 | 10 | 3 |
| Very poor | 25 | 18 | 11 | 7 | 5 | 0 |

# NORMS FOR 1 REPETITION MAXIMUM BENCH PRESS

*Instructions:* Warm up. Determine the maximum weight you can bench-press for 1 repetition (dynamic variable-resistance machine). Divide your max bench press (lb.) by your body weight (lb.) to determine your bench-press ratio. *Source:* The Cooper Institute for Aerobics Research, Dallas, TX, 1995.

| MEN | | | AGE (YEARS) | | | |
|---|---|---|---|---|---|---|
| *Rating* | *< 20* | *20–29* | *30–39* | *40–49* | *50–59* | *60+* |
| Superior | 1.76 | 1.63 | 1.35 | 1.20 | 1.05 | 0.94 |
| Excellent | 1.34 | 1.32 | 1.12 | 1.00 | 0.90 | 0.82 |
| Good | 1.19 | 1.14 | 0.98 | 0.88 | 0.79 | 0.72 |
| Fair | 1.06 | 0.99 | 0.88 | 0.80 | 0.71 | 0.66 |
| Poor | 0.89 | 0.88 | 0.78 | 0.72 | 0.63 | 0.57 |
| Very poor | 0.76 | 0.72 | 0.65 | 0.59 | 0.53 | 0.49 |

| WOMEN | | | AGE (YEARS) | | | |
|---|---|---|---|---|---|---|
| *Rating* | *< 20* | *20–29* | *30–39* | *40–49* | *50–59* | *60+* |
| Superior | 0.88 | 1.01 | 0.82 | 0.77 | 0.68 | 0.72 |
| Excellent | 0.77 | 0.80 | 0.70 | 0.62 | 0.55 | 0.54 |
| Good | 0.65 | 0.70 | 0.60 | 0.54 | 0.48 | 0.47 |
| Fair | 0.58 | 0.59 | 0.53 | 0.50 | 0.44 | 0.43 |
| Poor | 0.53 | 0.51 | 0.47 | 0.43 | 0.39 | 0.38 |
| Very poor | 0.41 | 0.44 | 0.39 | 0.35 | 0.31 | 0.26 |

# NORMS FOR 1 REPETITION MAXIMUM LEG PRESS

*Instructions:* Warm up. Determine the maximum weight you can leg-press for 1 repetition. Divide your max leg press (lb.) by your body weight (lb.) to determine your leg-press ratio.
*Source:* The Cooper Institute for Aerobics Research, Dallas, TX, 1995.

| MEN | AGE (YEARS) | | | | | |
|---|---|---|---|---|---|---|
| *Rating* | *< 20* | *20–29* | *30–39* | *40–49* | *50–59* | *60+* |
| Superior | 2.82 | 2.40 | 2.20 | 2.02 | 1.90 | 1.80 |
| Excellent | 2.28 | 2.13 | 1.93 | 1.82 | 1.71 | 1.62 |
| Good | 2.04 | 1.97 | 1.77 | 1.68 | 1.58 | 1.49 |
| Fair | 1.90 | 1.83 | 1.65 | 1.57 | 1.46 | 1.38 |
| Poor | 1.70 | 1.63 | 1.52 | 1.44 | 1.32 | 1.25 |
| Very poor | 1.46 | 1.42 | 1.34 | 1.27 | 1.15 | 1.08 |

| WOMEN | AGE (YEARS) | | | | | |
|---|---|---|---|---|---|---|
| *Rating* | *< 20* | *20–29* | *30–39* | *40–49* | *50–59* | *60+* |
| Superior | 1.88 | 1.98 | 1.68 | 1.57 | 1.43 | 1.43 |
| Excellent | 1.71 | 1.68 | 1.47 | 1.37 | 1.25 | 1.18 |
| Good | 1.59 | 1.50 | 1.33 | 1.23 | 1.10 | 1.04 |
| Fair | 1.38 | 1.37 | 1.21 | 1.13 | 0.99 | 0.93 |
| Poor | 1.22 | 1.22 | 1.09 | 1.02 | 0.88 | 0.85 |
| Very poor | 1.06 | 0.99 | 0.96 | 0.85 | 0.72 | 0.63 |

# NORMS FOR PUSH-UPS, MEN

*Instructions:* Assume push-up starting position by lying face down, body and arms straight and weight supported on your toes and hands. Lower your body until your chest touches the floor; then push up to the starting position. Do as many push-ups as possible. *Sources:* The Cooper Institute for Aerobics Research, Dallas, TX, 1995, and a survey of published sources.

| | AGE (YEARS) | | | | | |
|---|---|---|---|---|---|---|
| *Rating* | *< 20* | *20–29* | *30–39* | *40–49* | *50–59* | *60+* |
| Superior | 64 | 62 | 52 | 40 | 39 | 28 |
| Excellent | 49 | 47 | 39 | 30 | 25 | 23 |
| Good | 39 | 37 | 30 | 24 | 19 | 18 |
| Fair | 31 | 29 | 24 | 18 | 13 | 10 |
| Poor | 24 | 22 | 17 | 11 | 9 | 6 |
| Very poor | 15 | 13 | 9 | 5 | 3 | 2 |

# NORMS FOR MODIFIED PUSH-UPS, WOMEN

*Instructions:* Assume push-up starting position by lying face down, body and arms straight and weight supported on your knees and hands. Lower your body until your chest touches the floor; then push up to the starting position. Do as many push-ups as possible. *Sources:* The Cooper Institute for Aerobics Research, Dallas, TX, 1995, and a survey of published sources.

| | AGE (YEARS) | | | | | |
|---|---|---|---|---|---|---|
| *Rating* | *< 20* | *20–29* | *30–39* | *40–49* | *50–59* | *60+* |
| Superior | 50 | 45 | 39 | 33 | 28 | 20 |
| Excellent | 41 | 36 | 31 | 24 | 21 | 15 |
| Good | 35 | 30 | 24 | 18 | 17 | 12 |
| Fair | 28 | 23 | 19 | 13 | 12 | 5 |
| Poor | 22 | 17 | 11 | 6 | 6 | 2 |
| Very poor | 14 | 9 | 4 | 1 | 0 | 0 |

# NORMS FOR COMBINED RIGHT- AND LEFT-HAND GRIP STRENGTH

*Instructions:* Using a hand-grip dynamometer, measure your maximum grip strength for your left and right hands and combine the score (left hand + right hand). Make two measurements for each hand, measuring each alternately. Record your measurements in kilograms. Originally compiled from survey of published sources.

| MEN | | | AGE (YEARS) | | | |
| --- | --- | --- | --- | --- | --- | --- |
| *Rating* | *< 20* | *20–29* | *30–39* | *40–49* | *50–59* | *60+* |
| Superior | 137 | 136 | 135 | 128 | 119 | 111 |
| Excellent | 121 | 120 | 120 | 117 | 108 | 99 |
| Good | 112 | 111 | 111 | 108 | 100 | 91 |
| Fair | 105 | 104 | 104 | 100 | 94 | 84 |
| Poor | 96 | 95 | 94 | 91 | 85 | 76 |
| Very poor | 82 | 81 | 81 | 76 | 74 | 62 |

| WOMEN | | | AGE (YEARS) | | | |
| --- | --- | --- | --- | --- | --- | --- |
| *Rating* | *< 20* | *20–29* | *30–39* | *40–49* | *50–59* | *60+* |
| Superior | 78 | 78 | 76 | 74 | 72 | 67 |
| Excellent | 71 | 71 | 69 | 67 | 63 | 56 |
| Good | 63 | 63 | 61 | 59 | 54 | 51 |
| Fair | 58 | 58 | 56 | 54 | 50 | 47 |
| Poor | 53 | 53 | 51 | 49 | 47 | 45 |
| Very poor | 45 | 45 | 43 | 41 | 40 | 38 |

*Source:* Fitness norms from *The Physical Fitness Specialist Manual,* The Cooper Institute for Aerobics Research, Dallas, TX, revised 1996. Used with permission.

# Glossary

**abduction**   Lateral movement of a body segment away from the midline of the body.

**actin**   One of the contractile elements in muscular fibers.

**adaptation**   Changes in the body as a result of a biological stressor. For example, forcing muscles to contract against increased resistance causes them to increase in size.

**adduction**   Lateral movement of a body segment toward the midline of the body.

**adenosine diphosphate (ADP)**   A cellular energy compound that fuels biological processes and is used to make ATP, the principal energy-bearing compound in the cells.

**adenosine triphosphate (ATP)**   A compound that carries chemical energy in all living organisms. Its breakdown releases energy that is used to fuel biological processes such as muscle contraction and protein synthesis.

**aerobics**   Exercises that increase oxygen consumption, such as running or swimming, and improve respiratory and circulatory function.

**agonist**   A muscle that causes motion.

**American College of Sports Medicine**   The principal interdisciplinary organization of sports-medicine professionals. Represented disciplines include medicine, athletic training, exercise physiology, physical therapy, psychology, motor learning (study of how physical skills are learned), biomechanics (study of motion), chiropractic, and education.

**amino acids**   Substances that form the principal components of proteins. They are taken in supplement form by some people to enhance muscle growth, but there is no evidence that they are effective.

**anabolic steroids**    Synthetic male hormones taken to enhance athletic performance and body composition. (Anabolic: biochemical building processes.)

**androstenedione (andro)**    One of several hormones produced by the adrenal glands that is broken down to form testosterone. It is used as a muscle-building agent by some athletes but has many of the same side effects as anabolic steroids. Its use as a supplement is banned by most sports organizations.

**anorexia athletica**    An eating disorder related to anorexia nervosa. People with this condition add excessive exercise to their obsessive preoccupation with body weight.

**anorexia nervosa**    An eating disorder characterized by a neurotic fixation on body fat and food.

**antagonist**    A muscle that can move the joint opposite to the direction of movement produced by the agonist.

**anticatabolic**    Describes a process that blocks chemical breakdown processes.

**atrophy**    Decrease in size of a body part or tissue.

**balanced diet**    A diet composed of the six basic food groups: dairy products, protein foods, fruits, vegetables, whole-grain products, and fats.

**body building**    A form of weight training dedicated to improving the shape and appearance of the body.

**bulimia**    An eating disorder characterized by binge eating followed by forced vomiting.

**carbohydrates**    Organic compounds, such as sugars and starches, composed of carbon, hydrogen, and oxygen.

**circuit training**    A technique involving a series of weight-training stations. The weight trainer performs an exercise and rapidly moves to the next station with little or no rest. Circuit training develops cardiovascular endurance, though not as effectively as endurance exercises such as running, cycling, or swimming.

**circumduction**    Movement of a body segment around a point so that the free end traces a circle and the segment traces a cone.

**clenubuterol**    An anti-asthma drug that also causes muscle hypertrophy.

**collar**    A device that secures weights to barbells or dumbbells.

**concentric muscle action**    Application of force as the muscle shortens.

**constant set method**    The same weight and number of sets and repetitions are used for each exercise.

**cool-down**    A light exercise program done at the end of a workout to gradually return the body to its normal resting state.

**core**    Muscles in the central thorax that support and stabilize the spine.

**coronary artery disease**    A disease of the large arteries supplying the heart; sometimes called "hardening of the arteries."

**creatine monohydrate (creatine)**    A supplement taken to increase strength and muscle mass. It increases muscle creatine phosphate, an energy storage compound in muscle.

**cycle training**   A training technique that varies the type, volume, rest intervals, and intensity of workouts throughout the year. Also called "periodization of training."

**dehydroepiandrosterone (DHEA)**   One of several hormones produced by the adrenal glands that is broken down to form testosterone. It is used as a muscle-building agent by some athletes but has many of the same side effects as anabolic steroids. Its use as a supplement is banned by most sports organizations.

**dorsiflexion**   Movement of the foot toward its dorsal (upper) surface.

**dynamic**   Application of force resulting in movement. Also called "isotonic."

**dynamic constant resistance**   A form of weight training that uses a constant load, such as a barbell or dumbbell.

**dynamic variable resistance**   The imposition of variable loading during an exercise. Resistance is generally increased toward the end of the range of motion. Usually, you must use weight machines to do variable-resistance exercises.

**eccentric loading**   Loading the muscle while it is lengthening; sometimes called "negatives."

**eccentric muscle action**   Application of force as the muscle lengthens.

**electrical muscle stimulation**   Application of an electrical current to the skin over a muscle group for the purpose of contracting the muscle.

**endurance**   The ability to sustain a specific exercise intensity.

**ergogenic aid**   A substance or technique used to improve performance.

**eversion**   Rotation of the foot that lifts the lateral border of the foot upward.

**exercise physiology**   The study of physiological function during exercise.

**extension**   Movement of a joint that results in an increased angle between two adjacent segments; return from flexion.

**failure method**   Doing an exercise to the point of fatigue.

**fasciculi**   Bundles of muscle fibers.

**fat-free weight**   Lean body mass.

**flexion**   Movement of a joint that results in a decreased angle between two adjacent segments (bones).

**frequency**   The number of training sessions per week.

**functional training**   Specific training to develop strength and power in a movement.

**giant sets**   Use of multiple exercises in succession for the same muscle group.

**glycogen**   A complex carbohydrate stored principally in the liver and skeletal muscle. It is an extremely important fuel during most forms of exercise.

**high-power sport**   A sport that requires rapid, powerful movements. Examples include softball, soccer, tennis, alpine skiing, and field hockey.

**hydroxy-beta-methylbutyrate (HMB)**   A breakdown product of the amino acid lysine used to increase muscle mass and strength.

**hyperplasia**    Increase in the number of muscle cells (fibers).

**hypertrophy**    Increase in the size of a muscle fiber, usually stimulated by muscular over-load.

**inorganic phosphate (Pi)**    A salt of phosphoric acid used to make ATP, an important cellular energy chemical.

**insertion**    The place of attachment of a muscle to the bone, which the muscle moves.

**insulin-like growth factor (IGF-1)**    A hormone released from the liver in response to growth hormone. It has many of the same effects as insulin on muscle, including protein synthesis.

**intensity**    The relative effort expended during an exercise; also, the amount of resistance or weight used.

**interval training**    A series of high-intensity exercises followed by rest. Factors manipulated are distance, intensity, repetition, and rest.

**inversion**    Rotation of the foot that lifts the medial border of the foot upward.

**isokinetic**    Application of force at a constant speed. A form of dynamic exercise.

**isometric**    Application of force without movement. Also called "static."

**joint**    The place where bones intersect. Joints are often surrounded by joint capsules and are supported by ligaments and, to a lesser degree, by muscles.

**kinetic chain**    Movement sequence involving one or more joints; can be closed (foot or arm fixed against a resistance) or open (foot or arm not fixed against a resistance).

**lifting stones**    Large rocks used for functional exercises.

**ligaments**    Structures that connect bone to bone.

**load**    The intensity of exercise—that is, the weight or resistance used.

**lockout**    Full extension of a joint at the end of a range of motion.

**maximum lift**    The maximum amount of weight you can lift in one repetition of an exercise.

**medicine balls**    Heavy balls usually weighing 1 to 20 pounds and made of leather, rubber, or plastic. Some medicine balls have handles.

**mixed grip**    Gripping the bar with one palm toward you and one away.

**motor unit**    A motor nerve (nerve that initiates movement) connected to one or more muscle fibers.

**motor unit recruitment**    Activation of motor units by the central nervous system in order to exert force.

**multipennate muscles**    Muscles in which the fibers are aligned in several directions.

**muscle definition**    Property of having the size and shape of a muscle clearly visible. Best developed by decreasing surface fat and increasing muscle size.

**muscle fibers**    Cells causing contraction of the muscles.

**myofibrils**    Any of the small protein structures that make up the contractile part of skeletal muscle fibers.

**myofilaments** Small threads of proteins making up myofibrils in striated muscle. Thick ones contain myosin, and thin ones contain actin.

**myosin** One of the contractile elements in muscle fibers.

**origin** The point of attachment or end of a muscle that is fixed during contraction.

**osteoporosis** A disease characterized by bone demineralization that is most common in postmenopausal women.

**overload** To subject the body to more than normal stress.

**overtraining** Training too much or too intensely and not providing enough time to recover adequately. Symptoms include lack of energy, decreased physical performance, fatigue, depression, aching muscles and joints, and vulnerability to injury.

**parallel** A squat position in which the long axis of the thigh is parallel to the ground (i.e., a parallel squat).

**paused reps** Resting within a set.

**peak power** The maximum value for work/time. Practically speaking, the maximum combination of weight (amount of weight on the bar) and speed (time it takes to lift the weight). Most people are capable of generating peak power in a particular lift at a weight that is 60 percent of the weight they can lift for one repetition.

**periodization of training** A training technique that varies the volume and intensity of exercises between workouts. Also called "cycle training."

**plantar flexion** Movement of the foot toward its plantar (lower) surface.

**plyometrics** Rapid stretching of a muscle group that is undergoing eccentric stress (i.e., the muscle is exerting force while it lengthens) followed by a rapid concentric contraction. Sometimes called "implosion training."

**poleates** Resistive exercise routine using a pole, softball bat, or strong broom handle.

**power** In physics, power equals work per unit of time. In weight training, power is usually defined as the ability to exert force rapidly.

**power lifting** A competitive sport consisting of the bench press, the dead lift, and squat lifts.

**power rack** A device used to restrict the range of motion during an exercise.

**prime movers** The major muscles used to perform a movement.

**pronated grip** Gripping the bar with palms away from you.

**pronation** Inward rotation of the forearm.

**pyramiding** A training technique that uses increasing amounts of weight with succeeding sets. After a maximum weight is reached, the remaining sets are done with decreasing amounts of weight.

**rack** A structure that holds or supports barbells. Racks are often used in squats, bench presses, incline presses, and preacher curls.

**rehabilitation** The restoration of normal function through the use of therapeutic exercise and modalities.

**repetition** The number of times an exercise is done during 1 set.

**resistance**   A measure of force that must be exerted by the muscles to perform an exercise.

**rest**   The period of time between exercises, sets of exercises, or workouts.

**reversibility**   Decrease in fitness caused by lack of training or injury.

**rotation**   Movement of a body segment around its longitudinal axis.

**rotator cuff**   A group of muscles that rotate the humerus (shoulder). The rotator-cuff muscles are the supraspinatus, teres major, infraspinatus, and subscapularis.

**set**   A group of repetitions followed by rest.

**skill**   The ability to bring about some end result with maximum certainty and minimum outlay of energy or of time and energy; proficiency at a particular task.

**Smith machine**   A weight machine that includes a free-weight barbell that rides in a track, which restricts its motion.

**speed loading**   Moving a load as rapidly as possible.

**sports medicine**   A branch of medicine dealing with medical problems of athletes. Disciplines often considered part of sports medicine include exercise physiology, athletic training, biomechanics (study of motion), sports physical therapy, kinesiology, sports psychology, motor learning (study of how physical skills are learned), and sports chiropractic.

**spot**   To assist with an exercise. The spotter's main job is to help the lifter with the weight if the exercise can't be completed.

**spot reducing**   Reducing fat in a specific part of the body, such as the abdomen, legs, or hips. There is no evidence that spot reducing is possible. Except for plastic surgery (liposuction), it appears that body fat can be lost only by inducing a negative energy balance—expending more energy than is taken in.

**stabilizers**   Muscles that contract with no significant movement.

**strength**   The ability to exert force.

**stress**   In weight training, the resistance placed on muscles and joints during an exercise.

**striated**   Describes the stripped appearance of skeletal muscle.

**super sets**   Two sets of exercises performed in rapid succession, usually working opposing muscle groups.

**supinated grip**   Gripping the bar with palms toward you.

**supination**   Outward rotation of the forearm.

**Swiss ball**   A large rubber ball that provides an unstable surface on which to perform exercises.

**synergists**   Muscles that assist another muscle to accomplish a movement.

**tendons**   Rigid structures that connect muscles to bones.

**testosterone**   The principal male hormone. It is produced by the testes, is responsible for the development of secondary sexual characteristics, and plays a role in muscle hypertrophy. (The principal hormone in women is androstenedione, produced by the adrenal glands.)

**testosterone receptors**   Structures in the cell that bind with testosterone, the principal male hormone.

**thermogenic**   Describes an increase in metabolic rate and body heat production.

**vitamins**   A general term used to describe a group of organic substances, required in small amounts, that are essential to metabolism.

**volume**   The number of sets and repetitions in a workout.

**warm-up**   Low-intensity exercise done before full-effort physical activity in order to improve muscle and joint performance, prevent injury, reinforce motor skills, and maximize blood flow to the muscles and heart. In weight training, people often warm up by lifting lighter weights before attempting heavy weights.

**weight lifting**   A competitive sport consisting of the snatch and clean-and-jerk lifts.

**weight-lifting belt**   A belt, approximately 4 inches wide, used to support the abdomen and back and maintain proper spinal alignment during weight-lifting exercises.

**wraps**   Joint supports made of elastic bandages, neoprene, or leather.

**Z lines**   The cellular borders of the sarcomere, the contractile element of the muscle fibers.

# References

Aagaard, P., and J. L. Andersen. 1998. "Correlation between contractile strength and myosin heavy-chain isoform composition in human skeletal muscle." *Medicine and Science in Sports and Exercise* 30: 1217–1222.

"ACSM position stand on the recommended quantity and quality of exercise for developing and maintaining cardiorespiratory and muscular fitness, and flexibility in adults." 1998. *Medicine and Science in Sports and Exercise* 30: 975–991.

American College of Sports Medicine. 2005. *ACSM's Guidelines for Exercise Testing and Prescription.* 7th ed. Baltimore: Williams and Wilkins.

Andersen, L. L., G. Tufekovic, M. K. Zebis, R. M. Crameri, G. Verlaan, M. Kjaer, C. Suetta, P. Magnusson, and P. Aagaard. 2005. "The effect of resistance training combined with timed ingestion of protein on muscle fiber size and muscle strength." *Metabolism* 54: 151–156.

Berger, R. 1962. "Optimum repetitions for the development of strength." *Research Quarterly* 33: 334–338.

Berger, R. 1963. "Comparative effects of three weight training programs." *Research Quarterly* 34: 396–398.

Bergstrom, J., L. Hermansen, E. Hultman, and B. Saltin. 1967. "Diet, muscle glycogen and physical performance." *Acta Physiologica Scandinavica* 71: 140–150.

Bhambhani, Y., G. Rowland, and M. Farag. 2005. "Effects of circuit training on body composition and peak cardiorespiratory responses in patients with moderate to severe traumatic brain injury." *Archives of Physical Medicine and Rehabilitation* 86: 268–276.

Blackburn, J. R., and M. C. Morrissey. 1998. "The relationship between open and closed kinetic chain strength of the lower limb and jumping performance." *Journal of Orthopaedic and Sports Physical Therapy* 27: 430–435.

Brocherie, F., N. Babault, G. Cometti, N. Maffiuletti, and J. C. Chatard. 2005. "Electrostimulation training effects on the physical performance of ice hockey players." *Medicine and Science in Sports and Exercise* 37: 455–460.

Brooks, G. A. 1987. "Amino acid and protein metabolism during exercise and recovery." *Medicine and Science in Sports and Exercise* 19 (Suppl.): 150–156.

Brooks, G. A., T. D. Fahey, and K. Baldwin. 2005. *Exercise Physiology: Human Bioenergetics and Its Applications.* 4th ed. New York: McGraw-Hill.

Brown, C. H., and J. H. Wilmore. 1974. "The effects of maximal resistance training on the strength and body composition of women athletes." *Medicine and Science in Sports and Exercise* 6: 174–177.

Butterfield, G., and D. Calloway. 1984. "Physical activity improves protein utilization in young men." *British Journal of Nutrition* 51: 171–184.

Caiozzo V. J., F. Haddad, M. J. Baker, and K. M. Baldwin. 1996. "Influence of mechanical loading on myosin heavy-chain protein and mRNA isoform expression." *Journal of Applied Physiology* 80: 1503–1512.

Celejowa, I., and M. Homa. 1970. "Food intake, nitrogen and energy balance in Polish weight lifters, during a training camp." *Nutrition and Metabolism* 12: 259–275.

Chu, D. 1994. *Jumping into Plyometrics.* Champaign, IL: Leisure Press.

Costill, D. L., E. F. Coyle, W. F. Fink, G. R. Lesmes, and F. A. Witzmann. 1979. "Adaptations in skeletal muscle following strength training." *Journal of Applied Physiology* 46: 96–99.

Cotterman, M. L., L. A. Darby, and W. A. Skelly. 2005. "Comparison of muscle force production using the Smith machine and free weights for bench press and squat exercises." *Journal of Strength and Conditioning Research* 19: 169–176.

Cronin, J., and B. Crewther. 2004. "Training volume and strength and power development." *The Journal of Sports Science and Medicine* 7: 144–155.

Cronin, J. B., and M. E. Henderson. 2004. "Maximal strength and power assessment in novice weight trainers." *Journal of Strength and Conditioning Research* 18: 48–52.

Cronin, J. B., and G. J. Owen. 2004. "Upper-body strength and power assessment in women using a chest pass." *Journal of Strength and Conditioning Research* 18: 401–404.

Daniels, J. 2004. "Fad diets: Slim on good nutrition." *Nursing* 34: 22–23.

Department of Health and Human Services. 1996. *Physical Activity and Health: A Report of the Surgeon General.* Atlanta: U.S. Department of Health and Human Services, Centers for Disease Control and Prevention, National Center for Chronic Disease Prevention and Health Promotion.

Dunstan, D. W., R. M. Daly, N. Owen, D. Jolley, E. Vulikh, J. Shaw, and P. Zimmet. 2005. "Home-based resistance training is not sufficient to maintain improved glycemic control following supervised training in older individuals with type 2 diabetes." *Diabetes Care* 28: 3–9.

Evans, N. A. 2004. "Current concepts in anabolic–androgenic steroids." *American Journal of Sports Medicine* 32: 534–542.

Fahey, T. D. 1987. *Athletic Training: Principles and Practice.* Mountain View, CA: Mayfield.

Fahey, T. D., L. Akka, and R. Rolph. 1975. "Body composition and $VO_{2max}$ of exceptional weight-trained athletes." *Journal of Applied Physiology* 39: 559–561.

Fahey, T. D., P. M. Insel, and W. T. Roth. 2005. *Fit and Well.* 6th ed. New York: McGraw-Hill.

Fahey, T. D., and M. S. Pearl. 1998. "The hormonal and perceptive effects of phosphatidylserine administration during two weeks of resistive exercise-induced overtraining." *Biology of Sport* 15: 135–144.

Fleck, S. J., and W. J. Kraemer. 1997. *Designing Resistance Training Programs.* Champaign, IL: Human Kinetics.

Garhammer, J. 1980. "Power production by Olympic weightlifters." *Medicine and Science in Sports and Exercise* 12: 54–60.

Garhammer, J. 1991. "A comparison of maximal power outputs between elite male and female weightlifters in competition." *International Journal of Sport Biomechanics* 7: 3–11.

Glowacki, S. P., S. E. Martin, A. Maurer, W. Baek, J. S. Green, and S. F. Crouse. 2004. "Effects of resistance, endurance, and concurrent exercise on training outcomes in men." *Medicine and Science in Sports and Exercise* 36: 2119–2127.

Goldberg, A. L. 1972. "Mechanisms of growth and atrophy of skeletal muscle." In R. G. Cassens, ed., *Muscle Biology.* New York: Marcel Dekker.

Gollnick, P. D., R. B. Armstrong, C. W. Saubertt, K. Piehl, and B. Saltin. 1972. "Enzyme activity and fiber composition in skeletal muscle of trained and untrained men." *Journal of Applied Physiology* 33: 312–319.

Gonyea, W. J., and D. Sale. 1982. "Physiology of weight lifting." *Archives of Physical Medicine and Rehabilitation* 63: 235–237.

Hadzovic, A., E. Nakas-Icindic, E. Kucukalic-Selimovic, and A. U. Salaka. 2004. "Growth hormone (GH): Usage and abuse." *Bosnian Journal of Basic Medicine and Science* 4: 66–70.

Hartgens, F., and H. Kuipers. 2004. "Effects of androgenic–anabolic steroids in athletes." *Sports Medicine* 34: 513–554.

Haslam, D. W. 2004. "Male central obesity." *Journal of the Royal Society of Health* 124: 209–210.

Helge, E. W., and I. L. Kanstrup. 2002. "Bone density in female elite gymnasts: Impact of muscle strength and sex hormones." *Medicine and Science in Sports and Exercise* 34: 174–180.

Hickson, R. C. 1980. "Interference of strength development by simultaneously training for strength and endurance." *European Journal of Applied Physiology* 45: 255–263.

Hill, A. V. 1970. *First and Last Experiments in Muscle Mechanics.* Cambridge: Cambridge University Press.

Hoffman, J. R., J. Cooper, M. Wendell, and J. Kang. 2004. "Comparison of Olympic vs. traditional power lifting training programs in football players." *Journal of Strength and Conditioning Research* 18: 129–135.

Hortobagyi, T., J. P. Hill, J. A. Houmard, D. D. Fraser, N. J. Lambert, and R. G. Israel. 1996. "Adaptive responses to muscle lengthening and shortening in humans." *Journal of Applied Physiology* 80: 765–772.

Hu, G., J. Tuomilehto, K. Silventoinen, N. C. Barengo, M. Peltonen, and P. Jousilahti. 2005. "The effects of physical activity and body mass index on cardiovascular, cancer and all-cause mortality among 47,212 middle-aged Finnish men and women." *International Journal of Obesity and Related Metabolic Disorders* 29: 894–902.

Ibanez, J., M. Izquierdo, I. Arguelles, L. Forga, J. L. Larrion, M. Garcia-Unciti, F. Idoate, and E. M. Gorostiaga. 2005. "Twice-weekly progressive resistance training decreases abdominal fat and improves insulin sensitivity in older men with type 2 diabetes." *Diabetes Care* 28: 662–667.

Jurca, R., M. J. Lamonte, T. S. Church, C. P. Earnest, S. J. Fitzgerald, C. E. Barlow, A. N. Jordan, J. B. Kampert, and S. N. Blair. 2004. "Associations of muscle strength and fitness with metabolic syndrome in men." *Medicine and Science in Sports and Exercise.* 36: 1301–1307.

Kamen, G. 2004. "Neural issues in the control of muscular strength." *Research Quarterly for Exercise and Sport* 75: 3–8.

Karlsson, J., and B. Saltin. 1971. "Diet, muscle glycogen and endurance performance." *Journal of Applied Physiology* 31: 203–206.

Katzmarzyk, P. T., T. S. Church, I. Janssen, R. Ross, and S. N. Blair. 2005. "Metabolic syndrome, obesity, and mortality: Impact of cardiorespiratory fitness." *Diabetes Care* 28: 391–397.

Kawakami, Y., T. Abe, and T. Fukunaga. 1993. "Muscle-fiber pennation angles are greater in hypertrophied than in normal muscles." *Journal of Applied Physiology* 74: 2740–2744.

Kawamori, N., and G. G. Haff. 2004. "The optimal training load for the development of muscular power." *Journal of Strength and Conditioning Research* 18: 675–684.

Kemmler, W. K., D. Lauber, K. Engelke, and J. Weineck. 2004. "Effects of single- vs. multiple-set resistance training on maximum strength and body composition in trained postmenopausal women." *Journal of Strength and Conditioning Research* 18: 689–694.

Kleiber, M. 1961. *The Fire of Life.* New York: Wiley & Sons.

Komi, P. V., ed. 1992. *Strength and Power in Sport.* London: Blackwell Scientific Publications.

Kraemer, W. J., J. F. Patton, S. E. Gordon, E. A. Harman, M. R. Deschenes, K. Reynolds, R. U. Newton, N. T. Triplett, and J. E. Dziados. 1995. "Compatibility of high-intensity strength and endurance training on hormonal and skeletal muscle adaptations." *Journal of Applied Physiology* 78: 976–989.

Kruger, J., D. A. Galuska, M. K. Serdula, and H. W. Kohl, III. 2005. "Physical activity profiles of U.S. adults trying to lose weight: NHIS 1998." *Medicine and Science in Sports and Exercise* 37: 364–368.

Lawton, T., J. Cronin, E. Drinkwater, R. Lindsell, and D. Pyne. 2004. "The effect of continuous repetition training and intra-set rest training on bench press strength and power." *Journal of Sports Medicine and Physical Fitness* 44: 361–367.

Lemon, P. W. R. 1987. "Protein and exercise." *Medicine and Science in Sports and Exercise* 19 (Suppl.): 179–190.

Levitsky, D. A., C. A. Halbmaier, and G. Mrdjenovic. 2004. "The freshman weight gain: A model for the study of the epidemic of obesity." *International Journal of Obesity and Related Metabolic Disorders* 28: 1435–1442.

Linderman, J., T. D. Fahey, L. Kirk, J. Musselman, and B. Dolinar. 1992. "The effects of sodium bicarbonate and pyridoxine-alpha-ketoglutarate on short-term maximal exercise capacity." *Journal of Sports Science* 10: 243–253.

Littman, A. J., A. R. Kristal, and E. White. 2005. "Effects of physical activity intensity, frequency, and activity type on 10-y weight change in middle-aged men and women." *International Journal of Obesity and Related Metabolic Disorders.*

Liu-Ambrose, T., K. M. Khan, J. J. Eng, P. A. Janssen, S. R. Lord, and H. A. McKay. 2004. "Resistance and agility training reduce fall risk in women aged 75 to 85 with low bone mass: A 6-month randomized, controlled trial." *Journal of the American Geriatrics Society* 52: 657–665.

MacDougall, J. D., G. R. Ward, D. G. Sale, and J. R. Sutton. 1977. "Biochemical adaptation of human skeletal muscle to heavy resistance training and immobilization." *Journal of Applied Physiology* 43: 700–703.

Magkos, F., and S. A. Kavouras. 2004. "Caffeine and ephedrine: Physiological, metabolic and performance-enhancing effects." *Sports Medicine* 34: 871–889.

Matsakas, A., and P. Diel. 2005. "The growth factor myostatin, a key regulator in skeletal muscle growth and homeostasis." *International Journal of Sports Medicine* 26: 83–89.

Maugham, R. J., J. S. Watson, and J. Weir. 1983. "Relationship between muscle strength and muscle cross-sectional area in male sprinters and endurance runners." *European Journal of Applied Physiology* 50: 309–318.

McCall, G. E., W. C. Byrnes, A. Dickinson, P. M. Pattany, and S. J. Fleck. 1996. "Muscle fiber hypertrophy, hyperplasia, and capillary density in college men after resistance training." *Journal of Applied Physiology* 81: 2004–2012.

McGill, S. M. 2001. "Low back stability: From formal description to issues for performance and rehabilitation." *Exercise and Sport Sciences Review* 29: 26–31.

McGill, S. M., A. Childs, and C. Liebenson. 1999. "Endurance times for low back stabilization exercises: Clinical targets for testing and training from a normal database." *Archives of Physical Medicine and Rehabilitation* 80: 941–944.

Moritani, T., and H. A. deVries. 1979. "Neural factors versus hypertrophy in the time course of muscle strength gain." *American Journal of Medicine and Rehabilitation* 58: 115–130.

Parssinen, M., and T. Seppala. 2002. "Steroid use and long-term health risks in former athletes." *Sports Medicine* 32: 83–94.

Petrella, J. K., J. S. Kim, S. C. Tuggle, S. R. Hall, and M. M. Bamman. 2005. "Age differences in knee extension power, contractile velocity, and fatigability." *Journal of Applied Physiology* 98: 211–220.

Porter, M. 2001. "The effects of strength training on sarcopenia." *Canadian Journal of Applied Physiology* 26: 123–141.

Rhea, M. R., and B. L. Alderman. 2004. "A meta-analysis of periodized versus nonperiodized strength and power training programs." *Research Quarterly for Exercise and Sport* 75: 413–422.

Rogozkin, V. 1988. *Metabolism of Anabolic Androgenic Steroids.* St. Petersburg, Russia: Hayka.

Sale, D. G. 1988. "Neural adaptation to resistance training." *Medicine and Science in Sports and Exercise* 20 (Suppl.): 135–145.

Sallinen, J., A. Pakarinen, J. Ahtiainen, W. J. Kraemer, J. S. Volek, and K. Hakkinen. 2004. "Relationship between diet and serum anabolic hormone responses to heavy-resistance exercise in men." *International Journal of Sports Medicine* 25: 627–633.

Scott, S. L., and D. Docherty. 2004. "Acute effects of heavy preloading on vertical and horizontal jump performance." *Journal of Strength Conditioning and Research* 18: 201–205.

Shaw, H. 2004. "Healthy way to lose weight." *Alabama Nurse* 31: 14.

Shaw, J., K. Witzke, and K. Winters. 2001. Exercise for skeletal health and osteoporosis prevention. In American College of Sports Medicine, J. Roitman, ed., *ACSM's Resource Manual for Guidelines for Exercise Testing and Prescription.* 4th ed. Philadelphia: Lippincott Williams & Wilkins.

Silver, M. D. 2001. "Use of ergogenic aids by athletes." *Journal of the American Academy of Orthopaedic Surgeons* 9: 61–70.

Singh, A. B., S. Hsia, P. Alaupovic, I. Sinha-Hikim, L. Woodhouse, T. A. Buchanan, R. Shen, R. Bross, N. Berman, and S. Bhasin. 2002. "The effects of varying doses of T on insulin sensitivity, plasma lipids, apolipoproteins, and C-reactive protein in healthy young men." *The Journal of Clinical Endocrinology & Metabolism* 87: 136–143.

Sleivert, G., and M. Taingahue. 2004. "The relationship between maximal jump-squat power and sprint acceleration in athletes." *European Journal of Applied Physiology* 91: 46–52.

Snow, C. M., D. P. Williams, J. LaRiviere, R. K. Fuchs, and T. L. Robinson. 2001. "Bone gains and losses follow seasonal training and detraining in gymnasts." *Calcified Tissue International* 69: 7–12.

Szymanski, D. J., J. M. Szymanski, J. M. Molloy, and D. D. Pascoe. 2004. "Effect of 12 weeks of wrist and forearm training on high school baseball players." *Journal of Strength Conditioning and Research* 18: 432–440.

Taaffe, D. R., and R. Marcus. 2004. "The muscle strength and bone density relationship in young women: Dependence on exercise status." *Journal of Sports Medicine and Physical Fitness* 44: 98–103.

Tesch, P. A., and L. Larsson. 1982. "Muscle hypertrophy in bodybuilders." *European Journal of Applied Physiology* 49: 301–306.

Thiblin, I., and A. Petersson. 2005. "Pharmacoepidemiology of anabolic androgenic steroids: A review." *Fundamental & Clinical Pharmacology* 19: 27–44.

Thorstensson, A. 1976. "Muscle strength, fibre types and enzyme activities in man." *Acta Physiologica Scandinavica* 443 (Suppl.): 1–45.

Toumi, H., T. M. Best, A. Martin, and G. Poumarat. 2004. "Muscle plasticity after weight and combined (weight + jump) training." *Medicine and Science in Sports and Exercise* 36: 1580–1588.

Trout, G. J., and R. Kazlauskas. 2004. "Sports drug testing—an analyst's perspective." *Chemical Society Reviews* 33: 1–13.

Urhausen, A., T. Albers, and W. Kindermann. 2004. "Are the cardiac effects of anabolic steroid abuse in strength athletes reversible?" *Heart* 90: 496–501.

Vandervoot, A. A. 2001. "Functional and metabolic consequences of sarcopenia." *Canadian Journal of Applied Physiology* 26: 90–101.

Willardson, J. M., and L. N. Burkett. 2005. "A comparison of 3 different rest intervals on the exercise volume completed during a workout." *Journal of Strength and Conditioning Research* 19: 23–26.

Willoughby, D. S., and L. Taylor. 2004. "Effects of sequential bouts of resistance exercise on androgen receptor expression." *Medicine and Science in Sports and Exercise* 36: 1499–1506.

Yesalis, C. C., S. P. Courson, and J. E. Wright, eds. 2000. *History of Anabolic Steroid Use in Sport and Exercise.* Champaign, IL: Human Kinetics.

# Index

Entries in **bold** indicate definitions. Entries with page numbers in *italics* indicate tables, charts, or illustrations.